A MOMENT IN TIME

Finding Strength in a Pandemic

Dr. Jody Kussin

CENTRAL PARK SOUTH PUBLISHING

Publisher: Central Park South Publishing
www.centralparksouthpublishing.com

Non-Fiction

Cover Design: Estella Vukovic
Book layout: Victor Marcos

ISBN:
Hardback: 978-1-7370777-8-7
Paperback: 978-1-7370777-7-0
eBook: 978-1-7370777-9-4

This book is dedicated to Stan Pavey, Ph.D., *mentor and friend, and for all lives we lost to COVID-19.*

May their memories be of blessing.

ACKNOWLEDGEMENTS

Thanks to my dear friend Marci Robinson, who threatened for years to 'put all these writings into a book.' I am grateful for your enthusiasm and perseverance as well as for sharing in the journey with me for all these years.

Thanks to my friends, new and old, for serving as touch points throughout the months of not leaving the house. I appreciate the shared learning, humor, and support. I hope to hug you each in person soon!!

Thanks to my family – my parents, siblings, niece and nephews, aunts, uncles, and cousins. I cannot imagine my life without you all. I am inordinately blessed.

Thanks to my spiritual community, who enhance my life. You are expanding my world and world view every day and are a gift for which I am grateful.

Thanks to my teachers and mentors, some of whom have been my village since the 1980s and some I've met just this year. Your integrity, compassion, and brilliance set a high bar.

Thanks, of course to my three cubs and their partners. Everything I do as a parent is related to the loving care and hilarity and humility you bring to raising me up as a mom. You fill me up and challenge me, and my cup truly runneth over with you and the loves in your lives.

Thanks to my husband Steve. You inspire me, every day, 40 years and going strong.

And most significantly – thanks to the many families and individuals with whom I work and who have touched my life, profoundly. I am humbled to accompany you through the challenges, losses, and joys of your lives. You are each precious, just as you are. I am honored to know you.

CONTENTS

PRELUDE

What a ride. Twelve plus months of uncertainty, fear, pain, loss, confusion. A time of living inside out and upside down and topsy turvy. A year where I used up all my adjectives—how many times can one say 'unprecedented, unbelievable, impossible, inconceivable' before those words lose their impact? I am happy to now pivot to 'hopeful, inspirational, remarkable' and retire the prior list.

In the midst of it all, around the world, people continued to do what had to be done. Many 'groups' were especially hard hit by the pandemic—obviously those who lost loved ones, health care providers, teachers, teens, aging isolated adults, people of color in the U.S. Parents raising children were a group who sustained a tremendous burden. In the U.S. alone it is estimated that there are thirty-nine million parents with children under 18 years, all trying to figure out how to work from home AND facilitate at-home-learning for their children. Parents trying to design the perfect blend of privacy and family time for themselves and their kids, trying to adjust to the reality of an empty nest re-filling, trying to ascertain how a five-year-old does 'Zoom school.' It was also hard for grandparents, who could no longer hug and comfort their grandchildren, and who often ended up isolated while trying to figure out the gift of Facebook Portal.

Parenting is tough under the best of circumstances. Our children fill us up like nothing else—and—also, they suck us dry and drain us. We worry incessantly and they call it 'nagging.' We set appropriate limits and they call it 'oppression.' We provide them with things, and they call it 'smothering.' It's a hard full-time, life-long gig. And that's under the best of circumstances. When all things are going well, when you have healthy children, extended family support, no financial woes, no health problems yourself, access to resources, and an educational system that is able to not only provide education, but also, a place for the kids to be, physically, for eight hours a day. Throw into that mix parenting during a pandemic, and it's clearly 'the worst of times' with a challenge to find the moments, even in that mix, that are joyful and sustainable for your children and for your own sanity. Adulting is also hard, under any circumstance: It's hard when you have to 'go backwards' to move in with your parents, who had converted your bedroom into a gym, and who, while happy to have you back, also see you as a 15-year-old, not the 25-year-old you've aged into. It's hard when you are making your own way, and stuck in your own space, and not able to see your parents and family. It's tough.

As a clinical psychologist of 35 years and a mom of three young adult out-of-the-house children, I found myself writing during the pandemic. There was no particular rhyme or reason as to when I wrote—it was more that the words found me, and my fingers tapped on my keyboard and captured the moments. Often my musings were related to work, in providing therapy on Zoom, and in offering, hopefully, a safe and soft place for people to land, to reflect, to cry, to worry aloud.

This book is a collection of some of the COVID-19 pieces I wrote. They do not correspond 1:1 to cover the 15 months of March 2020-June 2021 but are presented in the seasons as we experienced them together—spring, summer, autumn, winter and back around to spring.

I ponder. Lessons learned? We are more resilient than we know, more connected than we thought, and stronger and kinder than we anticipated. We managed to move from strength to strength, despite the difficulties. Lessons yet to learn? Get along with those who are different and think outside your own box and bubble. Develop empathy and kindness at every age and stage, and practice using it, the way we practice breathing.

All in all, the little notes in this book are a reflection of a specific moment in time, during an unprecedented pandemic, and a time of many national challenges. May we continue to move about more and more freely, while also retaining the internalized sense of safety some of us felt inside our little household caves.

SPRING 2020

...in the beginning....

Preparing in an Abyss

And so, it began....

It is an upside downy time. There are breadlines around the block, in the rain, even in L.A.—not to buy tickets to an event, but to buy food at Trader Joe's. We are out of so many oranges and lemons I'm wondering if scurvy will come back to us, and not simply to the pirates who live among us.

More contagious than the actual virus, though is our fear. It is VERY CATCHY. We are not clear on what is going on, and on how we should we handle life. Mood contagion anxiety is a real thing. Google it. We both give and catch fear from one another. The information herein is NOT about the science of the pandemic. You can turn to the CDC web site or your local Department of Public Health or anyone who tweets (although, do not confuse personal tweets with tweets from the reputable scientists and researchers among us.)

As things are changing daily (hourly?) here is my attempt of a little 'parenting du jour' for those who are raising children or helping to raise children or who of late, feel they are regressing back into being children themselves. Let me offer a little bit of help, for anyone who is interested. Because, in this unusual time, where does this leave us? As individuals, as communities, as people at risk...and in particular, where does it leave us as PARENTS?? This for sure was not covered in that owner's manual we received when we brought those kidlets home.... oh wait, you did not receive one? Hmmm, me neither...

First, be patient. We have to stay calm, even if we are not feeling calm, because our tone sets the mood for ourselves and for our family. (Of course, if you have the television as well as Alexa and Siri talking COVID-19 all day, that contributes to the tone as well, but mostly, your children watch you and listen to you when you think they aren't, and then they internalize your feelings and take them on as their own. Just saying. Be mindful. They hear everything, especially you—the television is background noise, but you? You are a *fountain* of information, and they are *sponges*.)

So, walk as if you are calm. Talk as if you are calm. Breathe deeply as if you are calm. Make decisions from a place of calm, not calamity. Practice being patient. It's a learned skill. Here's our chance to master it.

Second, be prepared. If you live in California, you have been prepared for years. You have been keeping your gas tank half-full since the Northridge Earthquake of 1994 and you have been keeping snow chains in the trunk since you were stuck in the 'once in a life-time' third snowstorm going over Highway 5 on the Grapevine. Your kids all practice 'shelter in place' at school in addition to stop, drop, roll and where to line up on the yard after the fire alarm goes off. Preparation is not PANIC and it's not HOARDING and it's not crossing state lines to find toilet paper. (Note—if you run out of toilet paper—use a rag, or an old shirt, or a towel, or a dish cloth, or a Kleenex, or a baby wipe, or just about anything you can think of…just make sure you have laundry detergent—but—note—if your run out of that, take a bath and use soap!) Be prepared emotionally (practice acting calm) and medically (make sure you can access prescription meds for you, the kids, and your dog and that you have a list of all medications on hand for everyone) and financially (cash, cash, cash on hand) and nutritionally (soup, tuna, pasta, beans, rice, some fruits/vegies, repeat) and physically (make your home environment as clutter free as possible, not to mention clean…) and again, practice emotional stability.

Third, try to be lighter and funnier. Maintain (or find) a sense of humor and whimsy. Seriously. Lots of fun opportunities come along with raising children, it's just easy to forget and instead, go straight to MAJOR WORRYING. I appreciate MAJOR WORRYING, being very competent as a worrier myself. However, worrying results in emotional and cognitive paralysis and, it turns out, worrying does NOT fix things. Contrary to mom-belief, you can take off the backpack of worrying you've been carrying since you first became a parent, put it down in a corner, and leave it there for at least a few hours at a time. It will still be there for you, but, put it down. Give it a time out and rest. Feel free to pick it back up after you've had a belly laugh or two or three.

And last (for today), *fourth—be practical.* This is a marathon not a sprint, so do NOT use up all your good the first day and on the other hand, be aware that your children will reach a point, EVERY DAY, where they have used up their good. Let everyone have their moment and do not dramatize. Let some things go. Be gentle with yourself first, and then with them. And if you want to learn something cool, learn how and when to ignore. It is NOT EASY. But—in these times, it's a good skill to practice! Hum under your breath. Put your ear buds in. Listen to music. Be a duck and let some things slide off your back. Be an elephant and have tough skin. Be practical.

We do not have any clue as to how long this will last, or if this will become our 'new normal.' SO, be prepared, be patient, be funny, and yes, be practical.

Bracing Ourselves

Fake it 'til we Make It

I s this still happening? What is happening? If I'm not sure what is happening, how can I 'be?' How can I be patient and calm? Prepared? Patient? Practical? Well…I am NOT patient and calm. It's not my nature on a good day, let alone on a bona fide scary day. Will all days be scary days?

Can we teach ourselves to be calm? What's the trick? Well, you may not like this idea but…. lean in and act as if. A lot of parenting, for instance, is 'acting as if.' For instance, I recall acting as IF I knew how to raise a baby when they released us from the hospital with son #1, when in fact, I was terrified. What about that belly button umbilical cord thing that has to be cleaned and turned around until it falls off?!?! Really? No one warned me. No one. They never should have let us head out, baby in a car seat not securely fashioned. They were, I imagine, wearing baby clothes we had not thought to pre-wash. But I pulled off the 'act as if' and have been using that impostor trick ever since—33 years—act as if you know how to parent.

Act as IF you are calm is step #1, but don't forget step #2, which is, monitor yourself. Check in and monitor your worry level. Is this worry today, in this moment, on your "A", "B", "C", "Y" or "Z" worry list? If not on "A" or "B," note to self, you can revisit it later on down the alphabet and put your attention to today's worry. This may be a helpful move: Recall a worry you had from when your kids were younger, a worry that turned out not to be 'worry worthy.' Did you spend months worrying because your neighbor's baby walked first and you were sure you child would never walk? Did you invest sleepless nights worrying about toilet training, when actually, as everyone told you, your child did NOT go to first grade in pull ups?

I remember a time when I kept a journal, writing down how many minutes my infant son nursed on each side and how many minutes in between and then how many ounces he drank and if I forgot to keep the journal with me, I went bonkers because what if he was hungry and I did not know it?! I was so worried. That child is now over 200 pounds (at age 33, but still…) and probably he was getting enough nourishment back then. But—how was I to know? What seems incredibly significant today may not be as significant a few years down the line. So, in considering and ranking worries, try to see the bigger picture and remember that 'this too shall pass.'

Conversely, if the worry is REALLY big, feel free to allow yourself lean in time. Maybe 10 minutes to lean into your panic, call a friend, vent, sit in your closet and imagine the worst-case scenario. Then, look around and realize you actually SHOULD vacuum inside the closet and it's okay to turn your attention to worrying about locating that attachment for the vacuum you can never find.

For step #3, move toward working on feelings of patience and calm…think about how many directives or commands you give in a day (to your children, to your partner/spouse…) ("Get up, get dressed, brush your teeth, get your shoes on, hurry up, put your homework in that folder, get your phone charger, where are your keys?") versus how many nice things you say ("it's gonna be a good day today") versus how many questions you ask ("Why did you stay up so late? Why can't you keep your room clean? What is the matter with you? Why are you not like your brother?") Keep a spread sheet in your mind. I don't believe there is an app for this or an excel spread sheet program, but more significant than how many steps you walk each day is how much intention you give to the spoken words you use with your loved ones.

Take a breath. Write this down on your hand: WE ARE ALL DOING OUR BEST. Smile. Look in the mirror (or your phone's backward camera) and make sure the smile looks genuine and not like you're grimacing. And then mindfully say, 'We are all doing our best. It will be fine. Thank you.' You can follow that up with an everyday 'thank you, today I am grateful for _____' and now that you are all home together for a while, do it together. We are grateful for this day, for this time together, for the information we can access....

Patience and calm. Practice, practice, practice. And remember that thing when we all flew blithely about in airplanes and were told to 'put your own oxygen mask on first' (as long as you know it's been sanitized) and then procced with your child's? Keep that in mind in the days to come. You have to ensure your own health to assist others with theirs. Patiently, calmly acting as if, monitoring where you are and being mindful with your language and communications. You got this. I promise! You are doing your best.

Keep On Keeping On

You got this...yes, but also, as noted...it's best to be prepared. When we hear those two words, we think of many things.... like the Boy Scout Motto and like what your mom said when you headed off to (College? High school? Middle School?) regarding keeping condoms in a wallet and like what the 8th nutritionist I saw mentioned regarding cooking all meals in advance on a Sunday so as not to be tempted to eat down the house on a random Wednesday afternoon. Be prepared.

The aforementioned examples of preparedness are mostly physical preparations. And physical preparations are pertinent and helpful. (As most millennials know, it is not crazy, but rather responsible, to have a Zombie apocalypse survival kit in the closet. Check Amazon right now. They still have some in stock.) So being physically prepared in this uncertain time includes having food and supplies in the house or apartment, but not *re-creating* Costco or Smart and Final in your garage. It also means making sure you KNOW your neighbors, and that you've identified those with whom you are comfortable sharing various things. (You provide the smoker and I'll provide the last frozen chicken to be found in Los Angeles, something like that.) It also means clearing out your space, de-cluttering, and vacuuming under the couch. Face it, you have more 'free time' than usual. And when is the last time you checked out all the outlets behind the desk related to the computer, printer, speaker, and router? When did you clean your baseboards, even those behind the toilets? NOW is the time.

While physical preparations are underway, do not forget medical preparations. This means knowing the medications for everyone in the family, knowing the best way to contact your physicians/dentists/eye doctors/vets (Online? Text? Call? Website? Doubtful that right now anyone says, 'just walk right in if you have concerns.') and checking your stock of Tylenol, and cough syrup. Additionally, if you still have a thermometer that has MERCURY in it or even know what mercury is—then it's time for a new one. You don't have to break the bank, but you should get one that zips across a forehead and merrily gives you a number.

You also need to be financially prepared. Cash is not a bad thing to have on hand, but it does not do much these days and in fact, in China, they were worried it could hold onto the virus (this is being scientifically questioned, so, check your own facts on this one.) But for sure now is the time to be EXTRA careful with online shopping and purchasing. More time at home. More time on the computer. Less ability to get out. More friendly notes from my BFFs, Old Navy, Michaels, and Amazon Prime books than EVER.... watch your spending. Comfort spending is no better than comfort eating. They both work in the moment, but longer-term consequences are not so pretty!

Which takes me to the next area of preparedness—nutritional. I'm pretty sure I could easily gain 72-ish pounds in a few weeks. In fact, the company who advertises 'give us a week we'll take off the weight' could use me and my family for a promotional ad that instead says, 'give us a week and we'll put on the weight.' That came in handy with our malnourished rescue dog Ginger. Our vet was nervous about whether we could help her get up to a normal poundage (note–we're there already, and now have to worry that she'll soon be the most overweight dog in the neighborhood, and probably badly teased...). It's great to be baking and cooking, but let's keep in mind we are likely exercising less and sitting around more and that no, granola is NOT health food, even though it SEEMS as though it is and even though you may be making it to give to pals—it's not ok to nosh on it every few hours. When possible, less carbs/sugar and more dark leafy green veggies and people, do not forget to MOVE. You Tube has approximately 2 billion movement videos. As does Tik Tok (ask your kids.) No excuses. (And if you're in California and noting it's raining—a) you won't melt unless your name is Dorothy and b) see aforementioned plug for indoor You Tube segments.)

So now you are physically and medically and financially and nutritionally prepared. That leaves the hardest thing to prepare—your emotions. Turns out, your emotions are not 100% in cahoots with rationality, or facts, or data. We'll get to that tomorrow. For today, remember this one thing—YOU ARE ALREADY HANDLING THIS. YOU CAN DO IT. Si, se puede! Yes, you can!

Predicting the Panic

We left off on the topic of EMOTIONAL PREPAREDNESS. We can handle this! Yes, we can! By now, you are a few days or weeks into the 'new normal' and already you are rocking lots of these ideas. You have figured out how to be your own I.T. person (or how to ask Google or Siri or Alexa to teach you how to unplug, plug back in, re-set and start again) and you have figured out that your dog now believes you were put on this earth SOLELY to be with him/her, 100% of the time, around the clock. You have mastered little things, like saying, 'Mommy needs a break now. Please go do something and unless you are drawing blood from one another, do not contact me until this timer goes off.'

You are arranging virtual visits with grandparents, even if they live a few miles from your house. You are also figuring out why HOME SCHOOLING is less fun than anyone thought (not that anyone thought that.) You also may be noticing that for many of our teens, the world's pandemic is not decreasing their important concerns about whether it's a good hair day, why it's taking their BFF a full 10 minutes to text back, or how. even though their school said that this is going to be an 8-3pm school day albeit online, that is NOT going to work for them.

You are likely not gaining the Covid-19 (pounds) (like the Freshman-15.... this observation provided by my savvy niece, Sarah), and you are not headed to the six months from now predicted divorce court. (Note: Every day you shelter in place with your spouse gets counted like 'dog years'—so each day you are stuck together at home, counts as seven days—by the end of this, you boost your anniversary numbers by years!) So, all things considered, you are FINE and for the most part, you are rocking this.

However, there is still the occasional panic attack, that presents like a mini-heart attack. Or the occasional melt down in the broom closet, garage, or car. Or the occasional yelling at your partner even though s/he did not do anything other than chew loudly (which, believe me, IS annoying.) There are also the moments of self-doubt, fatigue, overwhelming anxiety and worry. Moments of 'this is surreal, but it *IS* real, and who knows who is carrying what germs when and how long is this going to last?'

So, let's take stock and see what you think works that does not, and what you have yet to consider trying because the sheer number of links you've received in your in box is too overwhelming to review.

What you think works is that now you can consume more than your one glass of evening wine. You've slowly begun drinking earlier in the day because 'hey, it's 5:00 somewhere and I deserve it' and thus you are drinking more. This may provide momentary relief, but actually, this is not an adaptive or healthy plan. It's bad role modeling for the kids and the 'it's not like I'm driving anywhere' statements do not fool anyone.

You may also think that taking the *ostrich approach* works. However, note to self, ostriches do not really bury their heads in the sand—they may look like they've done this and have thus gained a bad reputation, but truly, they are digging holes for their eggs and after they lay the eggs, they are sneaking a peak to ensure that their offspring are okay. So not only are they NOT not paying attention to life, but they are also, actually, intently studying their soon to be babies to make sure they are fine. So do not bury your head in the sand because truthfully, you cannot breathe while buried. And what we are all essentially trying to avoid right now is breathing problems.

What works, though, in terms of our emotions? For one thing, try every now and then to lean into your feelings and acknowledge this is a once in a lifetime scary moment for the whole planet. We are all in it together, and none of us WANT to be in it at all. Have a little pity party. Have a pajama day. Watch a sad movie and have a cry (I'd recommend the original "Homeward Bound.") Feel the feelings! And where possible, feel them with someone else—a neighbor walking the dog who waves from across the street will be highly sympathetic to you sitting outside in your bathrobe and having a few sniffles.

What works also is acknowledging that despite the sad, mad or worrying feelings, you know you can handle this. You've handled lots of things. And you can handle this. Not alone, mind you. To be emotionally prepared, make an actual written list of the people in your life. Maybe make 10 large circles on a page and fill in names from different times/places (school friends, college friends, neighbors, camp friends, work friends, sports/team/gym pals, family/cousin friends, old neighbors, etc.) You can also look through your 'friends' on social media and remind yourself of those with whom you have not connected in a while. And then set up times to connect. Participate in a Facebook international sing along with pals from Instagram. Encourage your college friends to do a You Tube yoga or line dance class together or make a Tik Tok. With our technology today, we can all stay connected. We can decide on the balance for each of us, so that introvert cat-like folks do NOT have to be overly connected and the social butterflies can set up multiple events per day. We know that helping our emotions along is decreasing a sense of loneliness and FOMO. (Note—we are not missing out on much these days as the whole planet is literally now engaged in sheltering in place.) Meantime, tiny reminder—we CAN actually use a phone to call people. It is a lovely way to connect. Try it. Call a favorite aunt you typically only saw at weddings. Call your next-door neighbor from 'the old house.' Call.

Here are the things you already know to be helpful. Keep a schedule/routine that includes flexibility, mixing up the day, and building in balance between sedentary and active, serious and silly, arts and music. Unplug things and engage in WATER PLAY (bath, shower, wash dog, wash patio furniture, wash car) because water is good—we literally grew in it, and it continues to be nurturing. For your own sanity, do something nice for someone else, every day. Practice a random act of kindness because it's good for the planet, and even better for you. And remember, you got this!

Re-Charging

So, I'm certain you all are more responsible than I, and you do not constantly find yourselves without a phone charger. I don't know how I manage, but despite there being *at least* four kinds of chargers (car, wall, computer, portable– all of which probably have actual names—ask your resident IT guy), I am always at a loss as to where mine are. Thus, I find myself searching for a (fill in the blank) Target, Best Buy, Walmart, Verizon, Sprint store, and then searching for a (fill in the blank) phone charger or computer USB port, or the kind that actually is so old school you plug it in to a wall socket. You would think, knowing how attached I am to a functioning phone, that this would be a non-issue, and yet, I find myself ill prepared to re-charge, even when I know and can anticipate that I WANT and NEED to re-charge my battery. Even now, when I can order anything online and have it here in an hour I am out of chargers.

And so, it goes with our lives.

What do you need to keep you going? What kind of charger? Where do you find it? And how do you remember to have it handy, in advance, so you don't run out of steam and simply fade out?

I remember when I was a young adult, and my grandmother, during her 80s and 90s, was living alone in her apartment in Hollywood. My grandfather had passed, and she wanted to stay put. So, every day my Auntie Esther went to visit. And a few times a week, my dad went. He went after a long day at work, driving through peak traffic, to arrive and sit down to visit. I'd ask my grandmother about the visits, and she told me that usually my dad sat down and napped, for about 20 minutes. "But what did you do while Dad was napping?" I'd ask. "Oh, I watched him", said she, adding, "and it was a pleasure."

She sat and watched her son nap. If she was 85ish, he was 65 or so. And that means I was 35ish. And I could not, for the life of me, understand this. She sat and watched him nap. And it was a pleasure!?!? Really!?

I don't recall exactly what re-charged my battery in those days. I was working tons and raising three busy kids with a very busy husband. I was writing and teaching and planning. I think bubble baths were my guilty pleasure—99 cent store bubble bath, 15 minutes behind a locked door. We didn't have cell phones or email, or any way for people to reach us (other than the pounding on the door of three offspring!), and that bit of peace and quiet and solitude went a long way.

Fast forward 30+ years. Funny how life and time changes some things, and not others. I still enjoy a nice bubble bath, and I'm still getting my bubbles from the 99-cent store (but note, they do NOT deliver.) These days—the thing that never ever fails to charge my battery is time spent with my three young adult kids. It can be long periods of time, or short. It can be a quick snippet exchange on Facebook (although NOT on snap chat or tik tok—snap chat goes too fast for my brain to process and the picture is gone before I figure out whatever it was I was supposed to be viewing!). Of late, it is a weekly zoom family visit. In the before times, it included time with the kids. Doing nothing or going for a walk. Eating dinner or making dinner. Doing laundry or walking dogs. Yup, funny things charge my battery these days. Honestly, I would love to watch one of my kids nap. Seriously.

This week, take time and remember to charge your battery, whatever that looks like for you.

Practicing A 'Whatever It Takes' Mentality

An apple a day keeps the doctor away. Hmmmm. Not in these times. And anyway, it's risky to have to go from store to store to procure the apple. Remember, whatever it takes. That's what we need to remember…W.I.T. Whatever it takes.

In these times, we are afraid. We are hearing an 'alert' every hour or so, and due to phone expertise, we may receive alerts every few minutes, depending upon which apps we have downloaded. So, here's a reminder—it will be what it will be—and it's ok to find out an hour (or an afternoon) later. We do not need minute by minute info. By now we know the basics—we have a virus among us and to decrease its potential impact we need to stay physically away from one another for some length of time.

But HOW do we do that? Here is a tip for moms (and dads too)— for crafts time, have your kids make *you* a SUPERMOM cape. Wear it when you're feeling strong and brave. Wear it when you're gonna tear your hair out. Wear it when you're feeling giddy and giggly. Just remember to take it off when you're feeling sad and nervous, because none of us is SUPER all the time. And it's okay for our children to see that.

And—not to get teachers mad at me but…it's okay (and highly likely) that your children are not 'learning their lessons' every day at home. I guarantee you they are learning LOTS of things. Every day. And also, I guarantee you that there is not one kid who is going to be able to cognitively take in all that is being taught in this new world. There is too much background noise, and I don't just mean the vacuum.

The world is upside down and our kids know it. So, they can study algebra and build their robot at home, but you have to assume their ability to take in and acquire new didactic information has its limits. Which is really, in the course of life on this planet, fine. We will all survive, if at this point in time grammar rules and spelling words and chemistry labs are not mastered.

Instead (or in addition), let's review those things that you do need to learn in order to function in the world (and perhaps go to college and not bounce back). It is not necessarily on the menu that you or your child are receiving on the online curricula from their schools, but it is 'back to basics' for life skills.

1) *Laundry.* Every child at home should be doing laundry. All steps of it. And they should be doing it every day, just as long as they can do to it in a safe place. Even a preschooler can do parts of it—separate out colors, choose the water temperature, press the buttons—take warm nice smelling things out of the dryer, fold clothes, put clothes back where they go. Yup. It is not the same as language arts of course, but it is good learning.

2) *Organization.* Every child at home can help get themselves and the family organized, even the littler ones. They can set a table. They can set an alarm for when to get up and figure out what to do first and what to do last in a day. It's not math, but it is a skill you need in order to do math.

3) *Responsibility.* Every child can learn responsibility. Clean up after yourself and offer to clean up after others. Call grandma. Teach your parents how to operate their new Zoom account. This is not history, but it is Civics/Civility and goes a long way IRL (in real life.)

4) *Communication.* While on hiatus from our old world, it's a perfect time for every child at home to hone their communication skills. That includes active listening as well as engaged talking. We have a generation who excel at texting and social media, but who

struggle in face-to-face situations. They even have a hard time on screen, unless they are putting bunny ears on one another and making 30 second tic tok dances or video memes that are hilarious, but NOT actual forms of communicating with live humans. I applaud the creativity of their endeavors and say, IN ADDITION, learn how to talk and listen, take turns, approximate mood and tone from cadence, and modulate pitch and volume. It's not a foreign language class, but it IS a foreign skill for many of our kids.

5) *Mistakes.* This is a good time to let our children make errors and to not pre-save them from themselves. They are in the nest and are safely cocooned, surrounded by family and really glued together. Let them mess up with a friend, and then let them be upset. They can debrief with you and figure out in re-winding, what they could have done differently. Then they make amends and move on. Let them be mean or disrespectful to a parent and then you can be upset with them in response and—repeat as above—debrief, figure out in re-winding what could have been done differently, make amends and move on. It's not an ethics class but—well—it really is an opportunity to teach ethics!

What our schools are attempting to accomplish is impressive. I applaud their efforts. I also say, let's be realistic and perhaps *lower our expectations* for academic mastery and *raise our expectations* for life's lessons. It's not school, but it IS experience, and in these times, that means a lot!

Teaching Our Parents Well

E veryone can help. Everyone in your nest, in your fishbowl, all ages, all hands-on deck. But let's get more specific. Who's rockin this crisis? Well, if you ask me, so far, it's the millennials. They seem to be the generation who has the best grasp on it. Maybe it's because they are the ones who mastered the 'find balance, work remotely, eat avocado on toast and pay lots of money for it with pride vibe' or maybe it's because they are better wired to roll with bumps in the road, having come of age basically when the economy tanked in 2008; having graduated college when there were no jobs.

I'm not the first to write about the generation gap differential response to this pandemic, but I will add my two cents. Human beings. Highly interesting. And lots of time to observe and study and contemplate ourselves in these times. 30+ years as a licensed clinical psychologist and I understand people much less than I did when I started out over 35 years ago! I was so much wiser then (or so I believed…)

So –it turns out—(and yes, I am generalizing, not using a control group, and basically not consulting science, so, read with caution) that some of our elders are laissez faire. My 100-year-old Uncle Marty, in Arizona, is busy baking bread and *shipping* it to family members around the country, bless his heart. My 90-year-old Auntie Esther is staying home, but that is only because her son, a science writer with 40-years' experience covering infectious diseases, threatened her and made her stop attending multiple mahjong games. My 85-year-old father finally stopped going to his 120 people 'older/seniors' bridge game where they shared cards AND snacks, but only because the church shut them down last Friday. In his current state of driving my mother nuts, he is filling his time with at home exercise (three hours daily), tinkering on house projects (two hours daily), and going from supermarket to supermarket (mainly, I believe, for something to do, not because they are out of supplies and need more paper towel.)

I applaud their sense of denial. I do; however, I wonder and worry that if this was Europe in the 1940s, these would be the folks to stay put, saying 'this will blow over, no need to move to America.' But what do I know? My inspirational relatives all have longevity on their side, so maybe the fact that they do NOT have extra cortisol free flowing through their veins and pumping them full of anxiety/adrenaline like the rest of us, maybe that works as a protective factor against the virus somehow. Maybe it always has and that's their collective secret. They lived through worse but sweated it out less. (Think, raising kids without seatbelts and drinking and smoking while pregnant and having a 'devil may care attitude.')

Then comes my group, the 'boomers.' We were born between 1946-1964. We are a mixed group, some of us of privilege. Some currently identify themselves as 'essential' workers but it's kinda questionable. I'm sure it's well-intentioned but…really—all you billiard and liquor store owners in your 50s and 60s. Are you SURE!? How do you define 'essential?' At some point law enforcement will step in, but this generation is smart, and 67% went to law school, so, good luck to our local sweet 19-year-old law enforcement officers who will need to do some convincing to the 55-year-olds to get them to stand down.

There are some of us boomers, on the other hand, who are freaking out and building a panic room and feeling bad we did not go along when our old neighbors moved to Topanga years ago to be off the grid. We have been prepared for disasters for years, having lived through many California earthquakes, 9/11, and some hurricanes. My lite assessment shows there are more boomers in light denial than in easy panic and probably most are in the middle. Most of us are hearing daily admonishments from our Millennial kids, yelling at us via Google hangout, WhatsApp, Zoom and Facebook video chat messenger. (Note, they do not appreciate that we've learned how to put the teddy bear ears on our faces during their lecture talks with us.)

Bottom line—we are not sure—there are mixed messages. Stay home, but the stores will open early for us to shop so, can we go to the market? (Probably not.) What about walking our dogs—who are like our grandkids/grand pups basically –do we need to walk in the middle of the street or on the bike path or on the sidewalk or just host front yard doggy playdates with owners outside the fence and many dogs running around inside the front yard? (In our family the person with the busiest social life currently is rescue dog Ginger—we are investing lots of time managing her social life and she appears highly appreciative! Also, true fact, we've met a ton of dog loving neighbors we'd never heretofore encountered, all walking around in the middle of the day at various times, some in masks, some not so much.)

Also, some of us (not me) have our empty nests filling up again, all of a sudden–which to be sure is a mixed blessing. The last time there were this many size-12 sneakers lying around was when the kids were all in high school and frankly, it's as annoying now as it was then. But on a plus side, our kids can cook. AND go marketing for us. And they also are VERY funny, and also, they know all kinds of games to play. Those hours and hours of Monopoly and gin rummy and Bop It and Apples to Apples with which we raised them paid off because our kids now come armed with games called Settlers of Catan, and Code Names and even PANDEMIC. Our kids are also handy because they are bilingual in technology, so when we need to use Zoom or YouTube or watch something stream live on Facebook, they have our back. (And often, our passwords. Do not over think that! Somehow, they realized we use their dates of birth way too freely.)

Then come the Gen X group of parents ...born 1965-1979. These parents have it pretty tough as many of them are living with multiple school age children, while in some cases also caring for their aging parents, and often, they are also working from home. This is a very challenging set of circumstances! I say hats off to them. They are taking things seriously, but most serious is how to juggle work from home demands with how to entertain and educate children's demands with how to convince boomer parents to not wait in line at Costco. This is a generation most in need of respite, or at minimum, Grubhub and Postmates remaining functional regarding delivery times and services.

Next is the BIGGEST group in our country—and so far, as I already mentioned, looking like the group best handling this historic time. First, they already know how to remote for work from home purposes. They have already created online and virtual huge communities and circles of friends. They know how to buy food that gets delivered to their houses and they have not set foot into a mall since their mom made them go buy a suit for their bar mitzvah. They got this. They know their Amazon Prime FedEx people better than they know their local clergy. These peeps are known as the Millennials, and there are literally hundreds of thousands of them across the country. They are admonishing their older relatives to stay in the house. They are organizing happy hours in large park settings where they mark off six feet demarcations for humans and do not share the wine bottles, just the info regarding which wine goes best with the dinner they smoked in their back yards earlier in the day. They are taking this time to work on home improvement projects and already have painted two rooms and a bathroom, ordered everything there is from The Container Store, and begun work on next year's virtual holiday cards. They are truly heroes. They also are Millennial-splaining the new world order to their boomer parents, who are both rolling their eyes at them while also secretly taking notes the old school way, with a pen on a legal pad.

Last, but not least are the Gen Z kids, born 1995-2012. This age group appears to be a little less engaged with the whole phenomenon, worrying still about AP tests (cancelled or not?) and college acceptances (how to choose if you cannot visit?) and college finals on-line and social life situations that continue whether or not school meets in person, online, or not at all. These guys have the intense self-focus all teens/young adults should have, and kudos to them. They rely on parents to handle the 'deets.' They can be helpful at home, especially with pre-arranged facetime with grandparents, but mostly, they are about them. As well they should be. Hats off. Let's not force feed them our anxiety or minimize their angst over all that has been cancelled in their lives.

A brief note on our babies—there are known as the ALPHA GENERATION—born 2013-2025....and they are our future. Some are literally infants and the oldest are only six or seven years. We are protecting them as best we can and projecting lots of hope onto them to really change the trajectory of the world. They are our grandchildren, great grandchildren, and maybe even great great-grandchildren. We do well to protect them and play nice games and have story time and singing time and walks with them. They love water play and bubbles and baths in the sink or tub or shower. They are entitled to be clueless about this part of the world and we'd do well to keep them from the free-floating panic as long as possible. It may break our hearts they cannot see grandma in person, but they also are fairly adaptive and soon can be happy 'having dinner with grandma, where grandma is on Facetime on a screen sitting next to the highchair every evening.

Final thought—do you remember that John Denver song from the 1970s about listening to and looking for the wisdom of the children? It's called Rhymes and Reasons. Whichever age group to which you belong, perhaps consider seeking the wisdom of the younger generation this time around.

Knowing Yourself and your Intellect

The expiration date on my sanity could be fast approaching. To ignore or not to ignore? I tend to ignore expiration dates on certain items.... toothpaste for instance—does it really 'go bad?' Also, salt. Seems to me that salt lasts across millions of years, so I do not throw it out even when the box indicates.

I have learned my lesson on other things though. For instance, do NOT ignore sunscreen deadlines—we did that once a few years back and then had lots of little kids (mostly mine, but perhaps also a niece...) break out in weird rashes which we initially also ignored—only later to be diagnosed by a laughing pediatrician friend who said you should ALWAYS adhere to dates on sunscreens. Live and learn.

Speaking of living and learning...now, as you literally become home schoolteachers and observant of each child's approach to learning, it's a good time to get to know 'types of IQ.' Why not? You've got tons of free time, right? (Just sitting around and eating Sees candies, are ya??) This may help you to not get mad, frustrated, and overly focused on what your kids are NOT good at—and to remind you to take a breath, pivot, and look at their strengths! Catch Them Being Good, so to speak.

Here goes. There is zero expiration on identifying and naming your child's strengths and unique aspects of self. We tend to focus on remediating their deficits (tutors, Kumon, extra drills, more homework) with less focus on celebrating what makes each one of them so very firmly them. Read on and identify their areas (and your own as well) of grace, excellence, and shine!

About IQs. Per Howard Gardner, Ph.D. and Harvard professor/developmental psychologist, there are eight types of intelligence. Most of us only think of one, and that is 'General IQ.' Even that, by the way, includes two types: **Linguistic-Verbal intelligence** and **Mathematical-logical intelligence**. We measure this type of IQ with standardized IQ tests that typically have 'the average' IQ ranging between 90 and 110. And by the way, MOST of us fall in that range of average. A few fall into lower ranges which can signify Intellectual Disabilities and a few fall into higher ranges, which can (at the highest numbers) indicate 'genius.' Mostly, though, 70% of us have average IQs. Scientists posit that these IQs are fairly stable across the lifespan, but there are many flaws in the tests we use to assess them, so remember, a number is just a number. It is not a definition of a human by any means.

Another form of intelligence is **kinesthetic** (as seen in football players, who can anticipate where all 22 players on the field are and who can run and catch a ball before it's even thrown, and gymnasts who can spot their landing with eyes closed and in kids who do great at dodge ball, handball, and jump rope.) There is also **visual-spatial intelligence**. Can you intuitively figure out how to drive from point A to B without Waze or your GPS? Do you recall how to get to a place you've only been to once, and that was years ago, in the dark? Or do you (like myself and my sister, Susan) get lost pulling out of your driveway even WITH a navigation system on your phone, car, and an old-fashioned print map too?

Another two types of intelligence are **Musical/Rhythmic** and **Naturalistic intelligence**. Musical intelligence has to do with sensitivity to sounds, rhythms, tones, and music. People with a high musical intelligence normally have good pitch and may even have absolute pitch, and are able to sing, play musical instruments, and compose music. They have sensitivity to rhythm, pitch, meter, tone, melody, or timbre. Naturalistic intellect is what it sounds—it pertains to those who basically 'can talk to the animals' and who can walk the forests with ease and comfort and who love to be outdoors or on a ship or in a hammock hanging from the rock they are climbing. It is often associated with Indigenous Peoples who knew the earth as well as (if not better) than they knew themselves.

Finally, there are **INTRAPERSONAL (emotional) intelligence** and **INTERPERSONAL (social) intelligence**. I mention these last as in some ways these are the most pertinent. *Intrapersonal or emotional intelligence* means self-awareness or introspection. People who have high intrapersonal intelligence are aware of their emotions, motivations, beliefs, and goals. Ironically, people with high cognitive IQ may have relatively lower intrapersonal IQ (think "Big Bang Theory" characters on tv.)

Some research suggests that *social intelligence* takes you farther in life (depending on how you define 'farther') than other types of IQ, and in fact, in predicting successful graduation rates from college, social IQ is sometimes seen as more significant than SAT scores or high school grades or socioeconomic background OR cognitive IQ.) Interpersonal/social intelligence is thought to be the ability to get along well with others, and to get them to cooperate with you. Social intelligence includes *social awareness*—primal empathy, attunement, empathic accuracy, social cognition, and social facility—synchrony, self-presentation, influence, and concern. And here is a GREAT thing—it is believed that, unlike other intelligences, social intelligence is something we can INCREASE and ENHANCE across the life span, especially our ability to have empathy. (So, if you're worried your child cannot learn long division or write a great essay while sequestered at home and being taught over a computer or telephone—consider this: (1) How easy is it to learn through those media? (2) Which is more fun—bugging parents and/or tantrum-ing and/or annoying a sister or sitting online from 8am to 3pm daily? And (3) Maybe your child's best IQ is social IQ, which at the end of the day, may be just what our planet needs most. Encourage and support their ability to 'walk in another's shoes' and take another's perspective, because that's called empathy. Just sayin....

While we are all busy 'staying at home' let's take time to observe and identify some of one another's unique characteristics. We can grow and embrace any of these and our likes/dislikes and environmental exposure to things (more time in nature, more time playing sports) can make a difference. The list is CONCEPTUAL. So do not over think it or sign up for formal IQ tests. Just use the aforementioned as a light guide—it is never time to throw away our sense of wonder at the amazing billion things that go into making each of us. Enjoy. The intent is to look at each of your children, your partners, your parents and find things you had not noticed. Instead of generating that list of 'here are the top 10 things you do that bug me', create the other list 'fun things about you that I appreciate.' No expiration dates about which to worry. In times like these, embrace all aspects and shine the light.

Witnessing Egg Dealers in Plain Sight

Well, it is starting to set in. The 'being here now' stuff, not working so well. The novelty (if there was any) is wearing off and we are wearing down but hunkering in for the long haul, that seems hard, too. For instance, on my first walk of the day, I saw an older couple yelling at one another on their porch, a mom screaming at three kids on bikes, and a young homeless man asleep on the sidewalk. It's not that I never see things like this, it's just that I normally would see one such image a month, not three before 10am.

Then, something I've never seen: two mini vans pulled up alongside one another in what appeared to be a drug deal, one facing north and the other south. Luckily, my dog really wanted to sniff the grass on her perpetual hunt.

Because I follow our Nextdoor app and am always on the lookout for our roving band of mythical coyotes, I had a pretty good view from across the street. Turns out I was a witness to a very serious 'egg deal.' One driver, the seller said she'd driven out to a farm in Ventura County and while she was already all out of Extra-Large Grade A, she still had Large, but as she was running low, it would 'be a bit pricier than originally promised.' Bartering ensued until the other driver, the buyer, purchased three cartons and the seller electronically opened the hatch for the buyer, in her gloved hands, to reach in to collect her 'contraband.' An egg deal going down in broad daylight! These are unusual times to be sure.

On the second walk of the day, I saw a few trees that embody our So Cal rarely experienced seasons of spring + fall—trees covered with leaves turning to red and orange and gold, while also sprouting buds and little flowers. I also saw many squirrels who seem to believe they own the roads, as the roads are deserted. Additionally, people are outdoors pulling weeds like never before, and little children are learning about the origin stories of tomatoes. No egg deals going down, but oh so many people out and about. Mid-day.

By the third walk, I encountered the life-affirming thing I've been seeing every late afternoon—family groups walking together. While I often will see one parent and one child on a walk, until the past two weeks, I essentially never saw the whole ensemble. Most likely it's because one or both parents were working and one or more kids were off playing sports, seeing tutors, or hanging with peers. However, it is quite lovely now to observe (from more than six feet away) all members of the party. They appear to be taking their time—sauntering, if you will—down the middle of the streets. They are laughing and pointing out the return of the bees and the hummingbirds. Sometimes they are walking dogs, sometimes not. Sometimes they are on bikes or scooters and most often, they are on foot. Lots of times they are laughing. And unusually, none appear to have ear buds in their ears or headphones on their heads. They are, dare I say it, communicating with one another as they stroll together through the neighborhood.

I'm sure that in the years ahead, we will all have take-aways and memories from this bizarre time, as will our children. Our fear, which is 100% understandable and justified, makes it too noisy in our heads at times to take in the still soft voices and the sound of the almost here spring breezes. However, as noted on every meme and GIF you receive, keeping a gratitude list in these times is immensely helpful. It does not mean we have to pretend we're not nervous—just that while nervous, we can also acknowledge the grace in our lives.... family groups walking have one another, and egg deals in the 'hood' actually indicate a sense of community and communication (how did they know to meet up at that time on that corner?) Neighbors are meeting one another for the first time. And while screen time, which had been vilified for years, is now getting its due, people time has become even more valued. Just check your NEXTDOOR app.

So, to paraphrase a beloved old song—let us smile on our brother, and on our sister, and on our (can't believe they are still having to walk door to door delivering mail) and on our 92-year-old next door neighbor and on the older couple mid-argument as well. Mr. Rogers would be very proud of us. When possible, smile on yourself too—you know you have lots of time to turn that frown upside down.

Being Human is Human

"Be gentle with yourself," I say, "Are you friggin kidding me?!' I think. The post-it stacks in my top drawer are lonely. And the pads of paper I have with the heading, "TO DO LIST" feel neglected and left out. A recent attempt at generating such a list included, 'Wash hair and go onto YouTube to learn how to blow it dry.' I have more free time right now than, possibly, ever in my life. Which is not to say that I do not have responsibilities—patients to help, reports to write, evaluations to conduct, Instagram and Facebook streaming live concerts to follow. I do note, however, that in these times, my sense of time is slowly slowing down. I am overly privileged in this new world, with no children or grandchildren living in my house and only myself, my husband, and our ecstatic dog sharing space. I can count not only steps, but also heart beats.

I was visiting with my 90-year-old mentor recently (YES, by phone.) He is a wise man and an incredibly well-respected clinical psychologist. I asked him if he thinks perhaps, I have attention deficit hyperactivity disorder (ADHD.) I said I have this sense that I should be doing things and producing things and making things all the time. He said that is called my 'drive' and not my diagnosis. He said he'd write me a note to remind me—no ADHD, just a personality that likes to keep busy. Sometimes I'd like to swap that temperament with a friend who mentioned that she is so comfortable 'doing nothing' she's sure to need to purchase a new couch, as she is creating a permanent dent in hers. I am aspiring to get to that point too. (And, by the way, West Wing has seven seasons on Netflix and I'm only on season three, so, this goal is getting closer to reality for me nightly.)

Anyway, this all got me thinking—with less structure and more 'time' many of us are busy diagnosing ourselves. We are diagnosing our family members with whom we are cocooned, and our pets as well. This pastime can be dangerous, so let's beware. Feeling sad does not mean you have a clinical depressive disorder. Children who are whiny at the day's end do not necessarily have anger management problems. Spouses who are cleaning every surface with Clorox wipes do not have obsessive compulsive disorder (ocd.) Having margaritas on weeknights does not mean you have a substance abuse disorder. Eating extra chocolate chip cookies is not bulimia. Being happy and sad in the same day does not mean you have a bipolar disorder.

We throw around diagnoses freely. The terms are part of our daily vernacular. It would do us well to remember that googling symptoms, medical OR psychological, never ends well. Even if you're on 'Pub Med' or 'Web MD', you need a licensed professional to let you know if you meet criteria (signs, symptoms, frequency, severity AND level of impairment as to how your life is disrupted) for a disorder. And please note, if you or your family members are genuinely concerned about your mental health, there are many resources available. In fact, counseling and psychotherapy lend themselves to telehealth care more readily than say, podiatry or pedicures (or, for that matter, gynecology.) Lots of support and coping skills can be gained through phone or computer conversations so if needed, please reach out. We have hot lines and crisis lines, and colleges are still offering free counseling to their student bodies.

In general, though, do you know the best form of modeling for our children? Showing them when and how to ask for help.

It seems to me that part of our current instinct to label ourselves with psychopathology stems from too much time looking in the mirror—and by mirror, I mean the little photo/video of yourself you see when you do all the virtual work—when you're doing school on Zoom or conference videoing on V-See or facetiming with your kids who live across the country or visiting on WhatsApp with relatives across the globe—up pops a very distracting (and often highly unattractive) visual of you, staring back at you. It's like HD tv. We see every self-perceived flaw—every wrinkle or zit, every errant eyebrow hair or nose hair or ear hair, all of our pores (who knew we had so many?), every forehead square inch that once had hair, every natural color root poking through years of work by our hair colorists, all our extra chins—we see an image of us and infer that it IS us. That our full sense of self can be boiled down into how we look. We buy into the tv and magazine notion that how we look is who we are and that everyone we see, we are seeing in their natural (versus made up, made over, photo touched up) state.

This, by the way, is impacting people from middle schoolers to aging seniors. Our littler kids seem oblivious, which is a relief. Self-consciousness has not come to them yet and they are not typically focusing on their looks. But our young almost-teens and adolescents are struggling. They are used to images of 'perfect people' including themselves. They are adept at using their own social media skills to photo shop and edit and promote (and product place) their best external selves. They delete unflattering photos and know which is their 'best side' when posting. However, in the world of live virtual conversation, they see, up close, the unfiltered version of themselves. So, while you may think they are learning and mastering biology with their teachers on Zoom, it's likely instead they are counting the pimples on their nose bridge and then 'feeling gross' about how they look. Which, by the way, is not all that different from adults who are working from home and wondering 'how young is too young to start Botox and is that considered an essential or non-essential activity' in these times? On the one hand, our obsession with how we look serves as a distraction from our worry about the "Brave New World" in which we live. On the other hand, it really does not get us anywhere (except adept at the touch up appearance settings on Zoom.)

Normally I'd say, 'unplug' and quit staring at yourself all day. However, that's currently not an option. So instead, let's maybe try to embrace our physical imperfections and model that behavior. A little humor can work. Some funny apps that plop on virtual bunny ears or turn you into a young Elvis are helpful too. And also, a serious conversation or two on the topic of the insignificance of whether or not one finger is 'too long and everyone is staring at it.' Note—no lecturing your kids on this topic—if you're talking longer than a segment of Sesame Street, you are talking too long and are annoying. (Second note—if they roll your eyes take that as a win—it means they heard you.) National Geographic has a great Instagram feed that includes photos, up close, of people around the globe, highlighting life affirming aspects of humans. Maybe getting a new screen saver or changing up all the screen savers daily with a different theme—and highlighting our strengths *as a* people versus *how we look as* a people, would go a long way. Including people of all colors, of all shapes and sizes, of all ages.

It will be hard to convince Los Angelenos that it's okay to not be camera ready. But it's worth investing the time. We cannot physically embrace one another these days, so instead, let's work on embracing ourselves. Feeling all the feelings, as my daughter the clinical psychologist says, is important and we need to leave lots of room and safe space. And also, we can demonstrate positive body image and lightness of spirit, even if our five o'clock mustache shadow is appearing as early as 11am.

Putting Worry in its Place

We are clearly living in a time when the seams of society are unraveling. And we have aspirations to create a new tapestry, together, and I appreciate that kind of optimism. But I also think we may need to lower our bar a little and start perhaps with setting up a goal more like needle point, or even something simpler, like maybe creating a pre-printed cross stitch. LOWER YOUR EXPECTATIONS, it should say. We should all stitch that up, or just write it on a post-it note.

We are all struggling with various questions that bubble up. Why are liquor stores 'essential' but See's Candy stores are not? Who decided that it's not critical to keep stores stocked with fresh flowers? If we're all stuck at home, and our newly planted gardens have yet had time to bloom, shouldn't we have access to the 'friendliest' of flowers, daisies, as noted by Kathleen Kelly, Meg Ryan's character in *You've Got Mail?*

Some of us are even starting to run out of things to do. Which in some ways is funny, because I know we all have items we've moved from one list to another, over a few years, never to be crossed off. No time like the present?? Or not so much? Do you have a current updated phone list in your phone or computer? Do you regularly sort your emails and put them into folders and delete and thin the herd? Do you wash your windows, indoors and out? My impressive friends are cleaning like nobody's business. One told me yesterday that in her zealousness, after hand washing all the floors, she detailed her doggy door. (Which made me think, 'ooops—should I be doing that?' followed by, 'I'll add that to the list of going through the large boxes in the garage labeled 'misc., probably maybe should shred someday.')

Here is something we CAN be doing though.

Safety planning.

Remember how we are supposed to have home fire drills with our kids and designate the spot we meet (next door? around the block?) and where our 'go bags' are stashed, ready to pick up in a moment's notice, containing our important documents and prescriptions and extra dog food? Remember that? And the schools even sent it home as homework in one grade or another.

Well, this is an excellent time for a few family meetings to do a few different types of safety plans. The main thing is to brainstorm, write things down, and hang things up where they can be seen. In case of an actual emergency, our brains freeze and it's hard to remember anything, let alone whom to call first.

So, just for fun here are a variety of less typical safety plans you can create:

1) **Social safety plan.** Each person living in your space writes out who they are going to call or text or Facebook messenger in moments when they notice they are feeling alone, lonely, or checked out. In the moment of sadness, we can't remember one pal, let alone the hundreds in our aforementioned phone contacts or on our social media sites, so it's good to write down actual names. Feel free to be expansive. Your children have teachers and mentors, coaches and grandparents, scout leaders, neighbors, aunts and uncles, and also friends. Let them generate a long list of people they can call or to whom they can reach out. They may never need this list, but it can be of comfort to see it hanging in their room or on the fridge. And they can keep adding to it. For their exercise, you can just tell them, 'Let's make a list of all the people who love you and then a list of all the people who like you and then a list of all the people you know.' This is also a fine assignment for young adults and adults and older adults. WHO YA GONNA CALL? Ghostbusters, sure, but also why not that high school friend you love but have not had time to visit for years? Put them on the list.

2)   **Mental health safety plan.** Typically, we think of mental health safety plans as established for life and death crises. We may design a safety plan for if we ever felt suicidal or at risk of relapsing from addiction. Or at risk for self-harm. In these times we can extend the concept and develop a list of resources upon which we can call in case of changes to mental health—mini panic attacks, chronic sleeplessness, noticeable lack of interest in things that used to be of interest, plus crisis situations. This list can include the name and contact information of a therapist or counselor, priest or rabbi, clinic, or counseling center. It can also include apps (which can be downloaded now, into your phones) such as CALM and Virtual Hope Box and MY3. It can also include contact info for crisis centers, including those with texting and phone and email options. It can also include 2-1-1 as a reminder about local resources.

3)   **Medical and physical healthy safety plan.** As noted, this plan can include resources we may need relative to our health and physical safety. First, look to science and research for education and information. If someone in our house has an underlying condition, do we understand it? Do we know the symptoms for the current virus? Do we own a thermometer? Do we know what our MD wants should a family member feel ill? (It's NOT walk into their office this week!) Do we know where the urgent care facilities are in our area and what their hours are? Do we have the information for all those in our care and heart, including parents, children, spouse, best friend if you're their emergency contact number? Do we have all health insurance identification numbers written down somewhere so if needed we don't have to go searching? Also, if you do not have health directives feel free to download a template and save that with your health insurance numbers. It's good to be prepared. On a lighter note, physical health safety planning is like when you first baby proofed the house. Do we have batteries and back up and those long, tall candles in the glass jars from the

99-cent store? Do we have flashlights? Extra charger cords or charger stations? Medications? Gas in the car? The most sought-after comfort item at the market—toilet paper?

What's your plan? I am not trying to scare you—just wanted to give you an idea of things you can do. Now is a great time to work on safety planning in whatever format works for you. It does not have to be fancy or lengthy. You won't be graded on the assignment. And there are comprehensive suggestions much better than mine available online. Check batteries and change filters and decrease clutter and stacks of anything flammable. Make sure you have emergency numbers in your phone identified as 'emergency numbers.'

In these times, some of us have time to tackle things we previously avoided. So why not plan for our safety? Meantime don't get me started about tackling the boxes in my garage. They are up there for the long haul. I've explained it to them, and we are good!

Relaxing the Rules and Decreasing the Directives

We're gonna try something new.

Don't worry about the old rules that governed your household. In these times, we all need to do whatever it takes to stay safe and sane. If you used to have a 'no tv on the weekdays' rule with your children, consider throwing that out the window. If you used to have a 'no screen time after 6 pm' consider replacing that with a 'we'll play it by ear every day and see how it goes.' Do not worry about 'after these times' at this moment. When the 'all clear' whistle is rung, you can slowly return to your routine and structure and reinstate. For now, if helping your preschooler find peace and calm includes time on dad's tablet, go for it. You are all wise parents, I'm sure, so of course you do not have to go overboard. You can still set limits, but you can also loosen limits on a case-by-case basis. No cell phones at dinner is always a good rule, whether you are sheltering in place or on vacation at a tropical location. On the other hand, if you have an agitated, surly teen, you may want to consider changing even that.

This is not a good time for power struggles nor is it a good time to throw up your hands and say, 'oh well, let total chaos ensue.' We can find the middle ground.

This applies to kids across the developmental range, as well as us adults.

Teens do not need to be given constant directives in these times. Y'all used to have at least eight hours' break from one another, where they had the freedom to figure out how to navigate their world.

Consider attempting an eight-hour window of NOT telling them what to do. You can do it before and after if you can't help yourself, but.... we do not like anyone issuing commands at US all day long, and guess what, neither do they! While theoretically this could be 'a good time' to.... write essays for college applications for the class of 2025 or finish an honors thesis or practice SAT and ACT flashcards, it's also possible that this is NOT actually a good time. It's not a good time for us, as parents, and it's not a good time for our teens. In our attempts to manage our anxiety, there is a pretty good chance we are micro-managing perfectly capable adolescents. You know what happens next? (1) They get mad and (2) They withdraw and (3) They regress. So, you may or may not get a draft out of them for their personal statement that may or may not be good enough to submit next October to some colleges, but you almost for sure will agitate your child, which in turn, will agitate you. Your good intentions thus, will not have a good outcome.

So—when possible—with children of all ages—repeat after me: **RELAX the RULES** and **DECREASE the DIRECTIVES**.

If needed, write those down on your hand (but use sharpies because given how often we're washing these days, the words will disappear quickly.)

And by the way, this also applies to us. Same deal. This is not the time to be overly critical of ourselves. You are doing the best you can, under challenging circumstances, which likely are going to get worser before they get worse. Relax your self-imposed rules. Decrease the directives and relax the rules you've created for yourself.

Rather than counting steps, count laughs. If you are not laughing at minimum hourly, make that a goal. And instead of worrying about watching too much tv, search out funny old things to watch, with your children, partner, or by yourself...those oldies but goodies—I Love Lucy is timeless and do your children know who Alex P. Keaton is? Find him.

In these times, make sure to celebrate the little things—did someone in your household:

- Get fully dressed?
- Trim their toenails? Trim the dog's toenails?
- Weed a garden?
- Surpass the laundry loads per week record?
- Have their daily meltdown in the bedroom and not at the dinner table?
- Make everyone crack up at a really bad joke?
- Remember to put the seat down and close the kitchen pantry door?
- Collect some caterpillars?
- Start on decorations for Passover? Easter? April family birthdays?
- Play with a sibling?
- Relax. Decrease. Celebrate little things.
- Repeat.

Celebrating the 'Wins.'

My neighbor and friend told me she has leaned into the 'shelter in place' order and that, in her words, 'if I get any more relaxed, I will be comatose.' RESPECT!

I, however, am not feeling relaxed. If anything, I'm starting to feel a constant sense of pressure. Not from life indoors, but from all the time I seem to be spending checking out what everyone else is doing, on every social media platform and app I have mastered. In these times, it now seems like we are slackers if we do not host a dance party for a thousand, play piano on the front lawn for our neighbors, or start an Etsy industry of home-made knit gloves. I want to let you know; underachievers unite!

It's lovely to see so much industry, creativity, and passion. I was impressed to see my nephew and his lovely girlfriend, for instance, create BEACH NIGHT in their place in Colorado—snow outside, margaritas inside, and all in Hawaiian shirts, including the dog. It is exciting and upsetting to find people who have taken to sewing masks who two weeks ago did not even know how to sew. And people who are volunteering to help others and are organizing fund raisers and grocery delivery for at risk shut-ins (although, I think at this point, aren't we all at risk shut-ins?) And all of our hilarious entertainers who are at home letting their very bright two-year olds film them doing mini stand-ups (although, to be fair, many toddlers know more than their parents when it comes to A.V. and I.T.) And there are all the singers offering concerts from their home 'studio' which honestly, is ten times the size of my home. And yoga instructors and Zumba teachers working from home, to help others, in their homes, potentially break a wrist or sprain an ankle. Hats off.

I know it should be motivating to hear from friends and colleagues who started a pod cast last week and already have 7,480 followers, or who are hosting a virtual nightly wine club for the state of California. It's like how theoretically, we should be touched to see our neighbors perfectly groomed and perfectly behaved children while ours look like we forgot them in the garage for a few hours and honestly did NOT hear anyone banging or pounding on the door.

I know it should comfort us when we reunite with a friend from middle school to learn s/he anticipated this pandemic and moved their family to the moon back in November. Or more likely, to Hawaii, pre-quarantine, and to the island with 'the good hospital.'

Then there is all the new essential knowledge we need to acquire quickly. For instance, per my friend Jane, per her daughter-in-law the scientist, per a video she received: "We should be washing vegetables and fruit in soapy water." And should also be learning the laws of refrigerating or freezing vegetables and fruit to make them last longer. Who knew that apples need to be in their own crisper drawer because they release ethylene gas? Or that celery, to make it last longer, should be washed, cut, and wrapped in aluminum foil before putting in the fridge? Who knew indeed!

We cannot escape the new normal. But we can either quit observing/lightly stalking others OR, keep on watching, like it's a new episode of *Tiger King* on Netflix. Be fascinated from afar, knowing our lives are our very own, and it's not a competition and humans are fascinating (as are tigers.)

So those of you who are taking this opportunity to enroll your teens in astronaut training programs with NASA, or who are ensuring your child's entrance into Juilliard at some point by taking time to teach them the tuba—kudos. For the rest of us—sit back and enjoy the show.

Creating New Traditions While NOT Taking it Personally

So, on our list of new mantras…whatever it takes, be gentle with yourself, lower your expectations, don't take it personally…

Remember TGIF? When it really seemed that Friday (night) was different than all the other days and nights of the weekend, welcoming in a few days of respite and change of venue from work life to leisure life?

Hmmmmmmmmmmmm. Our days and nights are getting mixed up and many of us are 'not oriented' (psychology speak) to the context in which we live. Day of the week? Date on the calendar? Time of day? It all seems fluid, whereas these are the very things that should anchor us and serve as the foundation.

So—maybe make some fun plans to differentiate Saturday and Sunday from Monday etc. Create a new family tradition to mark the weekends. If you've all been on the computer all week long, consider letting it have a break from you (before we break them all from over-use!)

I'm giving and collecting tips, and not just the ones for helpers in our midst. This time in history, is unprecedented, and surely there will be a chapter or more in the social studies and history textbooks yet to be written. What will they say about us and our experiences in these times? Sure, the scientists and politicians will have much to say about lessons learned, and for that we will all be grateful. But what will the parents say? What are the tips for and from parents regarding supporting their families when the world is not only upside down, but, as my patient told me today, inside out, as well?

In no particular order, here are a few tips:

1) Relax/revisit family rules. You can pick them back up again 'at some point' but many do not work for these times. RELAX RULES

2) Build in as much private time as possible (for you too!) Perhaps an hour in your car with the phone or time in the backyard or basement. Remember, an introvert is DEPLETED from spending time with others, and they/we need extra concentrated time alone.

3) Decrease directives. Our children used to go 8-10 hours away from us at least five days per week so now that we have them as a captured audience, it's human nature to start issuing directives right/left. Try not to! (This holds for kids as well as spouses!)

4) Try to agree on a lite schedule for weekdays vs. weekends. We are so confused—what day is today? What is the date? What time is it? To remain somewhat sane, we need to have some semblance of 'orientation' to time and space.

5) Avoid the temptation to make them do the long list of 'things to do' you had for summer.... yes, at some point they can clean out their drawers and bag up clothing to donate, or, or help clean out the garage. However, looks like we have AT LEAST another month in our little nests, so, refrain from doing big projects for a few more weeks. PACE YOURSELVES on PROJECTS

6) Consider a family 'chore wheel.' Or else let each person choose their chores. Or have each person responsible for their own laundry.

7) If the mess in their room is driving you nuts—close the door—do not look in there! Try to minimize battle grounds. (Make sure there is a de-cluttered space for schoolwork though.)

8) Practice the HARDEST of all parenting interventions—effective ignoring. So, so, so hard to do!

9) Allow them to feel their feelings—and use their words regarding feelings. If very angry, try to intervene with 'jump up and down'

'run around the backyard' 'throw a pillow' 'sit in the car and scream.' Do not feed them our feelings. They can be very sad—there are many losses going on—and very anxious—this is a scary time—or….they also can be enjoying time with the family and not having to adhere to school life and social drama.

10) Set up fun family activities that work but do not overdo it—your child does not want family game night every night…

11) Join them in their world—do they play games online - videogames in general—virtual reality 'stuff'—binge watch what you consider weird tv, but make sure it's tv that they enjoy. Learn the names of some of those anime characters or figure out what TikTok is all about.

12) dTIP—do NOT take it personally. We are all in this together, stressed, worried, and trapped. Our kids' (and partners') reactions and behaviors are not always about us. In fact, most often, they're not.

13) Prepare for regression (at any/every age/stage) and practice patience. This too will pass. Someday.

14) Make a social safety plan to ensure they do not become too isolated. Do the same for ourselves. Virtual playdates for kids, virtual wine parties for grown-ups.

Meantime—take good care of ourselves and our adult relationships. We need one another now more than ever.

Meeting Angels in Winnipeg

My Winnipeg cousins Sheri and Susan said they were being called heroes, and they/we agree that's too strong a word. We are reserving that word for all our direct care providers and first responders—physicians, nurses, physician assistants, maintenance workers in clinics and hospitals, and the hundreds of thousands of others walking INTO and not away from the virus.

However, I for sure think it's ok to call them angels.

While we in California are sheltered in place, experiencing the rare/occasional rainy day, we mostly live in the land of perpetual summertime. It's a challenge for us to not head to the beach, because usually, we can be at the ocean 367 days of the year. Assuming we can find a parking spot. So, while our ability to move around the state has been impeded, we are staying in place in a bright inviting space. We are still walking our dogs and having cocktail parties on the lawn while visiting the neighbors out having cocktails on their lawns. We are working on our base for the summer tan (yes, it's bad for us but.... really?!) We are jogging and training for marathons, or half marathons, or 5Ks, or to hit our 10,000 daily steps requirement. Our children can blow bubbles outdoors, wash their plastic furniture, and even, on many days, set up the blow-up pool or jump into the large pool.

In Winnipeg, however, literally deemed one of the five coldest cities on planet earth, it is actively snowing and freezing cold. Adhering to the COVID-19 rules and regs there means you are STUCK. There are only so many fires in your home fireplace that make you feel cozy— on the 28th occasion, you just are feeling smokey and stinky. There are only so many games of cards you can play until you're no longer impressed with yourself for beating your six-year-old at gin rummy, and who has the energy to actually learn bridge this week? Or even this month? And while online poker has its charms, even that becomes tiresome at some point.

So my cousins are making home deliveries of groceries, in the snow. They are distributing food not only to high-risk folk and 'shut ins', but also to vulnerable and marginalized folk in their area. So far, they've delivered to 50 individuals with a long list left. Some of the food is donated and paid for by the local First Nations community and some is paid for by my cousins. In their little TOUKS (knit hats) and massive jackets and sturdy boots, they drop off food, and visit from six feet away. and sometimes, they shovel snow for a stranger, providing a little sunshine on a more than blustery day.

While we have many heroes, who are the angels among us? Are we seeing them? Being them? Supporting them to come forward? Now is the time. If not now, when?

Little acts of compassion and kindness go a long way. Bonus— helping others gives us a sense of happiness. Win-win. Solitaire on your phone will be waiting for you when you get home.

Need an angel? Wanna be an angel? Now is the time.

Celebrating Something This Spring

S pring is here—we are having actual 'weather,' and it's fabulous to celebrate holidays together, albeit not in person. Along with spring, comes a few holidays, including Good Friday, Passover, Easter, and more.

If you had to make four promises, one to yourself, one to the people with whom you live, one to your local community, and one to the planet—what would they be?

Passover, the Jewish holiday commemorating the almost 6,000-year-old historic exodus from slavery to freedom, is celebrated with an organized meal, called a Seder. The story of Moses is told. You know it well. You've seen Kirk Douglas in 'The Ten Commandments' just last week on network tv, or if not, then perhaps 'Prince of Egypt,' or, most helpful, The Rugrats Passover.

Here is a different 'take' on the tale. Moses was an at-risk and traumatized youth. Moses was a foster child, of sorts—he was raised by the Pharaoh's daughter but maintained contact with his family of origin. He had many identity issues with which to grapple—where did he belong, who was his family? He was also a 'special needs' child, and today, most likely would be receiving Special Education services with an IEP (individualized education plan). He had a speech impediment, anger management issues, poor judgment, and impulse control problems. When he encountered injustice, he acted out, without thinking, killing a man who was abusing a slave, and then, he panicked and ran away. It took him until young adulthood (early 20s or so), to be ready to problem solve well. The story is told that one day, he was asked, by G-d, to lead the slaves out of bondage. Moses was highly reluctant, saying, 'I have a speech problem and am really not up to doing this.' His bio brother, Aaron, offered to help, and together the duo returned to Egypt to confront the mighty Pharaoh, with their sister Miriam contributing her voice and strength.

The theme is nicely summed up in "If you believe," best known from the Prince of Egypt movie soundtrack, performed therein by the late Whitney Houston. Basically, it's a reminder to us that miracles begin with us, but only, if and when we believe.

The four promises of the Seder go along with the four cups of wine (or, often, grape juice) that are blessed during the meal. There are also four questions asked, and a celebration of four types of children.

As the story goes, Moses and his brother confronted Pharaoh, who, after 10 plagues, agreed to release the slaves. In that moment, Moses had to decide if he should flee quickly, taking only the fastest and most healthy of the people with him. However, as any good leader knows, there is strength in community, and each of us is responsible for our 'brother.' Thus, he told ALL the people to pack up and leave—he took the babies, the old, the sick, the sad, along with the young and healthy and vibrant. Together, as a community, the people left slavery, and moved into freedom. There were many risks involved, and it was not an easy passage. The Red Sea reportedly opened up for them, and they made their escape together. The power of a reluctant leader, who worked with his brother and sister, who focused on community, is now a story we re-tell annually.

So, each year, at this time of renewal and of Spring, we remember what it is to be slaves, and how hard it is to be a leader, and how important it is to focus on community and what together, we can accomplish. We think about promises we can make. We become mindful of things to which we are all enslaved. We commit to taking on leadership roles even when we don't feel ready. We pledge our faith in one another, and it is all relevant in 2020, surprisingly, shockingly. May we work together and ensure no one is enslaved to another, in any way shape or form.

Indeed, there can be miracles when you believe. But also, we have to act. Step #1—believe. Step #2—do something about your beliefs.

Thinking Global, Acting Local

We left off on 'miracles.' It is truly miraculous that you are raising your children, doing your work, doing their work, and also mopping the floor and making three meals a day, EVERY day!? What is up with that?! So, who's tired? Any parent staying indoors with children, of any age, of course, is beyond exhausted.

But also, I'm pretty sure my appliances have never gotten this much use. I imagine the oven and stove chatting with one another ("AGAIN with the fancy cooking?") And for sure the washer and dryer are shrugging their shoulders at one another ("How can two adults make so many loads?") The same of course is true for every computer and tablet, mouse, and pad. Additionally, there are tv screens that had not been looked at for years, who are now being powered up and left on for hours. ("Can't they at least switch from news channel to news channel?") I have speakers who are shocked to discover they can be required to work on weekdays and during daylight hours. ("Dan Fogelberg!?? Are you kidding me?") And cleaning supplies who had thought they were forgotten, only to be rediscovered ("You DO need me!" said the silver polish cleaner, almost dried up in the container.")

The times they are a changing. That's for sure.

First, we learn we should keep our physical distances from one another. Then we learn to shelter at home and work and learn from home. Then we learn about gloves and masks. Now we learn we should not be grocery shopping. This has huge impact for people of privilege, but more significantly, also for people not of privilege. We are going to have to increase our ability to think global but act local. If you are not financially insecure, are you continuing to support housekeepers or babysitters or nannies who can no longer come to your house? Do you have an out of work dog walker these days, who counted on your gig to help cover rent? Some of us may have large refrigerators and freezers and perhaps even more than one. Others have a tiny dorm-like fridge, and they cannot store large amounts of anything. Food banks are facing shortages. Let's help fill up cupboards without entering Trader Joes. Start with those we know, move to those with whom we share our neighborhoods and communities.

With all this free time, there is more time to look up recipes based on what food you have in the house. With all this free time, there is more time to cook and bake food like pasta, beans, and rice. We can get creative and share ideas and use up the canned food sitting alone in the back of the pantry and if not, donate, donate, donate.

It is to all our advantage to help one another. Slow to use gloves? Not wanting to wear a mask until now? Still going places you should not? It's ok—whatever you did up until today, face the future and make the change. It's a new day. And while it does feel like Ground Hog Day, we are not reliving each day over and over, instead, we are moving forward slowly, slowly and we can do so with compassion in addition to fear.

We have the opportunity to change things up. Think global. Act local. One Day at A Time. We are making a difference.

Keeping Busy When the World Comes to a Halt

We people are busy. Busier than you'd think, during a pandemic. And I'm not referring to our heroes and angels, who indeed, are 100% swamped saving lives to make sure we have access to bread and eggs, and also those working in hospitals with sick and dying patients.

Not to mention you, your children, your 'den mates.' Everyone has a lot going on.

What are we doing with our time? Well, one exhausting endeavor happening the world over is research. It's serious work.

Twelve--year-olds everywhere are researching 'how to murder your parents in a safe way during COVID-19,' and 17-year-olds are googling 'how to surf porn, find a private moment, and clear my browser history quickly enough to switch back to virtual school in a second's notice.'

Long term committed couples are investigating sites like, 'how to prepare for a divorce even though you know that's not what you want, but researching it makes you feel better' and 'how and *why* to find your spouse attractive after 30 years and 30 days in quarantine.' Baby boom post shelter at home? I'm thinking not.

Melancholy is hitting. Despite our forthcoming lovely weather, we are starting to feel the blues, if not also sing them. Brittney Spears is experiencing a comeback (as is her loneliness) as are The Animals (who were trying hard to get out of that place and space.)

The Spring holidays of Passover and Easter are behind us. Ramadan has not yet begun. School has NOT been cancelled. Instead, academic requirements are re-emerging post Spring Break with longer hours and more assignments, given that faculty 'had time' during their 'vacation' to prep and create assignments that make sense in these times:

Briefly describe ONE specific historical similarity between the internal migration patterns in the period 1910–1940 and the internal migration patterns in the period 1941–1980 and why anyone cares about that when we cannot find Clorox wipes in 2020.

And

Although literary critics have tended to praise the unique in literary characterizations, many authors have employed the stereotyped character successfully. Select one work of acknowledged literary merit and in a well-written essay, show how the conventional or stereotyped character or characters function to achieve the author's purpose in 2020 when we essentially all are becoming stereotypes of ourselves.

And, for preschool:

How many birds are found below? Remember birds? They fly. Build nests. Lay eggs. Ok, never mind. How many rolls of toilet paper are found below? Ok, never mind....

So back to basics please. Do not sweat the small stuff, as 'they say,' and, at this point, it is either ALL small stuff or else we all are living some bizarre dream where nothing makes sense. So given the options, let's call it small stuff. And in our fear, let's just be still. Every now and then. Slow your own heart rate.

Adopt the concept of sitting still, and being still, where the music overcomes all senses and we are okay, in this moment. Strength. In this moment. Peace. In this moment.

Maybe not as good as Brittney Spears circa 1998 (?), but.... inspiring, nonetheless. Oh, baby baby.

Listening when Miley Sings Pink Floyd

Chasing away the 'meh.' Did you watch Saturday Night Live last weekend? Did you happen to see/hear Miley Cyrus singing Pink Floyd? O.M.G. If you are a certain age, you know Miley and if you are a certain age, you know Syd, Nick, Richard, Rogers et. al from Pink Floyd and if you're lucky enough to be an inbetweener, you're familiar with both. The song is dedicated to Syd Barret and was based on a poem that Roger Waters wrote about Syd Barrett's fall from reality. It was believed that Syd struggled with schizophrenia, for which he attempted to self-medicate. He died in 2006.

Miley sang this as a soulful, chilling song, specifically timed for us during this pandemic when we are living in fishbowls. While there are fun and funny memes going around ("A Panda eats 12 hours a day. An adult in quarantine eats 12 hours a day. That's why we call this a PANDEMIC.") there are also haunting and touching performances surrounding us, noting the death, the loss, the loss of public mourning of the death and loss. Perhaps we need a balance.

We are aware that it's important and helpful to find humor and laughter every day. It's also ok, and pertinent, to feel the sad feelings, the mad feelings, the scary feelings. It's ok and important to not bury all the stress under the house and frenetically try to put on a smiley face each day. I know it feels like 'if I give in to the sadness, it will overcome me, and I will not be able to come back up.' However, you can put aside time and space for own the sadness, and still later in the day, enjoy an episode of "Tiger King." It's not an either-or situation when it comes to our feelings. We can feel many things, sometimes, in one moment. You know how you say, "I don't want to start crying because I won't stop."? Well, that's not true. You will cry yourself out. Promise. You will not simply cry from now until the end of time.

Our feelings are not mutually exclusive—only happiness without sadness, only love but never hate, only mania and never giving in to fatigue. This is a perfectly fine time to feel all feelings. Parents, in particular, have it hard as they are swimming in a fishbowl with their kids observing every behavior and every emotion expressed. It's ok. They can tolerate seeing you have a bad moment or even a bad day as long as you don't take it out on them. You can own it—"Mommy is sad today. She will feel better later, but right now she's a little sad." "Daddy is feeling mad today. He's not mad at you, he's just mad. Give him some space. The mad will go away."

My memories of this Pink Floyd song date back to 1983-1984, when I lived in Oakland/Piedmont, California. I had a roommate in a small apartment building. It was the early 80s. My roommate and I were 'the odd couple'—me more of a 'rules follower,' him more of a 'we're young and can do whatever we want' guy. It was a good combo. We had a nice community of fellow grad students and neighbors with whom we hung out. We went dancing every week at a San Francisco gay bar. This was right before/as AIDS was identified, and little did we know that we would lose friends to the disease in short order. But for that time, what we all shared, was a deep love of music. We blasted our records and tapes full volume, and not only did the other apartment dwellers not mind, but they also came out to dance and hang with us. We had many favorites ("Who Will Stop the Rain?" anything by Bruuuuuuuuce, some funny Supertramp songs) but our all-time best was Pink Floyd. WISH YOU WERE HERE. WISH YOU WERE HERE.

This version, this 2020 version. Man, oh man. Miley sang it for 2020, when basically each of us, every day, has someone or someones we wish were with us. We share fears. We share longing. And for sure we are sharing a small fishbowl, in which we are swimming around, day after day. It's ok to acknowledge that. It would be kind of silly to pretend it 'ain't' so.

Noticing May Day

Wow. May 1. Amazing. Feels more like March 1, or maybe more like December 1999, when we were preparing for Y2K. Remember that? We were sure all electronics and computers would break down and we would be alone, not able to function. Of course, that did not come to happen, and we were far from shut out or locked down. If it were to happen today, however, that would TRULY be the disaster on top of the disaster. I'm not sure how we would function whatsoever. So, let's remember to thank all our techie friends and family members, all IT guys, all engineers, and those who can make your phone play a tik-tok from your niece even when you do not know what that means, and who can also make their own bitmoji.

Yes, it's MAY DAY. A day to celebrate workers. I have no need to do the traditional dance around a flagpole but rather, I'd like to stand up on a soap box. Express gratitude. Good for ourselves, good for your peeps.

Everyone I know is currently working harder than ever. It's important to note that there are a few kinds of workers—some are working and are receiving a paycheck and alas, many are working for no income whatsoever. The number of Californians holding jobs in March was 18,244,100, a decrease of 512,600 from February. This will be nothing compared to our numbers for April. And these numbers leave out many of our work force, who are not part of any counts.

I'd like to acknowledge and salute those not getting paid and likely not eligible for unemployment benefits. The nannies and housekeepers. Dog walkers. Nail salon workers, hair salon workers, bar tenders in saloons. People who still have to pay rent today, but who have no money coming in, and likely have had no money coming in since mid-March. That's seven-eight weeks of zero dollars coming. For families who were barely making it on their paychecks or under the table monies before the pandemic hit, in these times, they are running out of milk and eggs as well as any optimism.

I'm honestly not sure how they are managing, day by day. Many of them are unable to navigate the 'offerings' in our cities and counties, to find the food banks open to them, to access electronic opportunities without wi-fi or to get a solid grasp of our systems. We have many wide-open hearts and tons of volunteers, and the local news is covering all the clapping at 7 pm and the parades of teachers and the drive-bys of police and firefighters at hospitals. All of which is good, impressive, and well captured in John Krasinski's truly wonderful weekly episodes of "Some Good News." And it really all is heart-warming. But...

For 'working adults' (i.e., pre-pandemic) L.A. County had a higher rate of working poor than any other county in California. This impacts not only them and their family members, but all of us sharing community space. For instance, recent data from L.A. County Department of Public Health show that:

The greatest vulnerability, in the time of this pandemic, is being poor.

And being poor is more than just the amount of money a person has. Poverty is a multidimensional issue that concerns a person's level of health access and coverage, available educational opportunities, and quality of life.

Yes, our elderly, our people with cardiac conditions and diabetes and obesity—they are all at 'higher risk' for COVID-19. But the HIGHEST risk factor, it turns out, is poverty. And, it turns out, poverty is increasing hourly. Twenty percent of Imperial County is unemployed—that's one in five adults, out of work—not counting those who are not counted in the counting.

So today, on May Day, in honor of those working and those wishing they were working—reach out. Text your nanny and let your kids sing a song to her on WhatsApp. Host a little zoom meeting with the personal trainer who helped you last year who has been out of work now for a month+. Call your dog walker. Maybe she can walk your dog with a special leash reserved just for her. And if not, you can send her some photos of your dog, who misses her even though he is living a happy life at home with stay-at-home parents. Track down your housekeeper. If you have any means yourself, see if she can work for you outdoors one day per week. It will earn her some money and she may be happy to be out of her house and enjoying the mastery of working. And when she's at your house, send her home with some food from your freezer. Why? Because you can.

In these times, we all are facing malaise and fatigue. Let's remember those who are also facing life and death fears from the virus and those facing food insecurity, and potential homelessness.

This is me, getting off the soap box.

Deciding: What's Essential— What's Not?

Sometimes I think I really must live in my own little world. I am surprised by things that 'everyone' else seems to take for granted. It reminds me of when our eldest started playing high school football and I was amazed at how the whole school showed up for the games. The head coach and athletic director, for whom I had/have tremendous respect, said, 'How do you NOT know about Friday Night lights? Did you grow up under a rock?' Nope. I did not grow up under a rock, but I also did not grow up attending high school sporting events. However, I made up for it in the number of games I attended as a parent, when two of two sons played every Friday Night over an eight-year period....OMG.

I feel it's somewhat similar during our local pandemic efforts. The notion that the most essential and first things to open-up are those deemed 'essential' and 'low risk retail and restaurants' is fascinating to me. I had no idea that so many of us support and/or are supported by eating out. I'm in favor of employment for all and am not reacting against the plan, just kind of surprised that more pertinent than office worker jobs, are food service jobs. Wondering if my husband and I really should become more foodie-esque. I guess knowing the "good Denny's" from the 'bad Denny's' does not a connoisseur make. We seem out of the loop of the culture and community yet again, although we are mourning the closing of Steam Punk, our lovely quirky local café that had to go out of business due to the virus.

I'm somewhat relieved that our mayor is not rushing us back to some kind of 'normal' given the data on our County and the number of our cases. I'm totally OVER sheltering in place, but, on the other hand, I'm totally in favor of slowing deaths in our neighborhoods.

I'm over lots of things, including how small my world has become. On the other hand, I am really impressed with the athleticism of the children on my street. There are so many kids balancing so beautifully. I literally saw a child ride by on a unicycle, so that won the contest for sure. But I also saw a girl using two scooters, one under each foot, rapidly chasing her sister who I swear was 18-months-old, who herself was moving along on her own tiny little scooter.

Back to my unrelated ramblings.

For instance, should I not have some privilege regarding access to Clorox Wipes if I am an ORIGINAL customer and consumer, having started purchasing the product when it first emerged on the market over 20 years ago and not simply a Johnny Come Lately to the COVID-19 party of cleaning supplies? I feel that I should be given a priority number, like the wrist bands we used to get standing in line to purchase concert tickets.

Same with some of the things we need for baking. It's wonderful that so many are just now starting to take up with baking, but, for those who have long been making yummy treats, should we not have a leg up on the flour and chocolate chips supply?

The whole process is fascinating if we take out the life/death aspect to this, which just makes it horrifying and scary.

It's actually unbelievable how fast we've pulled off a complete stop to our usual society. It's like we had an 18-wheeler come to a screeching halt on the highway while doing 100 mph. In most places in the world, people complied, went inside, and stopped marketing. Now that the fatigue is setting in, it's not unexpected that we are getting tired and cranky. Nor is it surprising that people are protesting—in some bizarre way, it's good to have a place to put your anger (the government) versus turning it all internally against yourself, which ends up in lots of cases of clinical depression. On the other hand—my goodness people—sometimes we sound like teens complaining they cannot keep the car out all night and drive while on the phone and without a seatbelt....

the parameters their parents provided were established to protect their kids, not 'just to mess with them.'

I suppose in the end we need to learn from our children. It's all about balance. I have no intention of taking up roller blading or even bike riding, let alone using a scooter, electric or otherwise. But I respect all the zig zagging I can see from my front porch. And it reminds me, one foot in front of another, head held high, focus on the horizon, breathe, and keep your balance.

Romper room memory for boomers from Miss Mary Ann:

See me walk so straight and tall. I won't let my basket fall. Eyes ahead and don't look down, keep that basket off the ground. Watch me hold my head up high, like a soldier marching by, a back so straight and strong you see, helps to make a healthy me.

Mother's Day—2020

You know what makes a mother? Children. Plain and simple. Children you biologically make or carry or adopt or take into your heart. Children you nurture or discipline or both. Children who seek you out or who roll their eyes at you.

A long time ago a little musical trio named Parachute Express had this little song:

Who will draw a line around the moon?
Who will draw a line from star to star?
Who will pull down the sun with the golden glow?
Who will light for you, this candle fire?

This is a perfect song for any and all moms. We are worried for you, our kids. Who will protect you? Who will educate you? Who will help you? And who will light the way?

As you all know, a major myth of motherhood revolves around the age-old question, posed to all pediatricians: "When will s/he sleep through the night?" Any honest professional will tell you, "It does not really matter, because truthfully, YOU, as the mom, will never again sleep through the night. Ever never. Built in radar that goes to 'rest mode,' but not sleep mode."

You will always sleep lighter 'than before.' You will have one ear open for cries, when they are babies, bumps in the night, when they first learn to catapult themselves out of the crib, tip toe into your bedroom (and up into your bed), for years longer than you ever thought possible, fridges opening for late night snacks by middle school years, doors or windows opening at 3am when they are teenage drivers, and finally, phone calls or texts that beep and buzz just when you hit REM sleep cycles, for the entire rest of your life.

A mother is created and designed by all her children—those she raises in her house and those who frequent her house. She is shaped into a person she was not, prior to the role. She begins in a 'starring role' and later becomes a 'co-star' as that's the way it's supposed to go. As the little boy in the Carrot Song, she plants the seed, waters, and pulls the weeds—and then the carrot/baby/child/teen/young adult grows. There are lots of weeds. Such is the nature of growing anything. Mom cannot stop the challenges that pop up and interfere with evolution. She can be present, spot them, acknowledge them, and on occasion, indeed, pull the weeds. Sometimes she can plant other flowers nearby. On other occasions, she can sit outside and visit as her child tends to their garden.

I am personally incredibly grateful to my children for raising me up. Three young adult kids wandering the planet who inspire me mostly and worry me always. I cannot turn it off, although I do try to turn the volume down on their behalf. I also am grateful to my niece and nephews and to my kids' friends and to my friends' kids. I am deeply appreciative to the community's children as well, who fill my heart with concern and motivate me professionally to ensure that every child has someone who will worry for them.

Who will draw a line around the moon? The song ends:

I will draw a line around the moon? I will draw a line from star to star. I will pull down the sun with the golden glow. I will light for you, this candle fire.

On Mother's Day I give thanks to my bear cubs and to all the other mama bears on the planet. We will do whatever we can for you, for all of you, whenever we can.

Living with "I Don't Know"

There are three words we are hearing more and more—and I don't mean "I love you" or "Are you kidding?"

I had a long catch-up chat with a very dear friend. She is a medical doctor in a large teaching hospital in the East Coast. She said last week that 70% of every bed in their place was reserved for an individual with COVID-19. As an academic chair as well as a physician, she is in charge of lots of things—providing direct care and services to patients, training and supporting newer docs, organizing and coordinating protocols and procedures with the hospital and the Center for Disease Control, and balancing administrative responsibilities while demonstrating calm, composure and compassion as she serves as a role model to colleagues and staff.

It was her line, really.

She said, "I said I DON'T KNOW more yesterday than in my career to date."

Earlier in the week I heard the same thing from a father of three. "The kids keep asking me "Why?" and "When will this be over?" and "How do we make sure we are safe if we go outside?" and I keep saying, "I DON'T KNOW."

Health care providers and parents alike are interventionists. We want to fix things and offer solutions as problems are presented. And many times, we can. A parent can clean a skinned knee, put a band aid on it, kiss it and literally 'make it better.' A nurse can read a thermometer, diagnose a fever, and treat it.

However, in these times, many times a day, none of us can offer answers to what may seem like basic questions. "When can I visit my grandmother in the hospital?" "Why is this happening?" "Is it okay to go outside now? Why was it not okay last week to hike, but this week it is?"

We are in 'opposite' world—where the simpler questions are, the harder to answer. And that is a challenge for us all. We have moved into "compassion fatigue" versus "compassion satisfaction." This puts us all at high risk for burn out (both as health care workers and as parents) and it also puts us at risk for longer term mental health issues.

And there is actually no solution in sight. Or as Jackson Browne let's us know in "Before the Deluge" when we are trying really hard to understand things that are hard to grasp, we arc toward pessimism, thinking perhaps we are not meant to be around, after the mess clears up.

What to say when we don't know. What to believe in when we don't know?

For starters—believe that we are meant to live after the deluge. History is on our side. In these hard times, hold onto the fact that we are survivors, and this will ultimately pass. We want guarantees and 100%ers. And when we don't have them, it's even more important to hold onto our internal strength. It's not, it turns out, a black or white, binary world. And we can live in this gray.

In addition, when we don't know, we can (and do) say "I don't know." And then add a few other tag lines while remaining calm and reassuring. We can do this by being available and accessible, physically, and emotionally. My friend the doc says she is making sure to be highly visible, even when she is swamped with saving lives and juggling priorities. Same is true for parents. She also delivers messages with empathy,

"I don't know, but I will look into it and see what I can find out. I know this is hard/frustrating/nerve-wracking/challenging/impossible/ heart breaking/worrisome. Let's make our best decision given the limited information we have."

We can also be conscientious to not infuse our responses with our own sense of inadequacy or anger. It's not all that helpful to tell our kids, "I don't know and if only these horrible _____ fill in the blank (politicians, news reporters, teachers) would get their act together we could make some progress."

And of course, as we are already doing, we can share the information we DO know: "I don't know the answer to that question. But I DO know that we are all doing our best to keep healthy, wash our hands, socially distance, and be kind to one another."

At the end of the day, however, it is exhausting to not know. So, we need to remember to, as they say, to fill up our own wells. They are running dangerously low to empty.

Remember your right and need to vent—to a friend, colleague, clergy person, therapist—(outside the hearing range of your child/mother/patient) and that it's pertinent to actually SCHEDULE this into your calendar. Consider at minimum 30 minutes per day with another adult in addition to an hour-long session a few times a week.

Remember your right and need to establish some sort of boundaries and to avoid the toxic people in your life in these times, as much as possible.

Remember your right and need to exercise and hydrate and eat healthy and sleep.

Remember your right and need to have privacy and leisure time, which is harder than we'd think, in these times. And remember your right and need to use some positive self-talk...talk yourself up, out loud—"I can get through this. I am good at what I do. I am needed and necessary, but I am not in control of the whole world. I can focus on today and not on the rest of the week/month/year. I can and will honor ME and MY needs, starting NOW."

While there is a ton of 'I don't know' going around, we also have lots we do know. So, take good care of you and take some deep breaths and whenever possible, please take a break. You deserve it, need it, and are entitled to it.

Voicing for the Voiceless

Dr. Seuss's classic, *Horton Hears a Who*

As I'm sure you'll recall, the book tells the story of Horton the Elephant, who, while splashing in a pool, hears a small speck of dust talking to him. Horton surmises that a small person lives on the speck and places it on a clover, vowing to protect it. He later discovers that the speck is actually a tiny planet, home to a community called Whoville, where microscopic creatures called Whos live. The Mayor of Whoville asks Horton to protect them from harm, which Horton happily agrees to do, proclaiming throughout the book that "a person's a person, no matter how small."

In his mission to protect the speck, Horton is ridiculed and harassed by the other animals in the jungle for believing in something that they are unable to see or hear. He is first criticized by a sour kangaroo and her little kangaroo in her pouch. The splash they make as they jump into the pool almost catches the speck, so Horton decides to find somewhere safer for it. However, news of his odd new behavior spreads quickly, and he is soon harassed by a group of monkeys. They steal the clover from him and give it to Vlad Vladikoff, a vulture (formerly a black eagle). Vlad flies the clover a long distance, Horton in pursuit, until the eagle drops it into a field of clovers.

After a long search, Horton finally finds the clover with the speck on it. However, the Mayor informs him that Whoville is in bad shape from the fall, and Horton discovers that the sour kangaroo and the monkeys have caught up to him. They tie Horton up and threaten to boil the speck in a pot of "Beezle-Nut" oil. To save Whoville, Horton implores the little people to make as much noise as they can, to prove their existence. So almost everyone in Whoville shouts, sings, and plays instruments, but still, no one but Horton can hear them. So, the Mayor searches Whoville until he finds a very small shirker named JoJo, who is playing with a yo-yo instead of making noise. The mayor carries Jojo to the top of Eiffelberg Tower, where he lets out a loud "Yopp!", which finally makes the kangaroo, and the monkeys hear the Whos. Now convinced of the Whos' existence, the other jungle animals vow to help Horton protect the tiny community.

Horton Hears a Who! urges readers to 'be the voice and be heard'—as well as to be the listener and observer and advocate.

This a long review of a story you already know, just to make this one 'tiny' point: In these times, we need to listen closely, lift up those invisible folks who need to be heard, and be the voice of the voice-less.

Parenting in Times of Violence

So many calls from parents and a few from kids themselves, over the past few days. Is there a way to explain to a child *why* George Floyd died? Do we want to describe *how* he died, to our children? Do we want to protect our children, black or white, purple or striped, from seeing what is going on across our cities currently, with a mixture of protest and outrage sprinkled with violence and mayhem? Do we take them to candlelight vigils? To rallies? Back to churches or synagogues which we've avoided out of concern for our health and the health of our communities? Have we turned off our televisions and screens, thinking 'we'll watch this later, when the kids have gone to sleep' only to realize, none of us really goes to sleep these days, offspring included, three months into this mandatory nesting period of time, and truly, do we keep this kind of incident a secret from our children for some reason?

Because, by the way, even after we took precautions thinking our children would not 'have to be exposed to this,' they heard, as did we, when the public alert beeeeeeping sound let us ALL know we are now not just in 'shelter in place from COVID-19,' but now are actually under curfew from 8 pm until 5:00 am to not leave our homes under any circumstances. After that, we all had to explain something to our littles, and hopefully, we tailored what we said based on the age and stage of our children. And hopefully, whatever we said, we included information and truth. And, by the way, for many of our youth, while they did not know about this specific incident, they were already raised knowing way too much about safety and lack thereof on the basis of skin color.

What have you told your children? What dialogue are you engaged in that will hopefully continue not just for days, but for months to come? What is our role as parents regarding teaching children about racism, about disparity, about discrimination, about safety in society, and ultimately, about our ability or inability to keep our children safe? How much comfort do we offer and how much reality do we share with them and what is the mid-point? How is the discussion different based on our own skin tone, personal experience, affiliations, and background? What kinds of privilege do we have with which we need to be transparent when we engage in these talks with our kids? I cannot speak for anyone other than myself, but I can listen and be present for those who want/need to speak. I can be respectful and help parents when they have to share heartbreaking information with their young children.

I have a profound sense of sadness and a feeling of déjà vu from the days when I stayed up around the clock during the Los Angeles 1992 riots. The riots were terrifying and not surprising. I had a newborn who required feeding by eye dropper, around the clock, and that was the beginning of television coverage that went past midnight. It was horrifying, but not a shock, to see people put their collective sense of outrage into action.

There have obviously been many subsequent incidents of racism, both micro and macro, across our country, which are also terrifying, but not surprising. It is almost 30 years since Rodney King and the LA Riots, and it seems we have not made much progress regarding basic civil rights nor change regarding the inequities that impact our people. Is it irrational for there to be country wide outcries after we witnessed a police officer keep his knee on Mr. Floyd's neck and chest, despite Mr. Floyd being handcuffed and lying compliant on the street, clearly stating, "I can't breathe."? I think not.

"I can't breathe," Mr. Floyd said repeatedly, pleading for his mother and begging "please, please, please." For eight minutes and 46 seconds, police officer Mr. Chauvin kept his knee on Mr. Floyd's neck, the prosecutors' report says. About six minutes into that period, Mr. Floyd became non-responsive. In videos of the incident, this was when Mr. Floyd fell silent, as bystanders urged the officers to check his pulse. At 20:27, Mr. Chauvin removed his knee from Mr. Floyd's neck. Motionless, Mr. Floyd was rolled onto a gurney and taken to the Hennepin County Medical Center in an ambulance. He was pronounced dead around an hour later.

As a white woman of privilege, I cannot speak to anyone's experience with racism. I can, however, be outraged to have watched a murder take place in broad daylight, on the streets of Minneapolis, by a police officer. I can commit to work toward change, and I can stand beside those who are wronged and demeaned. So, given that we want to work to create a better world in which all of us can live, what can we do? The first step, of course, for white individuals, is to become clear about the basics of white privilege, what it is and how it works. The second step is to explore ways in which we can work against the racism for which white privilege is a cornerstone.

Have you seen this meme, going around social media? I am copying and reposting it and apologies for only including a tiny part of it:

I have privilege as a white person because I can do all of these things without thinking twice:

- *I can go jogging (#AhmaudArbery)*
- *I can ask for help after being in a car crash (#JonathanFerrell and #RenishaMcBride)*
- *I can go to church (#Charleston9)*
- *I can walk home with Skittles (#TrayvonMartin)*
- *I can read a book in my own car (#KeithScott)*
- *I can be a 10 year old walking with our grandfather (#CliffordGlover)*
- *I can run (#WalterScott)*
- *I can breathe (#EricGarner)*
- *I can live (#FreddieGray)*
- *I CAN BE ARRESTED WITHOUT THE FEAR OF BEING MURDERED (#GeorgeFloyd)*
- *#BlackLivesMatter* 🖤

And to think of another white person of privilege, one who was incredibly helpful during times of earlier protests in raising awareness and pointing out hypocrisy, we can look to find answers blowing around in the wind. **1963**

Bob Dylan, I wish this were true, and that by now, the wind would have educated us all. Until that time, however, we only have one another, to hold safe and raise up and support.

So, when our children ask us what is going on, let's tell them. Tell them, 'People judge others based on the color of their skin, which is not ok.' Tell them, 'In our family we expect you to be fair and kind and to get to know people who are different than we are and to share in their lives and celebrations and invite them to share in our lives and celebrations.' If you are raising children of privilege, point it out, because otherwise, it's 'just normal'—it is, as has been noted by academicians, like asking fish to know they are in water or expecting birds to know they can fly—it's their existence and they know of no other existence. As humans, however, and not birds or fish, we have the capacity to observe, reflect, and integrate information to change the lens through which we see the world. In raising all of our children, we must remind them to not sit idly by when they see acts of cruelty or witness the misuse of power.

We desperately need the next generation to make right where we have failed, and for us not to assume it's no longer our responsibility, but instead, to work in tandem with young leadership. Given their newly acquired skills in technology and their newly acquired sense of resiliency and forbearance, I have optimism that in partnership, they will lead the way for us. No individual should be publicly lynched, attacked, shot, murdered. Not on our watch. And not on the watch of our children.

Be safe. Be strong. Speak out. And empower your children to speak out. Speak truth to power, without violence, but with a loud, loud voice. Share your grief. Share your mourning. Share your outrage. Share your fear. Raise us up with your children's spiritual leadership and let us walk together and light a candle while we put our ears to the wind to see if there's an answer.

Zooming into Summer

Realizing…. We're Still Here

hatting with a friend last night, which is one of the perks of all this staying safe at home time, and we were comparing notes regarding all the virtual calls in which we are participating. She had great observations which I will share regarding 'Zoom' etiquette. Yes, there are books written on this topic in the business world, and many H.R. folk scrambling around developing policies and procedures for how to conduct oneself in cyber-meeting land, but most of those focus on the work from home (WFH) issues, and then the educators are focused on the so called 'distance learning' issues and no one seems to be addressing the issues of the ELECTRONIC PARTYING world.

For WFH meetings, of course, much as been made around the issue that while you CAN be on the call without your pants, it's best to put them on, nonetheless. (There is a hilarious video floating around where a call ends and the four colleagues believe it's all shut down, so one man gets up from his table and walks around his house, pant less, while his pals attempt to get his attention. I anticipate that soon there will be more of these videos circulating than lines at Trader Joes.)

For adults conducting business and teachers instilling wisdom, laws of the land include having one person able to mute all others ('the administrator or host') as well as managing the narrative, having an outline or curriculum to which all are adhering and reminding all participants to either close their video feed OR remove the beer bottles from the camera's eye. Another suggested rule is that colleagues/ students refrain from eating more in the 'distance meeting' than they would in a real meeting. A cup of coffee is ok—a margarita, not so much. Snack on something that is not crunchy, unless you are 100% certain you are muted, ok—steak and lobster dinner, not so much.

From the educator tips, columnist Mary Jo Madda notes that should teachers be having a hard time getting students' attention, they may consider visual changes, including 'shave your head—that will get them all focused on you.' It's hard enough to engage middle school aged kids (or any developmental stage child, for that matter) in 'figurative language, analogies, allusions' and 'slope intercept formula' when teaching in person, but once you take it to the pads and tablets, the task becomes almost Sisyphean.

What about conduct for the now very popular Virtual Parties? These are wonderful and innovative and are incredibly helpful in these times, but turns out, they too can benefit from some structure. It has been noted by adults and teens alike, that Zoom parties, like real life parties, can feel isolating and replete with ZPC…. ZOOM PARTY CLIQUES. Getting invited onto one of these calls is fun. However, it may seem like once there, there is no avoiding mean people or nice people who inadvertently exclude others. In fact, this has become a huge issue for our little zoom users, who are experiencing 'mean kids' on Zoom, which in real life, they had been able to avoid.

Good news though—because there IS a way to avoid this painful social drama which is harder when you're in real life—sign off!! If you find yourself in a party with anyone toxic, simply write a note in the chat section saying, 'So sorry, G2G, got to go, my chimpanzee just turned on the shower.' Then blow a silent kiss and shut it down. Yup, protect yourself. A great thing about this cyber land of connecting is that when it's not working for you, you can easily opt out. True for grownups and kids.

If you are hosting, you can also ensure less negativity.

1) Limit the number of invites and try to keep each gathering to one 'group' (i.e., don't mix your first cousins with your pre-school friends.)
2) Set a time limit and loosely adhere to it.
3) Consider a tiny bit of structure. Celebrating a birthday? Ask a few folks to make a toast. Hosting a reunion? Ask a few people to bring some old photos.

4) Share an activity. Have a person demonstrate a favorite recipe, dance choreography, guitar riff. Or make it a cocktail hour with grown-ups once the kids are asleep.

Bottom line—don't let a party become work! Virtual time together is not the same as in person time together, but it IS incredibly uplifting, fun, funny, and a perfect way to close our social distances, in these times.

Measuring Life

So, to re-cap....do not turn a party into work but DO try to allow your work to have some festivity and/creativity to it, albeit in the virtual world. And also, remember that great song from RENT— 525,600 minutes...how do you measure, measure a life?

Well—I have some suggestions of late. I am measuring it in loads of laundry (my large detergent bottle noted that it covers 160 loads— and it is almost empty- is that even possible on day #who knows?) I am measuring it in the decrease of vitamins in the vitamin container, because once these run out, I'm not sure I can get them, having yet to even ONCE master 'online ordering.' Sigh. I'm measuring in number of socks eaten by the dog, and no longer am I even attempting to wear matching pairs. And for sure, I'm measuring in the amount of bird food consumed, because despite (because of?) the rain, we are currently serving 525,620 birds daily.

Counting minutes, or even days, has its ups and downs. Most likely we should stop and focus on the day by day, as it's hard to remember the day of the week, let alone the date on the calendar. In these first days of April, I do wonder—is there such a thing as too much virtual celebrating? Passover—Easter- Ramadan—birthdays—anniversaries— quincenarios—sweet 16s—wedding showers...The online celebrations somehow make 'partying' feel more compacted and condensed than when we were back in the days of our real lives, in person, physically planning and participating in joyful events. Perhaps that's because in person, we limited ourselves in saying 'yes' to only so many invites, but in the cyber world, we figure, 'why the heck not?' and thus we attend more celebrations. It's both lovely and lonely as for some, scrolling through social media feeds and seeing that EVERYONE has screen shots of multiple person parties results in a sense of extreme sadness and pain and for some, being one of many tiny little squares on a Zoom screen feels more like life is a hologram than life is a cabaret my friend.

Times are tough. It's especially tough, of course, for those families in life/death situations. The rest of us are grappling with many fewer challenging things. For instance, on the non-life-threatening front, many things are quickly becoming 'toooo hard.' It's very onerous to keep up with the chores. Because do you know what happens after you wash the floor? An hour later your kids have spilled chocolate milk on it and your spouse has dripped wine on it and you tipped over the coffee, and it went into every crease and crevice in the hardwood in addition to specifically crawling under your built-in fridge that no one will ever move. And do you know what happens when you clean up the playroom? An hour later, the puppets are mixed in with the dolls and the Legos are spread out in no discernible pattern other than the one sure to result in stabbing the bottoms of your bare feet as you return to pick things up again.

On a plus note, let's remember another great song. By Crosby, Stills, Nash and Young, called "Teach Your Children." A fabulous, often overlooked, part of this song is that it's not only about the legacy we give in raising our children, but also about the role our children play in raising up us parents. This is particularly poignant in these times, when we rely on our kids to play IT techy teachers to us, when we need them to make it so the tv screen shows the Zoom feed and when we need them to translate texting letters into words (WFHWK—working from home with kids—has its advantages.)

As the mom and aunt of many young adult Millennial kids, I have been taught lots. And these 'kids' often express pride in my new-found skill set. The most recent influence was their encouraging me to 'drink a little.' Having given up alcohol AND coke zero over the past years, I had very few vices left. I gave them up due to sugar and chemical content, but honestly, I've never stopped missing them. My collective child mentorship group were very supportive when I opened a mini bottle of champagne located on the top shelf of the garage fridge, and when I not only drank it, but thoroughly enjoyed it. I sent a text. Or maybe a Snapchat. Or Instagram. For sure I did NOT make a TikTok dance, but after a few sips, I could have! Perhaps I posted it on WhatsApp and Facebook. Any which way, they were highly complementary and said, 'SEE—we told you—a little alcohol goes a long way towards peace of mind. Go for it!' Teach your parents indeed!

Slowing Down without Sinking Under

I have a cedar chest. My husband bought it for me up in a little shop on Main Street, in Ventura, in 1986. "We" were pregnant and anticipating the birth of our first child and we planned to fill that cedar chest, over the years, with memories and mementos.

In these times when we are suspended between paralysis and agitation, I have been thinking about cleaning it out. To pull off the many stacks of things living atop it for months (ok, who's kidding, years) and open it up and pull out the treasures, one by one. There are 33 years' worth of three children's art, poetry, and Mother's Day mugs.

Given all the time on my hands, you'd think I'd leap at the task. Instead, I sit and reflect. Typically, we move through our lives at an alarming pace, which is nothing compared to the alacrity with which our children pass through us. We expect immediate gratification and cannot wait or even recall the 'one-hour photo' shops as that is now waaaay too long a time period to wait. Our impatience is impressive, but only in that it cycles us to expect and demand and feel most comfortable with faster- faster-faster frenetic paces which lead us down the highway toward fatigue and internalized chaos.

We raise our children to anticipate and internalize the pace, and then we wonder why it is that they are addicted to Red Bull, Adderall, methamphetamine…. But what are we chasing? What's the rush? We used to wonder, when and how will we ever be able to slow down?

Hmmmmmmmmmmmmm. Guess what? Our time has come, and our time is now. It's harder than we'd think though, right? And we cannot/did not go from 120 mph to stopping still. It's amazing to see that currently, there, is no need to move faster than the speed of sound, and in fact, it's impossible. It takes a week to order groceries online if you are lucky, have a 'perfect zip code' and are up at 12:01 midnight. It takes a month to apply successfully for unemployment benefits if you are lucky and the site does not crash, and you are up at 12:01 midnight. It takes who knows how long for all of us to get over the pretty selfies we enjoyed posting and instead, embrace the truth of our images—we are not perfect specimens. Without all the enhancements, we look more and more like ourselves (or our mothers!) than ever before. We look 100% human. At some point we may find that refreshing and freeing.

Create a good, happy, positive moment. Capture it in your mind and feel it in your heart. Visualize it. Smell it. Hold it. Breathe in. Savor it. Breathe out. Ease your foot off the gas. Get down from 65 to perhaps 30 mph.

It may be the perfect time for me to go through the cedar chest, but so far, I'm still 'keeping busy.' I am not going 120 mph but I'm still around 65—fast enough for our empty freeways and safe enough to avoid a ticket (there are gazillion CHP officers on our roads right now, so beware.)

As Judith Viorst noted decades ago, some days are "Terrible, Horrible, No Good, Very Bad Days." Some days are like that. I guess the point for us in these times is to note that not every day is one of those. Some days are rainy and cozy book reading with a blanket. Some days are sunny and gardening and playing with the hose. Some days are family Zoom meetings where your young adult kids make fun of you (and then tweet about it, thinking you don't look at tweets, but—you do!) Every day gets to have its own chance and opportunity. So, let's allow for that.

Remember, there are terrible, horrible, no good, very bad days even in Australia, so we cannot avoid them. However, we can differentiate between them and the other days. We have wild canaries in our yard now every day. Is there a billboard somewhere directing them here? And the bees are returning, as are the hummingbirds. And the neighbors are almost all wearing masks and the dogs seem to know one another pretty well, with "wassup?" nods versus trying to break free to jump one another.

When it's time to unpack the chest, I will remember to do so carefully. Pull out the memories, re-arrange them, perhaps make space for some new ones. Take my time. Do it slowly, carefully. Maybe take a few photos and text them to the kids, living far from me, but close in my heart. Reflect on a life well lived (mine) and blessings provided (them.) There is a time (turn, turn, turn) to every purpose under heaven. Who knows what it is and what to name this particular time?

I think I'll call it Monday, for today, and then Tuesday, for the next day, and so on. And if and when I get confused, I'll take out the kindergarten calendar from the box and follow along with the days of the week.

Resisting Impulses

The time has come the walrus said....

Lewis Carroll had a great imagination and brought us *Alice's Adventures in Wonderland* among many others. He is quoted as saying (as Alice): "I can't go back to yesterday—because I was a different person then." Simple and true for us all. We can't go back. We are already different today.

One of my Carroll faves is the tale of the walrus and the carpenter, which actually, for those who know it, is a fairly grim/snarky long narrative poem about tricking oysters into becoming dinner. It all begins as follows:

"The time has come," the Walrus said: "To talk of many things. Of ships—and shoes—and sealing wax of cabbages—and kings."

So where are we in this time? What has the time come for?

For one thing...this is **NOT** the time to make any rash decisions. It may feeeel like 'the time has come,' but, trust me, in fact, this is not the time! For instance:

- Do *NOT* quit your job this month (unless you (1) have another lined up and/or (2) there is a safety reason for leaving.)
- Do *NOT* file for divorce this month (1) unless you have been planning on doing so for months/years and just did not have the time until now or (2) there is a safety reason for leaving.)
- Do *NOT* get pregnant (unless you (1) have had that in mind for a while but did not have the time until now or (2) you have some insider info as to how long this is going to last!)
- Do *NOT* decide to drop out of school this month....

- Do *NOT* break up with your 'BFF' this month....
- Do *NOT* send an aggressive letter to your boss or HR demanding they guarantee you will not be laid off this month....
- Do *NOT* impulse buy a new house/motorcycle/car this month....
- Do *NOT* send that naked photo to ANYONE....
- Do *NOT* booty call your ex............
- Do *NOT* order lots of alcohol online 'just in case'.............

I'm sure the 'time has come' for many things, but also, in these times, know our theme of the month: Impulse Control during Crises.

Thinking About Tomorrows

The world is getting smaller and smaller, literally, from the pandemic perspective, and literally, from the sharing of space to which we are adjusting. Some of us are adjusting better than others. Some are crawling back into the metaphoric womb, or mommy and papi's bed, or forming intense affection for our screens, experiencing separation anxiety when, well, we are apart. Others are finding little crawl spaces heretofore forgotten (the attic, garage, back of the minivan, side yard) in which to seek privacy and solace.

Our dog Ginger has taken over the front yard, where her dance card of play dates is full up and her private time is replete with lots of barking at any passersby. In our past, that was a few folks per day. In these times, it's a constant parade, so it keeps her very busy.

Some of us are developing important skills sure to help us in our next phases of life. Sure, it's a major loss for me to NOT be at any hotel conferences where I can collect free pens, but, on the other hand, I'm developing other abilities. For instance, with the help of my nephew Michael, I can make almost anything a background on my Zoom page, something to add to my resume for sure.

Additionally, my ability to make music and song 'playlists' is becoming impressive.

In fact, what is YOUR visual background for these times, and what is your musical soundtrack? Are you re-connecting with comfort photos and sounds, or are you taking time to explore and discover new things? (Japanese anime for anyone over 35?) I'm in the 'not quite nostalgia but almost' state. I'm not participating in the high school yearbook challenge, the first photo of spouse and self-contest, or the pet or toddler "see one post one." I enjoy voyeuristically observing others, but, thus far, I'm not a participant. That could change in a moment, however, based on levels of boredom…we shall see.

In terms of music, I am happy, happy, happy. I am reclaiming this first love and it fills up the well quite nicely. Somedays I choose a theme. My brother David passed away in Fall, 2018, way too young (in his 50s) and way too quickly (cardiac arrest.) He loved music of all kinds. I took him to his first concert (Fleetwood Mac at the Great Western Forum), and we sat in the top row, where we could actually touch the ceiling. In return, he spent decades playing guitar and singing with me and for me and with all his pals and for them all as well. He influenced his kids and my kids with his tastes. In his honor it's a day of Grateful Dead (early and late.) It's not a hard playlist to develop, and the sounds really do 'ripple.'

Indeed.

I know we are all wondering about 'when will this be over' and 'when will be get back to being normal.' Given we have no clear-cut answer to either, I recommend choosing a backdrop (Hawaii, perhaps?) and making a playlist (DANCE MUSIC) and attempting to keep your well as full up as possible.

Because it is true: No more free hotel pens. No more kids' concerts and musical theater. No more club soccer or park soccer or school soccer.

And it is also true: No more frenetic drives to get into the carpool line. No more 'did you leave your backpack at school again?!' No more 'wait until your dad/mom gets home!' No more 'I will pick you up late at karate because I have to get your sister at her piano lessons and your brother at the Model United Nations first.' No more hour commute from home to work on a good day. No more competing about which is worse, the 405 or the 101. No more 'we just don't have time for bike riding—or roller blading—or picking up trash in the yard.'

In honor of my brother David—hum a little about a fountain, perhaps, not made by the hands of human. And about where all our flowers have gone. And about the one tin soldier who rode away. Or just hum any ole melody that pops up for you.

Good Enough Parenting

Here is a great meme I saw this week (thanks Dr. Lisa Shadburn for posting):

Parents don't stress about schoolwork in September. I will get your children back on track. I am a teacher and that is my superpower. What I can't fix is socio-emotional trauma that prevents the brain from learning. So right now, I just need you to share your calm, share your strength and share your laughter with your children. No kids are ahead. No kids are behind. Your children are exactly where they need to be. With love, all teachers on the planet Earth.

It is so stressful to be a parent under 'regular' circumstances. There are so many tasks that go into parenting: nurturing, providing resources, being available and accessible, providing safety and advocacy, taking care of your own needs, meeting basic needs of each individual child, meeting sense of self developmental needs, discipline and providing a foundation for cultural/spiritual development, and education. No one parent can fulfill all these to perfection, we can only be 'good enough' parents.

Of late, however, we have become super focused on our role in the task of educating our children. For good reason, obviously, when your den/kitchen/living room/ bedroom alcove becomes a classroom, and your tablet/computer/telephone becomes a 'white board.' And we do what we as parents do best—WORRY. We worry our children are 'falling behind.' We worry that each of them has ADHD (they do not) and that each of them has zero capacity for learning (they do not.) We are sure they are bored or overly challenged and who they are failing everything, which, in parent speak, means WE are failing in our jobs as parents.

As noted by this anonymous public service announcement seen on Facebook, it's not true.

Your children will be fine academically. They will learn what they need to by the time they need to. It's true they may not master the finer points of geometry this month, but their geography skills, as they follow the maps of this pandemic, are going to be stellar. They may not master cursive skills, but their touch-typing skills and texting skills are impressive. They may not ace science, but they are making tremendous progress regarding application of technology and may just be motivated to learn coding and/or engineering sooner than later. Additionally, they have learned a whole new vocabulary, even though it was not on the 2nd grade list (pandemic, social distancing, false negative, briefing, alerts, quarantine, virus, antibodies, closures, shelter in place, flatten the curve, co-morbidity, etc.)

While there IS a such a thing as a 'permanent record' in school, there is NOT such a thing as our permanent records really being 'permanent' and following you around the rest of our lives. Have you recently been asked your Middle School GPA? Your class ranking in 4th grade? Your SAT or ACT score? How many AP courses you took? We all managed to get to wherever we are today, even though it's just possible we MAY have failed a final, bombed an SAT, messed up credits toward graduation. There are thousands of colleges in the U.S. for those college bound, and other than those 'for profit' institutions who take money and do not provide learning opportunities, the rest all have something to offer someone. It's okay. It's truly okay.

Our main job as parents right now, is to provide love, nurturance, support, structure, humor, whimsy and security. Our children are learning things all the time, every day, from you. They may also be mastering various academics, or not. But they will be okay. We will all be okay. It may look different today than last month, and different next month than this month. But we will all be okay.

Hug your kids—because we can't hug our friends or neighbors anymore. Celebrate one another. Mark little milestones (Can someone ride the two-wheeler now?) Watch your children grow and your garden (Did the tomatoes start growing? Are your roses in bloom?)

Teach kindness because that will always be useful. Teach appreciation and gratitude because they will be useful as well. Spelling tests will come and go (and we will use spell check and tracking and review.) Math tests will come and go (and we will use phones instead of calculators which replaced slide rules.) History is not going anywhere, by definition, so if they cannot memorize dates this year, they will do it another year.

Your children are exactly where they need to be. And so are you.

Moments in Time

As noted, we are all where we are, and that is where we are supposed to be, for this exact moment in time.

And, have you heard, the animals are taking back their rightful spots, be those in the meadows of Yosemite (per the L.A. Times, "bears have quadrupled,") the canals of Venice ("dolphins are seen for the first time in over 60 years") and the streets of Japan (where the sika deer are freely roaming?) What are they thinking? "Thank goodness those loud people and stinky cars are gone!" or "Where have all the people gone, long time passing?"

Headlines in print news (does anyone other than me still subscribe to newspapers that are delivered every morn?) and on social media sites declare "Animals are Re-Wilding Our Cities," "Animals Roam while Humans Shelter in Place" and "Nature abhors a vacuum." (I'm not sure I totally understand the last one—but I know I have been searching online high and low for a good vacuum….)

We are all, I think, strangers in a strange land—on our best days it may not feel that way, and on our worst, it feels that way x10. And in these times, the land that is strange to us, is starting to feel familiar again, to the animals. If we have learned nothing else, we are definitely learning It's not a race—our love can *seem slow*—but let's let it shine… we want it for the long term and we have lots of time for it in this short term.

We are meeting and knowing one another for the love we share today. The friends we have—the community we build—the people we meet and add to our collection. Day by day we are realizing that in this strange world, it is not our accomplishments defining us. It's not our weight, our income, our zip code. It's not our GPA, SAT, college acceptance letters. We are known, and becoming more known, for our kindness, laugh, and sense of shared adventure on an unknown ride.

We are for sure known for the friends we have, and the relationships we develop and the lives we impact. And thanks to our technology, we are connecting, literally, across the continents and around the globe.

Thank you all for creating that place, that space, even if that was not on our vision board.

It's also pertinent to keep perspective. Some of us are living with aggravations and some are living with life-threatening illness. Some are living with annoyances, and some are living with hunger. All are living with uncertainty.

And so, it goes with our lives. See the orcas take back Puget Sound. Watch the squirrels own the streets. Beware of the coyotes (primarily on Next-door App.) Take it all in.

'Love is like the galaxy—seems slow but it sure does shine'. Sure, does shine.

Lowering Our Expectations

Dr. Mona Delahooke is a clinical psychologist and author of many books, including *Social and Emotional Development in Early Intervention* and *Beyond Behaviors*, describing behaviors as the tip of the iceberg, important skills that we should address by seeking to understand a child's individual differences in the context of relational safety. To loosely quote her, she says "Currently, parents' expectations of their children far exceed their capacity to reach those expectations."

I have observed this to be true as well. I'm not sure what it is— we have more time to observe our children, for one thing. We are not necessarily education experts who know how children learn and how much they can take in and process in a given context. We are nervous about them 'falling behind' and 'not being able to recover.' And we are spending more time with them since their infancies. This combination, in addition to our shared free-floating anxiety, seems to translate into us earnestly believing our offspring should be 'first trial learners,' acquiring information on the first time it is presented, retaining it, and mastering it immediately. Our concept of how they SHOULD be functioning versus having empathy for how they ARE functioning is hard on them, and hard on us. It sets up a scenario whereby day's end, we believe we have all failed.

Internalizing a sense of failure day after day is obviously not healthy for any of us.

Combine this trend with another regarding 'loneliness.' The U.S. only recently started studying loneliness in children, but the data, PRE Covid-19, is alarming. In 2018 a major research project found that 11.3% of children 10-15 years said they were 'often lonely' and 9.8% of teens (16-24 years) said the same. 19.5% of children living in a city versus 5% living in a town or rural areas indicated they often feel lonely. The respondents in the study differentiated between 'being alone' and 'feeling lonely.'

In a time when we are all living in some form of isolation, it's especially pertinent to ensure we can connect with those with whom we share space. It seems 'obvious' but it's not. Scrutiny, criticism, judgmentalism on top of sheltering in place result in a sense of disappointment, sadness, anger, and loneliness.

In these times, cut yourself some slack, and cut your kids some slack. Yes, there is learning to be done and schoolwork to complete, but perhaps prioritize process and not product. In other words, mastery includes getting up and getting started, keeping some sort of organizational system in place, but not military precision. You are doing fine. Catch yourself being good. Your kids are doing fine. Catch them being good.

Lower your expectations regarding what is to be accomplished each day. Because the accomplishment, it turns out, is making it through each day, and sometimes, making it through each moment.

Making New Friends, Keeping the Old

Funny, the relationships we make along the way. This is a great time to rid ourselves of any 'toxic' people in our lives and to embrace those who are positive and loving. Make new friends and keep the old. And discard the mean and toxic ones. This is a very good time for that kind of intention. Look around. Embrace the good, let go of the bad.

Middle Schoolers are very busy with middle school drama. Lots of 'getting together' as well as 'breaking up' over the past few weeks. It's a good opportunity to play dress up and try on new friendships and relationships in a 'less risky' manner than while in person with one another in a school setting. However, young broken hearts take time to mend, even in the land of Zoom 'dating.' It's also a good time to experiment with identity and sexual orientation, given all the romance is in cyber land. Lots of discussions parents were not expecting—'Mom, two things—(1) I am pansexual and (2) Can you find the old Legos because I want to play with them.' Not time for parents to be derisive or dismissive, just good listeners.

Many High Schoolers, on the other hand, are managing social lives fairly well. They are mostly vampires these days, online in the night, sleeping in the day (when their parents give up attempting to rouse them before noon) and enjoying lots of social 'connections' from the safety of their beds. They have this down. Less 'hooking up' than you'd expect. More commiserating about oppression conditions in houses with siblings and adults under one roof for weeks on end, with no end actually in sight.

In addition to taking our temperatures in order to enter Trader Joes, I recommend you take your emotional temperature a few times a day and/or, take your kids'. Get a read on how everyone is doing. We have our ups and downs. This does not mean we have bipolar disorder, although some of us do. It does not mean we are clinically depressed or anxious, although some of us are. It means we are humans living through history and not happy to be totally powerless. Figure out where your children are regarding these kinds of fevers and respect their needs for privacy and anticipate when a good night is for charades. Better yet, your family versus your sister's family so cousins and relatives can 'see each other' and share some laughs.

In these times, I too am reviewing my 'contact lists.' I notice that my newest and closest friends include the online 'folk.' In particular, I reference here my sweet ties with *See's Candies*. Yes, we are on an 'email every few hours' basis, and I could not be prouder. This is a sustainable committed relationship for sure.

My relationship with See's goes way back, to childhood, where all festive events included See's. We are a family fond of scotch mallows (me) and Bordeauxs (most of the rest of my family of origin) and almost all varieties of See's (except truffles—no truffles for sure.) We rely on these treats not only for celebrating good times, but also, as companions in hospital waiting rooms and at funeral gatherings. They have been there for us. We ship them cross country to loved ones and carry their special lollipops in purses and backpacks. They are our go-to gifts for holidays, loved ones, and colleagues. Not to mention our go-to for a 'little something sweet' at midnight. Just sayin....

You can imagine how upsetting it was, therefore, when on day #11 of Shelter in Place, I received a personal note (okay, mass email letter) from the company stating they were not only shutting down the brick-and-mortar stores, they also were HALTING PRODUCTION. I was touched, of course, that they reached out to me. But also dismayed and astonished. I heard through back channels (Next Door app pals) that Oriental Trading Company would be carrying stock from their warehouses, so I quickly went online to make some totally pertinent purchases, to store in the house and freezer, 'just in cases.' I was thrilled to buy four boxes before the dreaded "OUT OF STOCK" sign flashed. Success.

Today I received a notice that they are BACK IN BUSINESS. Yay. That has got be a good sign, right? And honestly, I have zero need to buy more chocolates. All I needed was to know that I COULD, if I WANTED to.

Sometimes what we need is KNOWING we have choices, even if we do not exercise our right to participate in the choices. I like living in Los Angeles and knowing I COULD go to the opera, or one of many museums, or any number of clubs. I do not really DO any of those things, but I love the diversity of opportunity afforded me in this city of angels. When not staying safe at home, we have access to concerts across the musical continuum, sporting events of all kinds, snowy mountains for skiing and acres and acres of beaches.

Note: Don't hate on happies and for sure support the sads. Meantime, ☏ Your candy is calling order and pick up at select shops!

Radically Accepting

What's our main goal as parents? Yes, of course, to produce Ivy League wealthy gorgeous happy adults without a care in the world—but—really? What's your main vision for them as young adults? Picture your child at 22, 35, 56.... who are they in the world? And who are they relative to their relationships with you?

If we think about it, one objective, conscious or otherwise, is to establish a relationship with our children that is strong and sustainable across our lifespan. We'd like to know that during any of the aforementioned ages and stages, we are still 'a first call' on a best day and on a worst day. On a "Terrible, Horrible, No Good Very Bad Day" we hope to hear from them. On a day they are dumped by their girl/boyfriend. On a day they mess up. On a day they fail something or are fired from something.

Of course, we also hope to be called on the day they are excited about their school project/thesis/dissertation/Boards. We hope to hear directly when they realize they've 'found THE one.' We hope they introduce us to their friends and let us into the window of their lives on some days, and perhaps into the window of their souls on others. We do not want to guests or visitors in their lives, but rather, we'd like to be perceived as permanent, loving responders.

We also of course hope they have resiliency and grit and determination and that they can weather tough times and adapt to challenging situations. This pandemic will certainly serve as a foundation for them going forward.

In these times, it's hard to hold on to any big picture. Our perceptions keep playing tricks on us. It "SEEMS" like we are just about done with this and ready to walk the planet without a care in the world, and yet, if you follow the science, and not the politicians and relatives, we are not quite there yet. Not there yet at all.

This time is divisive because some of us are sheltering in place and being labeled neurotic church ladies, and others are walking about freely and being labeled as anarchists. Probably we are fall somewhere in the middle of that continuum, doing our best to navigate what feels safe and sound for us and our loved ones. Although it's easy, it's not particularly helpful to judge our neighbors, unless they are directly in your line of sight, in which case, cross the street.

The basic idea is to use Radical Acceptance, a term from a therapy model known as dialectical behavioral therapy. "Radical acceptance" means completely and totally accepting something from the depths of your soul, with your heart and your mind. Psychologists note the following steps toward practicing radical acceptance:

1) Notice that you are fighting reality. The first step towards radical acceptance is awareness that you are resisting reality. The next step is to let go and stop fighting it.
2) Turn your mind towards acceptance. Once you've recognized that you are resisting some truth in your life, the next step is to turn your mind toward acceptance.
3) Use your body to help you. Relaxing your muscles and unclenching your fists and loosening your jaw. Hum. A lot. It's a quick and useful little intervention.
4) Act as if. As if it's going to all be okay and that this will pass. Avoid judgment. Of self and of others.
5) FIND THE GOOD.

We are all getting tired of this reality and would love a new one, sooner than later.

As parents we realize, more and more, that we have little control over our children's lives. We cannot get them to walk faster by exercising little legs at six months and we can't get them to fulfill our dreams by insisting they apply to certain colleges we love. We can accept that we are here with them, and we can focus on enhancing our relationship with them while we have all this free time. Take a walk, one: one. Stay up late and learn the new video game. Ask if you can be in on a few minutes of their virtual playdate to say hi to their pals. Bake their favorite food, with them. Pay attention to what uniquely makes each of them, each of them. What makes them laugh. What makes them sad. You can't fix their lives. You can accept them, and yourselves, for where we are right now.

In These Times.... we need one another more than ever. And clearly, we can start/continue building relationships from home. We've got a lotta time together. Make a strong connection with your roommates—your kids.

Going Down to the River, or Lake, or Ocean, or Tub…

I miss water. Bodies of water other than my tub, that is. Do what is do-able, I think.

I miss a swimming pool, which I gave up five years ago when we 'down sized' and left the big house with the big yard and the perfect pool.

I miss the Merced River, and despite following Yosemite on multiple nature web cams and social media pages, it's not the same. I'm holding out for the fantasy that we really CAN go to the cabin we rented for 4th of July, as planned a year ago, but…it's so 'iffy.'

There are all the songs of the Beach Boys and even the Beatles sang about water and octopuses. Jack Johnson captured it: When this work is done, and this coat is dry…when this world is too much, it will be only the ocean and me. Do what is doable, I ponder.

So, I decided, why not? The beaches are 'open.' Why not go for a dip? Or even a swim? Many questions arose. Do we have to wear masks in the water? And if so, will that not contribute to a very quick swim and an early drowning? Which is of greater risk? Potential virus in the water or my purple gloves filling up with water and being impossible to get off later? Are there lifeguards out and about (no) or just police and sheriffs wandering the sand (yes.)

Not typically a risk taker, all this sheltering has made me a little more antsy than usual.

So—down to the water. Ventura Beach to be specific. Do this.

Looks like it's summertime in the city of Ventura albeit Spring in real life (which, given the L.A. Heat Wave, is not far from the truth, if not exactly accurate per our calendars.) There are tons of people out and about on this beach on a weekday afternoon. No masks in sight. I know their numbers are low but, am I safe to discard mine? No gloves to be seen. LOTS and lots of signs—no sitting or loitering or sunbathing...no picnicking or visiting with pals.... Also, notably, no signs saying, 'no alcohol' and I did witness many people 'exercising' with open beer bottles from local breweries—supporting local businesses for sure. Nowhere did it say no swimming, however, so I figured I was safe.

Amazing. Exhilarating. Perhaps even spiritually uplifting. I kid you not. Cold water. Beautiful view of surfers, local islands AND blue skies. And one oldish woman, with gray hair and hanging skin, floating on her back, looking up at the fluffy floating clouds, taking in the cacophony of sounds of the local wildlife—seagulls, dolphins, pelicans, and children laughing—and feeling restored.

I recommend a swim to any of you, in any means possible. Take a shower or a bath. Play in the sprinklers or the hose. Wash the cars and patio furniture with sudsy bubbly water. Or better yet, take advantage of why we live in California and head to the beach. Bring your children. Bring your partners. Where possible, bring your dogs. Wade in or dive in or jump in the waves at the shore. You can find shells, rocks, sand crabs in addition to reunited with that version of yourself you'd lost along the way.

Coloring Your Heart

I 've been doing a little exercise with some of my patients (kids and teens.) I've been having them draw a heart and then identify the top five feelings they are currently experiencing. They then match a color to the emotion and color in the heart proportionally. How much of the heart is now 'black' for 'mad?' How much of the heart is 'green' for nervous?" This is an old-time exercise, but in these times, the results are disturbing ('ruby red' for 'disturbing.')

I throw in another exercise or two depending on the needs of the specific child or adolescent.

In this one, I have them visualize the red balloon from the French story *The Red Balloon* or Winnie the Pooh's balloon from his blustery day. I let them know that the balloon comes to their house and offers to take them for a guaranteed safe trip, to wherever they want to go.

So—there's a balloon awaiting you. Where do you want to go? Where does the balloon take you? How do you feel up there? What do you observe below? Is it a blustery day? Cool? Chilly? Hot? Is the sky blue? Are there pretty clouds? Can you see forever? Or to the beach? Or to the desert? Or to your grandma's house, who you have not been able to hug or see in forever? This is your balloon ride so you can magically request it to take you wherever you'd like. Family in another country? No problem. Your school? Your summer camp you still are desperately hoping will open— even though you know it's a long shot....? The college you are supposed to start next year. Where will you go?

Again, this is not a new exercise but the results...the stories 'my kids' are telling are, well, disturbing.

We are in week #49 or #92, depending on what you and your family chose to count and while there are many reports of us 'returning to normal' there is no internalized, collective sense, that we can safely return to anything. There is a huge DESIRE to turn back time, for sure, but many of us seem to be moving from anxious to depressed.

Family members who are acting out and angry, in fact, may be 'healthier' than those who are internalizing the anger and becoming increasingly sad, listless, fatigued. The new rules that are starting tomorrow are mostly plans not revolved around meeting our kids' needs. Beaches will open but you cannot sit and schmooze or visit. Can you build sandcastles? Can you bury your little sister in the sand? Can you find a nice person walking up and down selling snow cones?

And what about parents, who themselves are overwhelmed and undercooked—not enough of anything of late—not enough financial security, not enough privacy, not enough fun, not enough distraction....

Everyone needs to master something or work toward mastering something, every day, across our lifespans. That means that in these times, many parents, in particular, are not experiencing a sense of mastery. They feel they are 'not good enough.' Not good enough teachers, not good enough workers, not good enough parents. Even with the focus on 'lowering the bar', they experience their children's angst as proof they are not doing their jobs well. Every child who acts out, who melts down, who can't sleep, who is failing geometry—their moms and dads internalize that as a sign they are failing as moms and dads.

As plans are made and summer is upon us, this is a good time to find some new crayons for coloring in our hearts. Let's mix it up. Let's cut all parents some slack, whatever that really is. Lots and lots of slack to anyone at home with kids, of any age.

Everyone gets to have their meltdowns, which will continue, as the heat and temperatures rise and the sheltering in place continues. There will be no one miraculous moment, like when the bell rings the last period the last day of school and everyone rushes out to freedom. This is not that.

This is a time to push the positive voices in our head forward, and to force them to drown out the negative ones, when possible. And when impossible, it's a fine time to find a little corner nook and have your own time out and your own weepy moments.

That is not a failure moment. That is a parenting moment. And lots of those moments together will weave the tapestry going forward. This will pass at some point. We will weather other crises. Your children will recall being cared for and will internalize that sense of being loved and valued. People live through horrible things and survive, and experience hearts full of love, friendship, curiosity, wonder, imagination. I promise.

You may not feel you are mastering every aspect of this, but I can tell you—you are.

In and Outing

Life in the nest. Feeling smaller and smaller. More and more confined. From sweet cozy spot to overcrowded falling apart at the seams site. We are purportedly coming toward some changes, so let's help everyone survive until then. Grownups—focus—kids are ALMOST done with the school year. Do NOT overwhelm them now with tasks outside 'finish the semester/term.' No studying for SAT and ACT. No practicing for the Olympics games. No new diet, exercise regime, required hour a day Facetiming with grandma. Let's just help them get it done. (We'll likely have a long summer for all those other tasks—don't worry—time is still going to be available to us, even in the next phase!)

It's likely good that we are headed to transitioning—not sure to where—but—the times, they are a changing….be patient, be practical, be mindful…

Which makes me wonder, speaking of changes—who was on the committee to choose what opens first? What was that process? It seems like the list publicized is somewhat bizarre and includes a list of fairly obscure establishments in our area.

Bookstores?!! How many bookstores do we even have left? Is that what we're clamoring for? Toy stores?!? Since the demise of Toys R, Us, I'd bet we have fewer toy stores than bookstores. (I'm surprised they did not include "Jewelry stores carrying only items over $500,000" and perhaps "Pet stores illegally selling tiger cubs rescued from Joe Exotic/ Tiger King." How did those not make the cut?)

I am not a scientist and cannot offer an opinion on our next steps. I can tell you that the patients I see are having a harder and harder time, and their parents are at the brink of snapping or cracking or popping—and not from making their 19th batch of Rice Krispy treats shaped as the virus. I'm not sure being able to pick up shorts curbside at Old Navy will help them. I'm also pretty sure that increasing risk for additional cases and potentially higher numbers of death won't help anyone either.

I think the re-opening of trails and beaches is a great idea and I'd recommend that every Angeleno get out of the house. Golf courses, meh.

Back to my mini rant. MUSIC STORES?!?! Really!? Is this pertinent or helpful to anyone other than our locals like Jackson Browne, Dawes, or the Jonas Brothers? And car dealerships and showrooms? Are we expecting a rush of people purchasing new vehicles right now?!?! Truly?

I've polled my family and pals to see what they'd like opened and here is their list IF these things can be classified into the same riskiness as the aforementioned approved sites. The top there are: dog groomers, day care centers, doggy day care centers. The next top three are hair salons, barbershops, and nail salons. Of course, bars are in their own category, despite the entrepreneurs who have started all the mobile alcohol enterprises (ice cream truck + Jimmy Buffet's Margaritaville.... yummmmmmmm.)

I've also polled 'my kids/patients.' The littles want to see grandma and have a hug from their teacher and have playdates with friends. The middles want to be able to hang out without grownups around, scrolling through their social media and saying, 'can you believe that s/he said that?!' The teens want to not have any more projects, essays, tests, APs, finals, or poems they are required to memorize. They are tired of 'make a video tape of you teaching us how to bake, in Spanish, or French, or Japanese, and then play it on our Zoom call next week.' And EVERYONE wants some privacy. Lots and lots of privacy.

Phase Two—here we go. Keep your seat belts buckled. We have a long way to go, and traffic is gonna be back before you know it.

Parent Planning

What's your plan? Your big picture parenting plan? I realize most 'little picture plans' have disappeared and been abandoned. But what's the overall context going forward? As Robert Burns said (and Steinbeck re-iterated:) "The best laid plans of mice and men, often go awry."

We are so far 'awry' at this point, I wonder again, what are your plans?

Have you considered that other old saying: 'Man plans, and God laughs.'

One dad told me this week: "The plan is for our kids to look back at some point and say, 'Wow, we really had fun at home with Mommy and Daddy when we all stayed home.'"

A mom said, "My basic plan is making it until the school year ends, and then really REALLY spend time doing nothing." I know you think we are not doing much, but this has been incredibly hectic to raise four children while crisis/home schooling them with two working parents."

Planning is like story telling—we need a beginning, middle, and end. That's one reason we can't do it right now. We only have the beginning and middle, with no clear end in sight. So how can we tell our stories? We just have to live them right now.

A dad said today, "We are less concerned about homework practice sheets and more concerned that the kids learn to get along with each other. Fewer formulas, more forts. Less lectures, more Legos"

Summer camps are being cancelled and/or switched to online (which seems an oxymoron—*virtual camp* is like *bittersweet*—two things that do not go well together.) Working parents are scrambling to figure out what in goodness's sake to do. Teens are angry and mourning 'the only hope I had of breaking out of this house.'

I know some parents hiring college kids now, to come to their houses a few hours a day and play with the kids. Some families are looking into the Belgium plan of 'joining bubbles'—where you choose four individuals, and they choose you and you all agree to be a part of the Venn diagram and to continue sheltering in place while expanding the home nest. (This is already causing relationships problems in Europe—it's like little kids on the playground—'Cut that out or I won't let you be in my bubble or come to my birthday party.' And 'I hear you are inviting your sister-in-law into the bubble but not your sister, for real?!')

People are going back to basics and more sour dough bread is being home baked now than during Little House on the Prairie days.

Many families are now avidly following animals (online)—National Geographic and webcams of baby eagles being raised and bears frolicking in the woods. You know who needs more attention? The reptile CHAMELEON. Lots to learn from those little guys. Adapt. Change. While also staying true to yourself. How do they do it?

Our joyful planning ahead, in these times, needs to be both limited, thoughtful, and huge, all at the same time. One day at a time planning. Harm reduction analysis for meeting your family's needs. And seeing the forest and the trees at the same time.

For the day: plan to be happy and kind.

For harm reduction: plan to be careful and conscientious.

For the forest: plan to raise yourself and your family up with gratitude and a sense of connection and attachment to the human race.

Life is definitely willy nillying all over the place.

Dreaming

Imaging, all of people together, sharing a dream or two.
Imagination is the ability to produce and simulate novel objects: people and ideas in the mind without any immediate input of the senses. It all starts in infancy (or maybe in the womb) and can include dreams, thoughts, and wonder. All it requires is 'time, doing nothing.' It happens when you leave the baby in the crib in the morning and can hear him or her cooing and babbling and later, looking up and reaching for the mobile overhead. It happens when the toddler is sitting with dolls and trucks and s/he starts making a story out of them, moving them here or there, giving words to their actions.

Storytelling is a major part of imagination. Thinking is too, as is contemplation and dreaming. Drama, acting, painting, art of any kind—it is an internal process that sometimes has an external presence and sometimes does not. Our authors engage in lots of it, as do our musicians and artists and our engineers of all kinds.

Although we have TONS of 'free time' these days, in some ways, we are still scheduling ourselves (to keep sane) and still keeping our kids 'busy' (to keep sane.) And now, summertime when we put on our shorts and flip flops and make Hawaii our backdrop on Zoom work calls.

We have been good about so many things—cooking and baking with kids, gardening with kids, walking and biking with kids. We have implemented game nights (in person and on the world wide web) and have been practicing loving acts of kindness—helping neighbors, painting rocks and distributing them, playing concerts for grandma.

What we have surprisingly lost, however, is the art of imagination and wonder. So, as summer takes over, let's remember to PRETEND. Let's set up some leisure time where children take the lead, and where it is unstructured and screenless. It seems contradictory to *schedule leisure*; especially given how much time we've been in our houses but.... it must be done! Trust me!

Imaginative play is when we are role playing and are acting out various experiences we may have had or something that is of some interest to us that we have never personally experienced. When children do it, they are experimenting with decision making on how to behave and are also practicing their social skills. Social development. When children engage in pretend play, they're actively experimenting with the social roles of life. Sometimes they are babbling and sometimes they are coherent. They are emoting—putting their feelings out into the world, without necessarily labeling the feelings and affect.

When our children engage in pretend (or dramatic) play, they actively experiment with the social and emotional roles of life. ... When they pretend to be different characters, they have the experience of "walking in someone else's shoes," which helps teach the important skill of empathy. It's great for them to be bored first, as it leads to creativity, time after time.

The ability to imagine things pervades our entire existence. It influences everything we do, think about, and create. It leads to elaborate theories, dreams, and inventions in any profession from the realms of academia to engineering and the arts.

Let's think about leisure in a few ways, and ensure we have it for ourselves, for our children as a unit, for us as couples, and for each child. We need to set it up—find the time, mark it, and put it aside, and then establish the space. For younger children, be sure to rotate access to various props—stuffed animals, blocks, vehicles, puppets, arts, and crafts materials they can use on their own, etc. For older children, include Legos and other more sophisticated building materials, as well as 'younger kid' stuff like the aforementioned puppets. For teens, access to supplies for making videos, writing songs, making mash ups of songs and movies—electronics, jewelry making, mask making....

So, let's get a huge poster board or white board and title it MY BIG IDEAS—and have each family member jot down one big idea per day (or week.) And then talk about them. They should be HUGE ideas. That generate creative conversations and questions. My first one is: All freshmen not able to move into their dorms and take classes in person come Fall 2020 should be offered the option of a YEAR OF SOCIAL SERVICE.... I'm happy to help organize it. I just need someone 'high up' to drop by my house and look at my big board of big ideas.

What's your idea? What about your child's?

A child in my life said her big idea is SWIMMING POOLS FOR EVERY YARD—they could be little blow-up ones, or hot tubs that are used as pools, or big in ground pools—but every house needs one this summer. Another told me, "My big idea is for us to really take the homeless off the streets near our underpasses (in the valley) and house them in the hotels, which are mostly empty. And make sure they can stay there a long time because just a few weeks won't help them." This from an 11-year-old.

Yup, let's use our imaginations and play and pretend and wander through the wonder.

Just Breathing

A year ago, I was spending one month in South Africa. I enjoyed time with my husband and colleagues who were/are working with locals to address disparities in health services and to decrease alcoholism and to treat and prevent HIV/AIDs. I visited with my favorite ostrich, the one with the broken wing, who lives in the wild down by the Cape of Good Hope. I spent time with leopards, multiple varieties of monkeys, and a large Southern Right Whale. Toward the end of the trip, I was gifted with a week with my youngest, who was returning from his summer in Zambia where he was studying malaria interventions for children. All in all, an amazing, privileged time.

Toward the end of the visit my son suggested we go online and book a cabin in Yosemite for the following year—for July 2020. He said we could celebrate my 60ieth birthday there, in a place we've been visiting for decades. We set it all up, from Africa. The plan was for my little group to gather—two sons, one daughter, one daughter in law, one boyfriend, one girlfriend, myself and my husband and his BFF, our dog Ginger. We would spend the week of July 4th together. Over the next few months airplane tickets were purchased and planning commenced. (Fly to San Francisco? LAX? Fresno? How many rental cars? Bring bikes? Who has the water shoes? Rafts?)

Then the world turned upside down, with COVID-19, and then inside out, with significant unrest due to a nationally witnessed cold-blooded murder. Yosemite was officially shut down for visitors on Friday, March 20. I checked websites and Facebook pages and listservs obsessively, hoping against hope that to meet my personal needs, the park would reopen. And, low and behold, we got the news– Yosemite is back in (limited) business and if you have your reservation already, you are granted access. I called to confirm, and the answer was 'yes, come on in—there may be some restrictions, but, come on in.'

If you've never been to Yosemite (book your trip for summer 2025 now!) it's hard to explain the magic. It is different than any other spot on the planet—not the same as other national park experiences or visiting polar bears in Churchill or seeing animals in the wild in multiple countries in Africa or time in Alaska in the wilderness. It is, as our daughter said at age three, 'the place where God lives.' Driving in, opening the car windows, there is a scent that is 100% Yosemite. I've never been sure what it is—some describe it as 'wild strawberries fused with soothing mists of mountain rain' but the more practical note that *Forest Floor, Tree Tops, Bark, Mountain Air, Fir Balsam, Juniper, Moss, Dried Herbs, and Cedar Tips,* are all present in Yosemite and combined, they create the unique smell. Whatever it is, it defies definition, and combined with the breeze, which is also impossible to adequately describe, caravanning up to Wawona, 'our spot,' has immediate impact. Therefore, you can imagine, that visiting, hiking, walking, biking, swimming in the river, eating on the patio, sitting on the porch, star gazing with the bats, seeing the local animals, climbing the waterfalls—it is an experience for all five senses. And when you can do it with your children, who live busy lives away from you, it has the added benefit of the extra sense—the 'fill mama's heart with joy' sense.

So needless to say, I was ecstatic.

And then more information came my way.

I had sprung into action and spent a day calling around trying to find anyone who would give me the decision I wanted. Turns out, no. For instance, shockingly, my cardiologist and the infectious disease specialists at UCLA...they seemed very firm on this topic. "STAY HOME." People said things like 'you can go next year' and 'it is not worth it to jeopardize your health for a visit' and all kinds of other things. And in my head, I'm sure they are correct. Explaining this to my heart though, that's another matter entirely.

I'm working on perspective. In the past months I've listened to many voices expressing outrage and grief, fear, and anger. Patients, friends, strangers. I've seen the viral images—of the three year old girl asking the police officer if he is going to shoot her because she is outside walking—of the African American dad, living not far from my neighborhood, who explained he can only walk around the block if he takes his daughter with him, so he will not 'appear suspicious' to his (mostly white) neighbors—of all the black moms represented beautifully by Atlanta's Mayor, Keisha Lance Bottoms, who noted "Above everything else, I am a mother. I am a mother to four black children in America, one of whom is 18 years old. And when I saw the murder of George Floyd, I hurt like a mother would hurt. And yesterday, when I heard there were rumors about violent protests in Atlanta, I did what a mother would do. I called my son, and I said, 'Where are you?' I said, 'I cannot protect you. A black boy shouldn't be out today.'

So, I got my perspective back in place. I felt my privilege of 60 years of life as a white woman, raising children in the U.S. And I decided perhaps it's not ok for me to throw a pity party for my lost family vacation. Instead, I should say a blessing and offer some gratitude. For being able to even make a decision about my safety.

We will go to Yosemite in the future. It will still be there.

Salam Al-Marayati, President of the Muslim Public Affairs Council, on a multi-faith town hall hosted by Representative Adam Schiff, said, 'God turned Adam into a human by blowing breath into clay. It is not okay for us to take the breath out of another. It is not okay.'

Breathe deep. Think of others. Be patient. Dig deep. These are hard times for some, but much harder, for others.

Summer "Vacationing"

A typical assignment for 'back to school' is for students to write an essay on 'what I did on my summer vacation.' I can only imagine what students will say in a few weeks, when they 'return' to schools in their pjs, online, in their bedroom or den or kitchen.

"On my summer vacation, I stayed in my pjs and played with friends online from my bedroom, den and kitchen."

"On my summer vacation, I saw my grandparents on the computer until finally, my grandma could not take it anymore, so she put on a suit she made out of hefty garbage bags, came over to our front yard, and insisted on getting a hug from me."

"On my summer vacation my mom made me practice schoolwork. The hardest assignment was being able to tell her the day of the week, each day."

Here are some highlights from the summer in my life:

Last month I received a package from our mail carrier. It was not from Amazon or FedEx, but hand delivered in an old fashion white box. It was from my friend Marci, in New Jersey, who had addressed it in her own handwriting and who clearly had gone to the post office to mail it. Just that in and of itself was incredibly touching.

It was not my birthday nor was there any other reason to be receiving gifts, so, puzzled, I opened it up. What to my wondering eyes did appear but—A HUGE cylinder container of Clorox Wipes. Yes, huge, the family size, the kind we used to take for granted and could find anywhere pre-COVID-19 but mostly at Costco or Office Depot. There was a cute card and it said, 'thought you could use a smile … and these wipes.'

Seriously.

Funny. Thoughtful. Practical. (You know you're an adult when….)

A rare commodity—not just the wipes, but a dear friend who was thinking of me from across the country and who took the time to send me a smile. I have been smiling ever since, really. I leave the container on the counter and smile each time I pass it by. Don't worry. I obviously have not opened it up or used any of the wipes…they are too precious for squandering!

That was a real summer vacation treat for sure.

Another summer trip is the planning going on for a COUSIN reunion. On my dad's side we are nine grandkids. July 24, it turns out, is NATIONAL COUSIN Day (who knew?!) and we decided to set up a chat for August. A few of us are chatting nightly (mostly on Facebook) in preparation of our visit. I have to say, my cousins are hilarious. As 'they say', 'cousins are your first friends' (if by friends, you mean the people who make fun of you, cajole you into doing things you wouldn't normally do, and)

There are still a few weeks of summer. Clearly, this has not been a hoot n holler kind of respite from a usual year. Parents are understandably dreading the advent of school. No major trips to Walmart and Office Depot to get back to school supplies. Mainly you need strong wi-fi connectivity and as much bandwidth for your house as possible.

However, reminder and note to selves:

You know how 'they" say that moderation is good, but too much a good thing is bad? Well—that rings true. Too much alcohol makes you drunk. Too much ice cream makes you sick. Too much sun makes you sunburned.

And too much time with family and loved ones?! Makes you… irritated, grouchy, mad, angry, frustrated, anxious, sad…. And, conversely, too much time alone makes you…irritated, grouchy, mad, angry, frustrated, anxious sad.

You know how they say that we, like our dogs, are 'pack animals.' That we need to be together and raise our young all in one den…. especially given the above 'law of moderation' let's re-consider.

I find it not at all surprising that the innovation of 'sending the kids to school' dates back thousands of years (originating with private schools and then the advent of public schools) and the home school movement never completely took off.

I find it not at all surprising that until recently, most American residents who work for a living, did so out of the house, with under 6% working full-time remotely. (See New York Times Sunday magazine, June 14, 2020.) Now that we are in the midst of a pandemic, however, the estimate is that half of those employed are now working from home, and obviously that is regarding those in privileged occupations. And of course, regarding schooling, the estimate is that in the past months in the U.S., close to 100% of our children moved from attending schools out of the home to hosting schools in their own bedrooms, which will now be continuing in most of California in Fall 2020.

So, while it's evolutionarily possible that we are meant to hang out together, it's also historically true that we have put many systems in place to create a balance and mitigate the 'altogether, all the time' rule. That was true back in the day too—hunters and gatherers had to leave family members to, well, hunt, and then, gather.

In these times, therefore, we have likely been together waaaaaaaaaaaaaaaay too much. Normally, in summer, we think, 'ah, time to get back together and re-connect as a family and decrease the frenetic pace of running hither and yon and enjoy some pajama days and down time.' This year, not so much. The notion of family game night once a week is less appealing if you've been playing games nightly. According to many lovely parents and teens, the idea of sitting around lounging together seems more punishment than pleasure.

What to do? Change venues and seek privacy and time apart in whatever way is safe for you and your family. Also, turn to your adult friends and empower your children to turn to their peers. This is a perfect time to do something for someone else.

Telling Two Truths and Some Big Lies

There are two questions being asked right now, one of which is impossible to answer, the other of which, has a meaningless answer.

The first query is, 'how are you doing?' This is an impossible question to answer unless you answer with another question: 'So how CAN I be doing?' or 'How are ANY of us doing?' or the basic teen response, silent eye roll. (Remember, if they roll their eyes, it's a good sign because it means they hear you—it's the glassy eye stare back that should concern you.)

Yes, honestly, "How COULD we be doing?"

However, conversations are conversations and we all can use ongoing chats and zooms and old school phone calls with pals. So, despite the hardship of answering that question, it is worth it. Go for it.

Then, once that initial pleasantry salutation is exchanged, inevitably, the next topic of conversation is COVID. We could have aliens invading this week, but we would bury that information until after we deep dive into the virus holding us all hostage. "Are you healthy? Everyone you know, ok? Do you have any family or friends who tested positive?"

Until, finally, "are you following the rules and staying safe?

Almost everyone I know, from family, to friends, to neighbors, to patients, to colleagues, offer this foundational statement, or a variety thereof:

"I have not left the house." ("I've done nothing. I have not gone anywhere. I am not doing anything.")

I do not believe that we people are consciously lying with our emphatic statements, but I have observed that we are all defining 'going nowhere' in largely divergent fashion. The platform of 'what I am doing now versus what I used to do, when I lived my normal life' is a huge context. It is the glasses through which we currently see our world.

So, with some exploration into the comment "I do nothing," comes the caveat................ I am not going anywhere EXCEPT...........I have not left the house at all EXCEPT...................

I say with zero judgmentalism, that, like Gregory House used to say in his tv series, "HOUSE," 'everyone lies.' I do not see these as lies of malice or evil intent. I do not see them as conscious attempts to manipulate others. They simply are our versions of what makes sense to us.

In that every one of us is currently doing so much less than whatever it was we were doing B.C. (before Covid), in contrast, of course we feel we are now doing nada, zip, nothing.

So, it's true, from the viewpoint of the grandparent who says, "I am not going anywhere" (except to fill prescriptions and to my doctors' appointments) because B.C., they were going to their Zumba class, playing bridge, volunteering at the shelter, and baby-sitting grandchildren. Today, when this Granny says "I'm not going anywhere" from her perspective, in comparison, she is not going anywhere today, compared with where she used to be going.

Same for the 17-year-old who says, "I swear, I am not going ANYwhere." She truly believes this statement and offers it emphatically. Because she is currently not a CIT or counselor at summer camp, and she is not at parties on the weekends. She is not in hell week for her school sport, preparing for her senior year. She is 'not going anywhere.'

I have a neighbor who insists they do not go anywhere, and yet I see them walking our block, no masks on their faces, attending religious services (outdoors, yes, but cramped together under a tent to avoid the hot valley sun.) I don't think she is consciously lying. She believes she is going nowhere because she has not taken the family annual vacation and she has not been hosting summer dinners for which she is well known. She feels trapped, understandably, and feels she is not doing anything. (Feelings are reigning the day, for sure.)

Back in the day, Pod People (also known as Body Snatchers) was the colloquial term for a species of plantlike aliens featured in the 1955 novel *The Body Snatchers* by Jack Finney. Of course, pods also refer to many things. Marine mammals, for instance, live in pods—dolphins, whales, walruses, seals—all our favorites. They make life under the sea look very appealing, collectivistic large family communities, taking care of one another and traveling together.

IRL (in real life), in 2020, pods are gaining popularity in a grass roots attempt for us humans to set up life where we can gather together with others who share in our observances of safety. Families are setting up pods for educational purposes, for physical activity and exercise purposes, and for the basic intent to decrease social isolation. It is impressive to follow along on the various Facebook pages or listservs across many diverse groups.

I am not a scientist so cannot comment on the cost-risk analysis for these groupings. All I can tell you is, make a list of questions to ask yourselves and potential pod mates before you get started.

"I never leave the house" does not mean "I never let anyone *into my* house—not my housekeeper, visiting nurse, mother-in-law, hair stylist, handyman, masseuse, grandchildren, son's pals, etc."

"I do not go anywhere" may not mean "I stopped driving and am no longer pumping gas into my car without wearing gloves."

"I am totally 100% stuck in my house" may not include "I do not let the neighbors in for cocktails when our Sunday lawn visits get toooo hot outside to handle."

"I have not left the house in months"—other than to get groceries, drop off things at my office, attend a few exercise classes when we were able, eat at the outdoor restaurants, etc.

By all means, let's become pod people. I am a fan.

However, let's have a check list of questions, so we can enter into these new covenants with one another with our eyes open to minimizing risk. I don't think any of us can eliminate risk. But let's reduce potential harm wherever possible.

Me? I don't go anywhere. I swear! Except.............

FALL ....

Falling Forward? Falling Backward? Keep on Falling? Keep on Keeping On?

Our Children are Watching Us

D o something nice for someone else?! Seriously!? Every day....hmmmm....
Do you know that song—by Julie Gold—*From a Distance*....?
Well, since you have some free time, check it out on any music app.

I'm not going to write it all out here. It's a beautiful song and timely for all sorts of reasons. But for the purposes of my missive today, let's take the refrain and change it to 'OUR KIDS ARE WATCHING US.' More than ever, with all this togetherness, our kids are watching us.

Yes, our kids are watching us. They are watching how we treat others, from nannies and housekeepers and gardeners and neighbors to cashiers and grandparents and pets. They are watching to see if we can protect without smothering (i.e., how many carts have you filled up at Costco and how many do you really need?) and they are watching your interactions with your co-parent/partner/spouse. Also, they are listening to everything. There really are no secrets in your house right now, so be especially conscientious about exposure (from you, from Rachel Maddow) to the children and teens. They do not need hourly updates from CDC or WHO or the President or Governor or Mayor. We can let them know *what they need to know*: they are safe, you can handle this, we are in it together, they are loved, and we are all doing our best.

It's good to keep repeating that we are all doing our best. Across our life span, there are two things we need to have or do to be able to grow and evolve and develop or deepen our sense of self. Only two things to continually contribute to our ability to do our best:

1)   We need to have a sense of being valued, loved, appreciated, heard. All of us. So, make sure your children know that and feel it, and

ALSO, make sure *you* take it in from others. Expand your world from your den to reach out to old friends from camp and cousins with whom you have not spoken in years. Fill up your well with lots of loving folk and nicely distance yourself from those who are toxic. You can do it for you, model it for your children, and help them do it as well.

2) We need to continually work on mastering things. All of us, not just our children. So, in this new era, in times like these, we have more opportunity for mastery experiences than we'd ever anticipated. You are fast mastering the internet and on-line shopping and skooology or moodle or whatever those things are called. Soon you'll have down 4th grade math even. Really! Don't sell yourself short. You can master things, demonstrate it for the kids, and then also help them master things.

There are many lists being shared with 'things to do' and 'links and apps' and it is amazing, this thing called the world wide web. Try to not to feel overloaded. Save them in a file somewhere. For right now, we are at the very beginning. Think "Gilligan" and the 'three-hour tour' and the first week on the island. (And if you're too young for that reference, one bonus is you are not an at-risk older adult!) Pace yourself. There is wisdom in the 12-Step motto ONE DAY AT A TIME.

Feeling the Free Time? Really?

Anyone feeling like they have free time, as we live our lives, one day at a time? Perhaps, some of us more so than others, eh? There are loads of lists of what we can be doing with this 'free time.' I suspect that any parent with children home from school are not quite conceiving of this as 'free time' and rather, are already longing for the days when their stress came from locating the tear off to sign and return to school with a bizarre dollar amount ("Please sign this trip slip and send $7.34 for next week's lunch for our trip to The Getty.")

So rather than a list of suggestions of what to do, here is a nice list of things of what NOT to do, even if someone suggests otherwise:

1) Organize your garage from top to bottom. Nope. This is not the week for that. Maybe when we are all desperate in a few weeks, but not now. It's coldish out there. And be real, you've let it go this way for so long, it's not even clear where to begin. We in California are already known for keeping our fancy cars on the driveway and our 'stuff' in the garage. So—no garage cleaning. Repeat after me, "LET IT BE."

2) Scan all your photos. Nope. While that sounds like a nice idea, it's really not. Too overwhelming. Too exhausting. Too many photos you cannot identify and then it makes you obsess over 'Why DID we take 89 pictures at each t-ball game, birthday party, school play?' So no, save that task for a time when you are God forbid recovering from foot surgery which you scheduled for a time when all your kids leave the house for school daily and you feel okay, but you literally cannot get out of bed. Repeat after me, "JUST BE STILL."

3)   Check for expiration dates in your spice rack. Nope. Do not do this now as you will ascertain that 85% of what you own is expired. You will then feel a need to google what it means to have expired spices. And that will motivate you to want to discard everything on your shelf/rack and purchase new spices. BUT…you cannot be going marketing for spices when there are still lines around the block, and you have to collect more toilet paper and Clorox wipes. Repeat after me, "JUST BREATHE."

4)   Deep clean your stove. Nope. Too many fumes. Not enough satisfaction when you're done because, aren't you just going to cook dinner and bake a lot of stuff now anyway? And does all that burnt on granola every REALLY come off? I think not. Repeat after me, "IT'S FINE AS IT IS."

5)   Go over all your financials to prep for retirement. Now, IF you are about to retire, ok, but if not…. NOPE. There is really no point in it. You have already just paid taxes or are about to pay taxes or are about to ask for an extension on your taxes. This is not the time to go through all the paperwork for what you need to do in 10-20-30 years. There will be time for that soon enough. I swear. Repeat after me, "JUST SAY NO."

In these scary times, let's get back to basics. "Be gentle with yourself." "Kindness counts." "Hey, hey, we're the Monkees." (Ok Boomer.) "One day at a time." "Si se puede." "You got this." "This too shall pass." "Keep calm and carry on." (Or "Keep calm and eat chocolate.") "Be like a duck." "Be like an elephant." "You can handle this." "Assume positive intention." "We are all doing the best we can, under the circumstances."

My favorite of all mantras, though, is WIT—WHATEVER IT TAKES. As long as it's not child abuse or illegal, we now all sign up and agree to use the WIT method of parenting. You are the expert on your children and your household. You know what works with each kid and what does not. You know who needs more alone time and who needs more physical activity and who needs more social time. You know who has less frustration tolerance and who could lie in bed and chat with friends all day and all night. Use that knowledge. It's your secret power and it will last you across the lifespan. Whatever it takes to move toward health and safety, in these times.

YOU GOT THIS ~ WHATEVER IT TAKES!

Regressing, Together

At any age, for all stages…I wonder, approximately how long until we start regressing? I'd hypothesize that we've already begun.

By the way, it's bound to happen to us all, regardless of our age or stage (even our pets are going to return to previous behavioral challenges from when they first moved in with you…) Our little ones will go back to thumb sucking, refusing to sleep alone, exhibiting signs of separation anxiety, and wetting the bed, even if they've not done so for years. Our middle ones will likely become whinier, clingier, more irritable, and 'less capable.' They may need help for things they mastered years ago—shoe tying, hair braiding, bike riding, computer proficiency. Teens—well—teens may be a little less likely to regress initially, as many will be able to make this crisis 'not about them.' That's a protective factor although it can present to you as a parent as selfishness. It's developmentally appropriate so maybe enjoy it until it passes and no judging. Once their self-focus dissipates, they too may regress. And their regression may look like withdrawal, isolation, and/or irrational irritability and anger. Depending on the person and their innate temperament, regression can present uniquely for each individual, so knowing yourself and your children is helpful.

Which means, what about YOU? You the young adult or young parent or middle-aged boomer or aging adult? What will regression look like for you? Well—think of the areas of mastery in which you've made progress and for which you are quite proud. Exercising well? Getting out and about and sustaining friendships? Doing well at school? Doing well at work? Eating healthy? Feeling proud of your work performance? Keeping your space clutter free and clear? Getting along with members of your family? Roommates? Significant others?

Staying on top of work–life balance and not having more than 20, 200, 2000, 20,000 emails in your email in box? Regressing looks like slip sliding backward and falling into old behavior patterns. Regressing is not life/death, but it is disconcerting because once you start down that spiraling path, you think, 'well, I had two donuts this morning so, why not the box this afternoon?' or 'what the heck, I haven't gotten out of sweatpants since Monday so why bother today, on Friday?'

Resilience has been defined as the maintenance of healthy and/or successful functioning or adaptation within the context of a significant adversity or threat. So that's the question—can we adapt? Can we move outside the comfort zone and fit into the new world regs and rules? Time to access our inner chameleon and increase our flexibility skills.

Currently we are a country attempting to cope with a new stress—*sheltering in place*. It's unheard of for most of us, unless you are a survivor of the Holocaust or Japanese Internment or Armenian Genocide or Native American/Indigenous peoples forced reservation round ups....so, actually, it's new for *most of us*, but not all of us. And for those of us for whom this is new, we may be lacking the ability to tolerate frustration at the levels we need—so not only can we not cope, but we are upset to discover we cannot cope!

So, what to do? Is it too late? Should we just accept the inevitable and assume this is as good as it's going to get? Or, if not, what are the protective factors toward resiliency that we can adopt now, and which behaviors should we prioritize?

There are many wonderful studies on this topic (Google, Siri, Alexa, pub med) so I am not going to provide those here. Instead, here is a summary of what we know. Remember that resilience is 'the ability to manage and bounce back from all types of challenges that emerge in every family's life. It means finding ways to solve problems, building and sustaining trusting relationships including relationships with your own child, and knowing how to seek help when necessary.'

The Center for the Study of Social Policies lists five protective factors: (1) Parental resilience; (2) Social connections; (3) Knowledge of parenting and child development; (4) Concrete support in time of need; and (5) Social and emotional competence of children (i.e., building and sustaining secure attachments.) All you need to do is choose one on which to focus. One a day or one a week, your call. If it's parental resilience, make this the week you prioritize you. Go back to jogging. Or gardening. Stake out a claim for at least an hour of 'you time' (which may look like six different 10 minutes of 'you time' depending on your current responsibilities.) Or if you choose 'concrete support in a time of need', WRITE out a list of needs, like you write out a grocery list, and keep it handy and add to it. Then have a brainstorming session, including people in your house or friends online, and start writing out resources. If you are not on 'next door app' this may be a good time to download it. Check out your local public health pages. Join Facebook pages even if you have not done so before. Collecting concrete support is manageable, if not intuitive. One protective factor at a time.

I know this is HARD but y'all, it is not IMPOSSIBLE. To quote from Alice in Wonderland: "Alice laughed: "There's no use trying," she said; "one can't believe impossible things." "I daresay you haven't had much practice," said the Queen. "When I was younger, I always did it for half an hour a day. Why, sometimes I've believed as many as six impossible things before breakfast. *Alice in Wonderland.*

In these times, let's believe in six impossible things before breakfast. Or, given that we are all stuck at home, we can give ourselves all day to believe the impossible. Try it out as it pertains to you. You will find that the impossibly, improbably, IS possible!

Typing our Personalities

We each have our roles to play in these times, including doing the impossible, during the time it feels as though we cannot even do the bearable. My husband, for instance, is on one ZOOM meeting/ call after another, figuring how to help vulnerable populations like those with addictions or those with HIV/AIDS or the homeless. Me? I have perfected the game of indoor tag with our dog, Ginger. Ginger picks up something she is not supposed to have, usually a New Yorker magazine or one of our slippers. She then runs frantically through the house. Our house has that 'open floor plan' feel for the most part, with a clear circular run from kitchen to dining room to hall to den/ living room and back to kitchen. So, when she starts to run clockwise, I run counter- clockwise until we run into each other. This may not be helpful in terms of providing help and resource and leaving a significant footprint on the world, but it is highly useful for the sanity of one dog (oh, and me too.)

In light of what else we can be doing in case of TMFT syndrome (too much free time) ....

Here's a fun idea—figure out who in your family is most alike and who is most distinct, and in what ways? Be it biology or environment, it's a good time to take stock, because there is a good possibility that the people with whom you share space who are most like you, are also the ones more likely to drive you insane, and vice-versa. This is not always the case of course, but—if you're an extroverted, loquacious chatty Cathy—you'd think your seven year old who is also outgoing would be the one with whom you'd bond, while bonding together in the little nest/prison called home.....or, if you're an introverted person, cat not dog person, who likes nothing more than time alone, peace and quiet, soothing solitude—you'd think the child who shares those traits would be the one you'd respect and 'get,' but instead, they are the one most often making you want to climb a tree (literally.)

In these times, we have the opportunity to get know ourselves AND our roommates (children, grandchildren, spouses, children's boy/girlfriends who have moved in....) There are lots of (not scientifically based) online questionnaires (think BuzzFeed, not Cosmo or Teen....) and of course there are also tons of science and evidence-based personality inventories available as well.

What are we talking about when we talk about temperament? There are 'the big nine' so consider these, relative to you and relative to your relatives:

- *Activity level* (Does your child innately have high or low activity levels? And you?)
- *Biological rhythms* (Does your child have regular or irregular internal drives related to sleep, appetite, routine? And you?)
- *Sensitivity* (Does your child have high or low sensitivity to stimuli, such as noise, light, chaos, etc.? And you?)
- *Intensity of reaction* (Does your child react with high or low intensity, in general? Can they modulate their reactivity? Can you?)
- *Adaptability* (Is your child highly adaptive or low to adapt? And you?)
- *Approach/withdrawal* (Does your child easily openly approach new situations or does your child back away and withdraw from newer situations? And you?)
- *Persistence* (Does your child have high or low persistence? What about you?)
- *Distractibility* (Does your child have high or low distractibility? And what about you?)
- *Mood* (By nature, is your child more like Eeyore or Pooh—more negative and pessimistic or more naturally positive and

optimistic? And what about you? Which Winnie the Pooh character are you?)

We are all somewhere on a continuum regarding these traits, and neither side of that line is 'good' or 'bad.' We are what we are (or, as Popeye used to say, "I yam what I yam." OK Boomer.) The question is, where do you fall on that continuum and where do your significant others land? And once you have some sense of you and yours, what does it mean for you? Hopefully, the bottom line is empathy and compassion. Wherever we each fall on our continuum, we are not alone. And the lesson for these times is—we need one another to survive and thrive, even when it's with a six-foot social distance between one another.

Thinking We are All Now Sleepless in COVID

F unny times. Stay safe and stay sane seem incredibly challenging as mantras. Hard to anticipate which will be a good day and which will be a bad day. Mostly the days are in between days, with peaks and valleys. We are like new puppies being crate trained—we spend time in our crates and get to come out and play in the yard a little, and then for some reason, back into the crate. We have not figured out the wheres and whens of the process. However, the crates are often warm and feel like nests now, and less like prisons. Weird.

One challenge many of us are having in these times is sleep. We are sleeping too much. Or not enough. Or at the wrong times. Some of us (newborns, 12–22-year-olds, 82–92-year-olds) are mixing up our nights and days. Sleep changes in and of themselves are not necessarily a problem. The problem with our sleep problems is that we are obsessively focusing on the issue, and worrying about the issue, and sure that of all currently impacting us, this is the biggest disaster AND the area we can/should/ought to be able to control and fix. Thus, thinking about not sleeping has become much more distracting and devastating than not sleeping.

So, let me share some information with you.

1) You cannot force your child to sleep. At any age. You can introduce or reinforce nice sleep routines and habits. You can increase physical activity each day (cardio, cardio, cardio) for your child. You can sing pretty songs, tickle backs, set limits, threaten to take a phone away—but –you cannot make your child go to sleep.

2) Some children (and grownups) need less sleep than others. We are each wired differently. You probably are aware of your own sleep patterns and those of all with whom you are sharing space (the crates are kinda tiny, after all.) If someone is prone to insomnia, assume that will continue and/or worsen, in these times. If someone loves to sleep and can nap anywhere, anytime, assume that will continue and/or worse, in these times.

3) Unless the under or over sleeper is not functioning in one or more areas of their lives (work/school/independent living skills) then cross this off the worry list and file it under the 'hmmm, I guess it will all work out ok' list. Adding worry to the sleep problem does not help with sleep and, most likely, you already have plenty of things on your worry list.

4) If you want to try a few things just for fun, i.e., scientifically assessing yourself in a little at home experiment, then make a change once a day and see if/how it impacts sleep. Give up caffeine. Or, conversely, drink a lot of caffeine. Give up sugar. Do not drink any alcohol. Or, conversely, have a cocktail or two or a glass of wine or two. Exercise. Spent at least two hours outdoors. Try meditation. Practice breathing skills. Create a list of nice visuals and then visualize things. Do some yoga. Take a nap. Do not take a nap. Music, music, music. Read in bed. No screen time before bed. Screen time with grandma reading a story to grandpa? in bed. We have all the time in the world so, try the 'WIT' method—whatever it takes.

5) If you want to try medication, ASK YOUR M.D. There are over the counter sleep aides, but for children, get your pediatrician's okay first. Melatonin, for instance, may be helpful, but get professional advice prior to implementing the self/child study.

6) And if it's the middle of the night and someone cannot sleep, generate a list of 'what I can do in the middle of the night' and leave it in a prominent space. Slow laps around the house? Warm

bath? Read a book? Do a comparative analysis of our late-night talk shows to see who can function without an audience/laugh track and who cannot. Decorate and write cards to send to hospitals to thank responders. Change venues—sleep on the floor, sleep on the floor in a sleeping bag, sleep in another room on the floor, make a fort to sleep in.

This missive is not to minimize challenges with sleep. Sleep deprivation is dangerous and bad for us, for sure. And hypersomnia is not good either. However, for most of us, sleep changes in a time of tumult and crisis are to be expected. So, in these times, try to 'ride it out.' Deep breaths. And maybe, it's not a bad time to stop counting 'days in' and rather, count blessings....backwards from 100—sometimes it helps for sleep, and when it does not, it helps our hearts.

"Building back better."

Lonely shoes in the closet.

Worried canned goods in the pantry who survived years in the back, now sure they will be the next to be plucked out of obscurity and cooked into some dinner found by googling, 'what can you make with artichoke hearts, pitted green olives, and chicken breast in a can?' are chatting among themselves. "Stay low. Fall through the cracks. We've been here long beyond our expiration dates; we can hold out a lot longer!"

Clearly my mind hates a vacuum. Well, not REAL vacuums, those I've been researching all month long now—looking for a magical one that is cordless, holds the charge long enough to clean up every last piece of dog hair (can you say, 'weather changes = massive shedding activity?'), and does not require an engineering degree to figure it out. The kind of vacuum I do poorly with is the one where there is an emptiness of certainty. Life in the gray. SIP-fatigue is what I'm calling it. Being fatigued from all this sheltering in place. Shelter in Place fatigue.

Leads the mind to fill in the space with some rather 'out there' thoughts. Like the talking canned goods. Or these random thoughts:

1) Are doorbells obsolete?
2) Are my shoes sad and lonely without my feet?
3) Why would a dry cleaner be open?
4) Are doggie playdates ok when playdates for children are not?
5) Can we really 'build back better?"

The last question makes more sense given our lives today. I like to be hopeful. And when possible, helpful. Which reminds me to first be grateful. And then intentional. Which is a lot for this brain to remember.

Over the weekend I sent notes to my medical providers—to my internist now and to the internist I'd seen for years back when I worked in Ventura County, to my cardiologists (two, just in case, always good to have a backup), and to my dentist. I wrote to ask about their health and well-being, to see if they are holding up ok, to let them know I have zero intention of visiting them anytime soon, and to thank them for all their hard and dangerous work. As I know their nurses screen their emails, I thanked them too. A tiny gesture. Made me feel useful. Turns out, they were touched—despite their busy days and nights, they each wrote a little note back saying thanks (and that I should behave myself and NOT give into my SIP-fatigue.)

What are your fantasies for when we build back better? I wish for long vacations for health care providers. And for my mail carrier. And for truck drivers and cashiers and bus drivers and TEACHERS. And for sure for parents. A long vacation—where the children are all IRL classes for at least eight hours a day. And you can go about your life and still be a loving parent, just not on-call in person 24/7.

In these times, it's good to dream big.

Remembering 9/11

Today is an anniversary. It's not a happy anniversary. It's not a joyful anniversary. But as is true for any anniversary, celebratory or sad, it's important to mark it and acknowledge it and take a moment to remember.

My family's part of 9/11 was very small, in the scope of things. It was not even a blip on a radar of a nation in shock, in mourning, and in fear. Nonetheless, it is part of our family history, and so, while we reflect back on the state of the world, many years ago today, I cannot help but remember what went on for my group of five.

My husband, a scientist, was in Washington D.C. He was there for a 48-hour meeting of researchers. He was at the Doubletree Hotel, in Arlington, Virginia. This was before the time when the mention of the state of "Virginia" brought up images of grief and tragedy. This was before our world was turned upside down, and before we'd seen photos of planes crashing into buildings and of people jumping from skyscrapers to avoid death by fire and explosion.

Anyway. My husband was giving a talk when a plane crashed into the Pentagon. Being a Californian, he assumed it was an earthquake, so he kept on talking. It was, as we know, no earthquake. Back in LA, all attempts to reach him were futile. We were watching, along with the world, as the buildings pancaked like accordions and as the smoke billowed into the streets. However, since we couldn't reach him, we went on with our day—I drove kids to school, and I went into work. The enormity of the situation had not sunk in. I was supposed to be teaching a seminar on 'assessing children' to a group of mental health students—instead, I sent them all home and told them to find their family members and hug them. I figured we'd learn child assessment on a different day...on a day when we were not busy trying to assess reality and national security.

An hour or two or three passed. Still no word from my husband. I checked my emails. There was a piece of new email from a person named Ed Jaranksy, U.S.M.C. I don't know any Eds, any Jaranksys, or any Marines. I wondered, 'can they send you bad mail via the internet?' I got a good friend to sit with me and I opened the email: "See you later in LA when I can get there."

I found out later that it was sent from a wireless internet device (now quite popular, then, quite unheard of), and that during serious war-like conditions, a nice Marine offered to help a man stranded at 'the other ground zero' to contact his wife in Southern California.

It was, of course, a great relief and comfort to know that he was 'fine.' Healthy, alive, functional. Fine. Of course, he was also, as it turned out, stuck. There was simply no way to get from DC to LA that week of September in2001. So, he was as fine as anyone could be, given that he was across the street from a global war zone, with no place to stay, and no means of getting home. Fine is relative. Fine is alive. Fine is a blessing.

I know that our story of those days is mundane, compared to the real life and death tolls. My three children and I didn't have to print fliers with his picture on them, hoping against hope that someone had seen him and that he wasn't buried under the debris or scattered across the sky. We didn't have to await a call or visit from a government official or an airline representative. We didn't have to worry that he'd never come home—we only had to worry, how would he make it back home?

Sometimes he'd get a land line and call, from the floor of the local hotel, where he and others had taken up temporary residence, asking, "How are the dogs?" Sometimes he'd call with information about how he was helping to do triage with shell shocked citizens, as part of the mental health teams who were in the area. Sometimes, he'd call to say, "Guess who else is sleeping on the floor with us?? The pilots who are grounded from flying!" Mostly, he'd call to check in, though, to see if our world had crumbled. Our children were nine, 11 and 13. I was 132.

He had a very hard time imagining that in the San Fernando Valley, everything was 'fine'. Our eldest handled the event with his usual aplomb, helpful around the house, directing younger siblings here and there. Our middle, the only girl, struggled verbally with myriad fears: "Is Dad really, okay?" "What if there is a draft, will he have to go into it and fight in a war?" "Will I have to be a soldier some day?" "What if somebody crashes a plane into LA?" "What is a hijacker, exactly? What is a terrorist? Why does someone want to be a terrorist?" She became most concerned, however, the day her dad told her, over the phone, "Don't worry about your math homework. You can skip doing homework this week. There are things in life more important than homework." She had NEVER heard him speak that way. It had her totally unnerved for months. We could hear her muttering to herself, "There are things in life more important than homework—dad said. Hmph!"

The littlest one went silently to work. He took out huge maps of the United States and mounted them around the house. He pinpointed the action. He stuck push pins in various places. He colored out various routes his father could use to drive home. He slept fitfully, ate poorly, and mulled things over to himself, as was (and is) his way.

It was a very long week. On Friday, my husband called to say that he had procured "the last rental car available in the East Coast", and that he and a few strangers (many of whom had met hanging out at the rental car office) were going to drive home. Luckily, the little kid in our house had already figured out various routes home. This was a time, mind you, before global navigational systems.

They started driving. They headed south and west. They met nice people along the way and met many others who were trying to get home. Somewhere in Atlanta someone mentioned that the flights there were no longer grounded, and that they were flying into LA. So, they returned the car at the airport and did something that none of us will ever take for granted again—they 'hopped on a plane' and flew home.

When I heard he was coming home, I did what every good mom does—I prepared platters and platters of food. All day Sunday our friends, neighbors, and family dropped by to see him and talk to him about his experience. Everyone ate and chatted about the world—and how it had changed irrevocably, and would we ever fly again (yes) and would we ever feel fully safe again (no, not really, and especially now, during a pandemic, for sure no).

At one point, my youngest sister arrived with a red-white-blue cake. My nephew said we should sing something, but 'Happy Birthday Uncle Steve' did not seem like the right song. My then nine-year-old explained patiently, that while we were not celebrating birthdays, we were celebrating freedoms—he said we were celebrating being Americans and being able to find good people and helpful people, all across the country. My daughter added, 'we're celebrating that dad made it home—a lot of kids' dads and moms did not.'

"Ah", said my 6-year-old nephew, Noah. "I know what to sing then. And he started singing, and we joined in, and while it was a hokey, syrupy moment for a group of people who are typically cynical and sarcastic, it was too poignant to miss—"God Bless America. My home sweet home."

We ate the red-white-blue cake. We took down the crinkled maps. We sang some other songs. We ate and we visited. And we kept hugging and touching one another. We had found a tiny, tiny, moment of peace—and we'd all realized, moments of peace must be marked, and commemorated, and celebrated, inside the home, and outside the home as well.

May you all find some peace on this anniversary day. And may it sustain us and flow from us to the world at large, at a time when unity seems so far away. And sometime soon, may we all be able to hug and touch one another. And may God bless us all.

Misplacing, Losing, and Loss

When our daughter was little, she and my husband used to play a board game called *Pretty, Pretty, Princess.* You 'earned' jewels and tiaras and the individual most decked out as royalty the soonest, won. If I could locate the photos of the two of them, sitting on the floor, looking earnest with their crowns and long gloves, I would post them. Instead, I am delighted to have located the memory (as of this moment) and to pull up the visual in my mind's eye.

What have you misplaced of late? For what are you searching?

Keys to the car, for instance? Nail polish remover? Hand-written recipes? The 'good' shampoo? What else? A specific photograph? An old friend?

Which memories sustain you? Which are too fuzzy and are evading you?

Then again, in these times, what are you missing, if you are privileged enough to not be missing health and security? I miss audiences for talk shows. It's just not the same, although kudos to them for their adaptations.

I miss frozen yogurt very, very much. I miss walking with my friends. It has been too long. I'm worried I'll lose the 'walkie-talkie' ability following so many miles of solitary sojourning. I hope you will be patient with me when we are back on track beloved partners.

I also miss missing my husband—this is the longest stretch I can recall with him NOT traveling hither and yon for his science work. Funny. After years of complaining about him being gone, I kinda miss that he's never gone now!

Here, however, is what I do not miss:

Traffic. Over scheduling the calendar. Bad air quality. The mall.

So, to combat my worries over what I've misplaced, and what I'm missing, I focus a tad also on what I'm happy to have right here in my lap:

My appreciation for family and friends.

My thanks for those with a sense of humor. Y'all crack me up. Thanks. A little irreverence goes a long way. Yes, old I Love Lucy episodes are funny, but so are texts and posts from my kids.

My belief in things that are invisible—love, time, viruses that can be fought.

And finally,

My optimism—people are good—the 'bad ones' dominate our social media pages sometimes, but overall, people are good, and we will move through this and come out the other side.

I have not misplaced my faith in us. Not even the tiniest bit.

Those Tears, Coming Again

I t's hard to predict what will 'trigger us' or set us off, scrambling to catch up to the emotions we were not aware we were experiencing, trying to corral them, and put them back in the box under the bed where we feel they best belong.

Chris Erskine's departure from the L.A. Times, for instance, hit me hard. If for some reason you never followed him, check out his Facebook page or google him. He has been writing about family and life in Los Angeles for 30 years. No, I don't know him. But I feel like I do. He lost a son to a car accident a few years ago, followed by the death of his beloved wife "Posh," to cancer, a year later. His pithy observations and basic love of humans and dogs (and alcohol and tailgating and the LA Dodgers) has been far more than entertainment. It makes me weepy to read some of the goodbyes being posted on social media. And then it surprises me each time that happens. Why am I weeping?

The same thing happened with recent video footage I saw of Yosemite National Park. The Park Rangers remaining, and the nature web cams capture an emptiness (of humans) that is nothing short of magical. The waterfalls are full, the bears are frolicking, and the deer have taken over the meadows. I was not prepared for a little cry when I watched today's footage. What was that? Overwhelmed by beauty? Majesty?

It's hard to say. Sweet moments start water works, sure. Bad and sad news of course does the same. But listening to Kelly Clarkson sing Madonna? Really? How deep is this reservoir of my tears? I'm not sure I'd ever heard Kelly sing before I stumbled upon a video she filmed from her bathroom in her cottage in the woods where she and her kids and husband are sheltered. She sang "Like a Prayer" and honestly, it did feel like a prayer.

Less surprising for me is that this evening I had more waterworks when I listened to Jackson Browne's new release *A Little Soon to Say*. In essence he reminds us that we are not out of this yet, but ultimately, we're pretty sure we'll be okay...it's just, as the song titles says, perhaps too soon to know for sure.

That's the gist of it. Not sure whether everything will be alright. It's just a little soon to say.

Well, in my HEAD, I'm sure we will be ok. We will weather this pandemic and come out the other side, because that is how the world works. But this historical fact is not always evident to my heart, clearly.

So, I do what any of us would do. I distract myself with random thoughts. I wonder, what was your 'last _____ before' this storm?

Who was the last person you saw before you bunkered down with your current roommates (son, daughter, spouse, two dogs and a cat)?

Which was the last restaurant you visited before your family room became your Open Table go-to for dining?

When were you last in a mall and which mall was it? What was the last sporting event you saw live? Who was the last artist you saw live in concert? Which was the last museum you visited in person and not on your tablet?

What was your last trip other than the major walk around your block? In which hotel or Airbnb did you rest your head before you realized your own house WOULD make a great Airbnb, if/when we ever get out of here.

I also attempted to distract by working on re-learning the steps to FOOTLOOSE, by Kenny Loggins. The dog, Ginger, laughed for hours, and I could not master it, despite years of attending bar and bat mitzvah parties weekly and having that as the du jour dance. Age? Concentration? Heat wave in the valley? Hard to say.

Random questions, random dances.

Then I remember. Sometimes, it's just ok to give in and let the grief wash over. To not think. Not ponder. Not dance. Just be. Sad. Lonely. Empty. Scared. Sad.

As we turn our hearts to one another, sometimes the connection is so intense, that even with zero physical contact, we connect—deeply, intimately, innately. It is so intense it ignites a spark. Or sometimes, it trickles a tear.

Teaching Our Children Well

"I can't wait until this is over. I am so sick of this. The first thing I'm going to do when we get back to normal is...." Of course, we hear, and say, these sentences all day long.

How refreshing it is, therefore, to spend time with various people who have somehow not yet internalized the inertia and pervasive sadness that has come before our usual May Gray and June Gloom.

Is it a coincidence that I most often hear "This is kinda fun. I'm mostly happy all the time. I like dinner time together every night. It's okay if things are cancelled because we find new things to do." From the littles? Teaching us about gratitude and enjoying what is in front of us, where we are, even amid loss, fear, challenge. Yes, the littles.

I'm finding that the age group weathering this with the most optimism is the six to ten-year-old group. This is not science mind you, but, of the tiny sample in my practice and in my life, the 1st, 2nd, 3rd and sometimes 4th graders are pretty perky.

As a child psychologist, I tend to ask lots of questions. "What's the biggest feeling you had today? Who's bugging you the most? How much sad is inside you on a 1-10 scare? What dreams are you having when you're asleep? What dreams are you having when you're awake?"

The preschoolers seem to be struggling with having regressed to younger ages and stages, craving more touch, rocking, babying. Some have gone back to bed wetting even though it had been two years since diapers were last a part of their lives.

Older elementary school and middle school students seem to be struggling (still) with school and with the lack of access face to face with favorite teachers and favorite friends. "ZOOM sucks," said one

12-year-old. "I don't like having to be on it for school and then later in the day, on it some more for my virtual playdates."

High schoolers are pretty (understandably) upset, and often able, albeit reluctant, to express it. "I am so pissed off. No prom. No graduation. No tours of colleges." Some are even mad about the cancellation of the SAT and ACT standardized tests ("I'd already been studying the vocab flashcards for months!") and the schools who moved to pass/fail grading ("My GPA was going to be the best ever, and now it will just look lackluster." Nice use of SAT word...)

But the 6-to-10-year-olds, many are faring well. Back in the day we referred to this age group as 'latency,' meaning 'not motivated by psychosexual desires.' Freud thought of it as a time when children repress sexual urges and Erik Erikson thought of it as a time when children are on a continuum of 'industry versus inferiority.'

It appears that these children are far from 'latent' or 'dormant.' Contrarily, they are not waiting for their lives to begin or to get better, they are stepping up and stepping into it and already inhabiting themselves. Nothing to wait on from their perspective.

For one thing, they often are in what appears to be constant motion. This is not an attention deficit disorder, it's simply that their sense of energy and wonder comes out physically and kinesthetically. They are still equally as likely to do a cartwheel or throw stuffed animals up in the air, as they are to play the drums on the breakfast table and stack up whatever is in front of them on the dinner table.

In addition to their activity level, these kids also tend to be fairly expressive. They use the words we see in comic books and graphic novels. "AWESOME, Mom!" "AMAZING class." "HILARIOUS, Dad." They may actually become so animated they lie and cheat, but they do so with more of a sense of innocence than sociopathy. And they are not yet good liars, so you can almost always tell, and call them on it without prosecuting them too heavy handedly. Self-consciousness has often not quite set in. It's coming, sadly, of course, but not yet.

Our children are not waiting for fun to begin at some point, they are making their own fun or discovering it every day. They are not counting the days. They are not sitting this one out until these days are over. Our children are more like TIGGER than EEYORE. They are bouncy and they jump right in. Sometimes it annoys us. But let it instead inspire us.

If you observe them, you may see this: When going to sleep, they snuggle in, lie down, stretch out, and smile. When they wake up and are just becoming conscious, they stretch out and smile.

Worrying—a Privilege

Lots going on the world—some of it inspirational and some of it deeply distressing. How to stay sane in an insane time? Sometimes that means focusing on one foot in front of the other and keeping the little worries alive and the big worries, well, if the gremlins have not overtaken all your computer systems, store them in the Cloud and then shut down the tablet.

Little worry #1—Should we 'put up' our cherry liqueur this year? Every year since we married in 1985, my husband and I have made my grandfather's recipe for Russian 'vishniak.' It requires taking plump sweet cherries (usually out in June), vodka, and sugar and putting the ingredients into jars and leaving them alone for approximately six months. We collect bottles year long and then in December, we take out the alcohol infused cherries and pour the pretty liquid into pretty containers. We then gift our friends and family and colleagues with a container of nightcaps for the December holidays. This year however, it occurred to us, we have no idea what we will be doing in December. Working in an office or sitting at home? Able to host dinner parties or perhaps gathering together on tired Zoom calls?

So, we contemplate. What if we prepare the gifts, but have no one to whom to gift them? Not a huge worry obviously but.... Then we think, 'well, let's act with optimism' (and honestly, we have some free time in these times), so we answer our own query and yesterday we made 50% of what we usually prepare and put it into storage.

Little worry #2—What to do with the dog regressing to pooping in the street versus on the grass? We made great progress with her over the course of her first month with us, teaching that as a suburban loved dog you politely poop on a neighbor's yard and not on the sidewalk.

But of late, all bets are off, and Ginger has taken to doing her business on asphalt, cement, or concrete. It's like the previous seven months disappeared and her old anxieties and behaviors are back. Cesar Milan teaches that we need to better train humans, not dogs, and that the human needs to act the role of the ALPHA. In our family that used to be my husband. However, with our rescue dog Ginger, acquired during our empty nest and being raised in our shelter in place household of two humans/one dog/one annoying squirrel, she is now my husband's best friend. This means that on one of many daily walks, he allows her to poop literally in the middle of the intersection (of Coldwater and Burbank) and tells me, 'When she has to go, she has to go.' 'Clearly someone has to go,' I think to myself.

I Google dog behavior and again, am reminded that this is a matter of teaching the human, not the dog. So, I decide that tomorrow I'll bring some Skittles in my pocket on our walk. My husband is a huge fan of any candy, and especially, of Skittles. I will work on getting him back into the role of 'large and in charge' and see if the treats work. Stay tuned.

Little worry #3—There is no elephant in the room. There is only a large herd, in every space. It's the gathering of the obvious among us the oblivious and it's harder and harder to try to ignore it. So perhaps this is not a little worry. It's the underlying foundation of all worries. How safe are we and how do we know? You know what, never mind. I think I'll stick to rounding up the little worries and indeed, store those big ones elsewhere. Elephants? What elephants?!

Doing Fall

So, while it's evolutionarily possible we are meant to hang out together, it's also historically true that we have put many systems in place to create a balance and mitigate the 'altogether, all the time' rule. That was true back in the day too—hunters and gatherers had to leave family members to, well, hunt, and then, gather. We were not necessarily wired to be part of the pack, all of the time.

In these times, therefore, we have likely been together waaaaaaaaaaaaaaaay too much. Normally, in summer, we think, 'ah, time to get back together and re-connect as a family and decrease the frenetic pace of running hither and yon and enjoy some pajama days and down time.' This year, not so much. The notion of family game night once a week is less appealing if you've been playing games nightly. According to many lovely parents and teens, the idea of sitting around lounging together seems more punishment then pleasure at this point, and the notion of 'stay at home schooling' with an indefinite timeline, well, it is pushing some of us over the brink.

I'm not suggesting we all abdicate our roles and responsibilities and run away (Because, honestly, where would we go? How would we get there? I actually looked into how much it costs to charter a plane— and turns out, it costs TONS AND TONS…. go figure!)

But I do think in our pivoting (spiraling) we have to plop lots of numbers into the equation of 'how to do Fall, 2020.' We have to consider many aspects of each family member, such as educational and academic needs, medical needs, social needs, emotional and psychological needs, behavioral needs, and physical needs. This would become an algebra problem too complex for me to even write out, let alone solve, but it IS something we can each draw out—maybe on a white board. (In addition to the plexiglass producers and delivery industries, I think the white board people are going to really 'make bank' with this upcoming academic year—because, yes, google and outlook calendars are fine, but we all need some huge visual cues, especially ones where we can continually erase and then re-write things, preferably with cool markers that smell good.)

Therefore, consider drawing a grid. This can be a fun family meeting or just you, locked in a closet, by yourself, counting this sadly as today's 'self-care.' Put each 'need' category across the top and each family member's name on the left side. If you can do it in three-D, then also have it spread out for each of the days of the week. (See why I'm neither a mathematician nor an artist?) I think you get the drift here. Write down what needs to happen in each of these arenas because as we panic about one area of need (for instance, literacy for 3rd graders, a legit worry) we may forget another area of need (for instance, exercise for 10-year-olds, who, like puppies, need 45 minutes twice per day of cardio activity to be health and to not drive you nuts.)

Something to think about as the days of summer wane. (Do they, wane? What is wane? Decrease? Decline? If that's the case, then have we not all been waning since about March, 2020)

However, Fall does bring with it some good things, even in these days, during the time of the pandemic.

Maybe take back some of your old Autumn traditions and buy everyone a few 'back to school outfits' even though we all may be living in shorts and tees for months to come. Or buy some school supplies online and let everyone pick out a lunch box or backpack even if they won't be using them as they would have, were things 'regular.' Take out your box of Fall décor (unless you threw it out while Marie Kondo-ing the garage last month) and start putting sunflowers all over the house, as preludes to pumpkins and pinecones.

Any which way, the time passes. Let's try to pass it with panache, by practicing random acts of PRIVACY whenever you can arrange for it, so that we can enjoy our time with the pack. Set up Plan A and Plan B and Plan C. Make a chart or a grid or a table. Use a chalk board or a white board or your sidewalk sense. And remember, distance *does* make the heart grow fonder, so make sure to set up sometimes when you are in the back yard, and they are in the front yard, or vice versa!

It's Not Personal, It's Parenting

I took a totally non-scientific poll of the many adolescents, tweens, and teens I 'see' in my weekly therapy sessions. I have major respect for these young Gen Z folk and feel confident that at the end of the day, they will surpass our current generations and will be able to get the world 'back' while also establishing some permanence in the fields of humor, whimsy, and plain old-fashioned fun.

I asked them, "WHAT SHOULD PARENTS KNOW IN THESE TIMES?"

They had many suggestions, of which many are quite on the mark. (I changed genders and details of each of these and they are a conglomerate of many kids to protect the privacy of the speakers.)

"Please remind our parents that we know we are NOT Anne Frank. We are not being rounded up and incarcerated in Manzana. We are not being sold as slaves nor are we being sex trafficked. And we know the difference. Our world views are probably larger than you'd think.

So, when we whine and carry on about being trapped:

1) Do not remind us we are lucky to not be living in Darfur. Perspective, not helpful. We know. We still wanna whine.

2) Do not join in and tell us how horrible this is for YOU. Honestly, in that moment, we do not care if it is hard for you. We are whining about how hard it is for US.

3) Do not offer some lame activity, like, 'I know honey, let's play BOGGLE tonight.' Do not do NOT put out one more jigsaw puzzle. Just, please, do not.

4)   Finally, do not offer platitudes about how 'this too shall pass.' Yes, we know. What we'd prefer is a nice, 'Oh, dear, so, so, sorry about this. Yes, it sucks.' And then please please, please, PLEASE—walk away and give us a BIT OF PRIVACY for goodness's sake!"

Smart kid, I'd say. Then there is the one who told me:

"I wish my parents would be better at both being sympathetic about my friend drama and then not overly interested in my friend drama. It's my drama. They should stick to their own friend drama. You don't see me getting all up in that business, now do ya?"

Granted, this is a hard request for us parents. We think 'So, you want your cake and eat it too!??!' And the answer is, 'yes, we do, thanks much.'

Then there's a lovely 17-year-old who told me:

"My mom needs to back off a bit. Now that we are together, like, ALL THE TIME, she needs to quit constantly asking if I've finished my summer reading, written all my essays for college applications, called grandma, written out a gratitude list, and cleaned out my closet. Honestly, it's enough. I know she loves me and cares about me, but.... I'm 17! I will either do this stuff (which most likely I will—I mean, in the past, it's not like I did NOT complete summer reading) or I will not, in which case, bad on me. She should live her life and let me live my mine."

Actually, that's probably the main theme—teen to parent—"Live your life, let me live mine." (Except, also, "Can you pick up that great color purple so I can color my hair before school starts?!")

And here is a good one from a 14-year-old boy.

"I'd like my dad to know that I am not my sister or my brother. I'm not a jock. I'm not a whiz kid. I'm fine being me, but, both lower the bar and raise it and encourage me to be the best me, not a knock-off of them. My feeling is that when life was normal, no one was staring at me for so many hours per day, adding up how I'm not good enough. But now that we are ALWAYS together—all bets are off. You have too much free time on your hand. Maybe YOU should start jogging, dad, because honestly, I don't see that in my future, no matter how many times you mention it."

On the mark, I'd say. And how about this:

"I like that you are interested in my life mom/dad, but please be more interested in your life than in mine. I like that you like to problem solve for me, but please just be a good listener, nod your head, and go back to solving your problems, not mine. If we don't have prom, and I want to make prom in the backyard, I will figure it out with my friends. We love your support and help at some point, but this is for us to do. Not you. You can go back to figuring out taxes, and if we can afford college still, and where we will all be a year from now. Please, do not board my roller coaster, even if it's tempting. This is my ride. With all due respect, find your own."

And I like this one:

"Parents, take note—not everything in my life is COVID related. I have lots of other stuff going on, so let's change up the topic of conversation every now and then, ok?"

Very bright, loving teens, struggling with their own stuff, attempting to be respectful on a good day and to fly below the radar on another day—but, on almost every day, they have lots to say!

When asked by me "Can you tell this to your mom or dad?" the answer is pretty much always, "'No way.' It will hurt her feelings, make her more anxious, and start a fight of some sorts. I just want him to keep his anxiety to himself. I don't want to freak them out. It's better to keep quiet and just work around them."

Perhaps in some instances these kids are right, and it's best to not say everything you think or feel. On the other hand, I know parents, and I know they are trying hard and want to be the best they can, for each of their children. Perhaps a little bit of getting the teens to speak up will help?

And if not, here's a note from me, one parent to another—it's not personal—it's parenting. Hold onto your adult support system, because the road ahead is going to continue to be quite bumpy!

Long Time Passing...

So, did you know that following the big shortage of Clorox wipes and toilet paper, we are now encountering a new challenge—DESKS are the new toilet paper. Yup, if you live in California and recently realized 'oops, the kids WILL be learning from home and oops, my spouse and I will NOT be going into our offices for, fill in the blank, weeks/months/years?!' then you are not alone. No one has desks. And people selling them on Craig's list or eBay are getting double what they are worth, because even IKEA cannot get enough of them. Because warehouses are having to social distance their staff to ensure safety, there are often less than 1/3 the number of builders who produce things like, well, everything—furniture, appliances, clothing and yes, desks. Unlike with the TP and sanitizer shortages, however, this is not due to hoarding (although, if ANY of you have hoarded desks in your garage, call me, I'm on the hunt!). We are demanding for the manufacturers to supply but in this new upside-down world, supplying our demands that were not anticipated is impossible. So, we'll continue balancing laptops on laps while sitting on old recliner chairs in the den and pretend this is what 'going to work' looks like. Or, as many teens are doing, we will be sitting in bed, in pjs, with a tablet, which now constitutes 'going to school.' Please take selfies and save to the cloud because this is all going to be in the history books starting let's say, next year.

The funny thing is that as the world revolves, our lives become simultaneously both smaller, and larger. Smaller as we stay indoors, primarily, or walk our neighborhoods, and larger, as we zoom with people all over the planet. Smaller, as our private space feels less private with family members observing (and commenting on) one another. Larger, as our life cycle events are now attended by relatives across many time zones. On a plus note, WHEN we remember to schedule social time, even virtually, we enjoy it. And WHEN we remember to take a drive up the coast, we enjoy it. Hiking, swimming, biking, scootering (the three-year-olds on my block put us all to shame), surfing, rollerblading, yoga-ing, dancing, we enjoy it.

A new high or low for me has been the indoor games I play with Ginger, the rescue dog. She finds something she's not supposed to have (my fuzzy socks from the dollar tree, of which I am running low) and I chase her. My house has 'flow', so we have a circular path to take. At one point, I turn and go the other way and surprise her face to face. We have yet to tire of this game, and if I am really being good, I find a pair of shoes to put on so there is a loud clicky clacky sound, which makes the game even funnier.

And now schools are starting. I could write about school and education every day of the week, but there are others who do that for a living. (Check out *edsource@edsource.org* for instance, or *https://www.edusourcedapp.com/* for great reporting and easy to digest information for educators and parents.)

But any which way, school is starting. Or, as the case may be with many a school, it has already begun.

What is that experience going to mean to the littles, who do not have a bank of prior knowledge of 'school'—raising your hand, taking a turn, handling anger management, making a new friend, playing nicely, asking a teacher for help, learning by watching peers master things you have yet to master, playing on the yard, feeling praised for effort and success, being exposed to handball and foursquare and jump rope followed by kickball and tether ball when a bit older. How do six sessions of 30-minute Zoom segments work for kindergarteners. Remember Sesame Street? The longest snippets are far less than half hour in length. And who is helping the five-year old get Zoomed up and running, then turned off, then turned on again? And what about the other three plus hours they used to be in school? What to do with those hours? How do littles learn without the yard and indoors for some learning and outdoors for other learning? How do they build a community with blocks when home alone? How do they study 'people in my neighborhood' when trapped in their room all day? And what about when the sound on the tablet didn't work, as was the case for many last week. And what about when there is not enough Wi-Fi to go around for all four, five, six people working or studying at home? And what about when three students share one bedroom, and no one has headphones or ear plugs?

What about the experience for the kids who will now be deprived of building a California mission out of sugar cubes? What will happen to that 'special talk' in 5th grade when the boys go in the auditorium with their dads and the gym teacher and the next day, the girls go into the auditorium with their moms and the gym teacher? What of starting middle school and mastering, after much trepidation, both your hall locker AND your gym locker? Or high school with photo IDs and sports teams and clubs, like robotics, or community service, or Key Club? What of orchestras and marching bands and jazz bands? What of teacher office hours? Yes, they are offering them virtually, which would seem ideal, but—I wonder, how many students are going to take advantage of those? I'm sure someone is keeping track, but the first effort goes to tracking COVID-19 cases across counties, so, things like how many kids are attending which classes when and which students we lose on day #8—sigh.

Then also, what about basic learning, rudimentary skills, and critical thinking? How well does it happen when there are rolling black outs due to the heat wave, sisters having PE on zoom in the same bedroom as other sisters studying Algebra II, and brothers practicing their recorder in the kitchen with the other siblings practicing language drills in the den?

Overcoming the Challenges

If there is a parent who is rocking this, I want them to have a platform like the speakers at the political conventions and tell us all HOW DO WE DO THIS? On the other hand, if you saw Brayden Harrington give a speech while overcoming a stutter, you realize, we really can overcome all kinds of challenges, even if they seem unsurmountable. (If you have not seen this, please Google it AND have your children watch it. Amazing.)

As a psychologist, I'm lightly tracking it all, wondering how the intersection of learning and mental health (or mental illness) is forming. The stressors are impossibly high for every part of this algorithm— teachers, administration, parents, children, grandparents, community members. We are all certain we do not want to put anyone in harm's way by being together in person too soon and we are also certain that for the good of the whole community and society, in addition to medical health, we still need to raise up our next generation into people who are literate, thoughtful, reflective, critical thinking humans. We need the youth of today to have both breadth and specificity of knowledge that comes not just from enriched homes and cultural dens, but also, from graded, sequential, well developed and well tested curricula, so they can grow into the leaders of our future who will better handle crises like pandemics, wildfires due to climate challenges, disparities, and violence.

At this point, all I can figure is that we have to do a few things at the same time:

1) Lower our expectations for ourselves as parents and quiet the inner critical voice we hear AND quiet the critical voice we are using when addressing spouse or parent partner or in-laws. Cut yourself

and the other members of the village some slack, assume positive intention (API!) and keep in mind that saying snarky things, albeit gratifying for a few seconds, is better saved for talking back to your tv, and not to your people.

AND

2)   Raise our expectations. See, that's where the 'do a few things at the same time' comes in—lower your expectations in one regard and keep them high in the other. Keep your expectations high when it comes to practicing kindness and patience, when it comes to using humor (levity and brevity) in your interactions with those with whom you share space. Expect yourself and your family to learn things during this time and do not give up on that objective. Use whomever and whatever is available to you—niece who is now doing college remotely? She likely has free time on her hands and is stuck at home going nowhere and seeing no one. Hire her. Next door neighbor who is 70 and healthy and going nowhere? She may be helpful to you and yours. If you don't have easy access, try signing onto Next Door App—a free app for neighbors to share ideas and resources.

We do not have to understand all the terminology (synchronous versus asynchronous instruction??) but we do need to know that in the local public schools, our littles get 180 minutes, 1st thru 3rd grade kids receive 230 minutes and grades 4-12 will have 240 minutes of instruction a day. So that's three hours for littles, less than four for middles, and four hours for bigs. Thus, requiring us as a society to make up the difference.

We can do this. We can take deep breaths and know our limitations and ask for help when needed. And then teach our children, reach out for help when needed. Warning signs things are going poorly are when your children withdraw, want to sleep all the time, revert to old behaviors (bedwetting, thumb sucking, fingernail biting, temper tantruming) and when they look 'checked out.' Take those signs seriously and look for them early in the semester so we can try to help them sooner than later. They may not learn all the advanced math you'd like this year, but we need them ok for next year, and the year thereafter, etc.

Furniture Swapping

I can't tell you how many times a week a parent, most often a mom, tells me, "I'm such a bad mother." Sometimes they say it in jest, but most often...it's with an underlying sense of failure, despair, and sadness. I remind them that 'bad moms' do not wonder or reflect on their parenting skills and that no mom has a child and then wants to do a poor job. However, the task is so ginormous, it's hard to keep perspective. And no parent, ever, can be great at every aspect of parenting. Maybe use the 80:20 rule.... during pandemic, maybe make it closer to the 50:50. Are we doing ok at least 50% of the time? And by what measure?

In these times, of taking on burden and task upon task, to be nurturing and kind, to be organized and efficient, to keep everyone healthy, to oversee and help teach, to master technology, to be frugal and adhere to a budget, to continue to make a living or support those in the family bringing home the income, to put together pods and bubbles, but then dismantle them because of new phases or tiers or alerts or color warnings....it's amazing any parent is at all efficient and that more are not staying in bed binging all the Disney channel has to offer!

I too find myself succumbing to this thought process. It's a slippery slope.

I KNOW I'm a bad mom because in the last month, we took out the 'guest beds' in our house and substituted in desks and office chairs. There was no room for cohabitation of beds and professional space, so something had to give. My husband and I managed the first six months of the pandemic by working from a reclining chair (him) and from a large Costco folding table (me.) We continued to have faith in two things: We will go back to work soon. Our children will be able to come visit soon.

Turns out, we are wrong on both accounts.

UCLA is going back 'maybe sometime mid 2021' and my beloved small office space may not be safe for in person therapy sessions for a year or longer. And, given health concerns and access to science and education, our sons, ages 33 and 28, are not traveling from DC to LA to hang out with us. They are highly conscientious regarding keeping themselves safe, and especially worried and careful to 'not come to LA to kill the parents.' It may sound extreme, but they study the Hopkins data, first-hand, and let us know it's too risky. We are all behaving cautiously and judiciously and enjoying weekly Zoom visits and more phone calls and texts than were previously part of our long-distance family norms. Our local daughter is also hard to see, as she is an essential worker, exposed every time she goes into work, which is at least three times weekly... so, no daytime guests and for sure no overnight guests. Although, when they are our kids, they are not 'guests.' Which makes this decision seem more heart breaking than perhaps it really is.

While it is practical to not house beds when there is no indication of children's sleep overs, it still feels weird. There has never been a time we didn't have a house situated to accommodate children, even though we have been empty nest folk for at least ten years. We liked our house to be ready at all times (which is our excuse also for having so many treats in here—even though the kids are healthier eaters than are we....still—chocolate raisins from Costco in the cupboard, just in case an East Coast offspring suddenly moves in and craves the comfort food of youth!)

Parenting during a pandemic is hard at any age and stage, and I am in the easiest of all stages—post-kids in the house, pre-grand kids on the planet. I feel guilty and am well aware of my privilege. Nonetheless, my role as mom has always been of paramount importance to me, and the home we had during those first 25 years made it easier. The physical comforts of multiple rooms, swimming pool, band room, basketball court—they all were so helpful. They really raised up the kids. And now, here we are—not many bedrooms, no pool, no place (thankfully) for the drum set....and, it appears, no beds.

It makes me sad and nostalgic for a different time. Or maybe I'm just sad and nostalgic for a different time in general. Maybe I'm full up of the larger sense of loss, as well as the littler losses. Maybe I'm missing the ability to hug children and do their laundry and take them to that most religious place of all—Costco. Maybe I'm missing 'before the pandemic' and somedays, it's harder than others. Maybe, maybe, maybe.

I'm setting up these home offices now, organizing closets and realizing I somehow have enough supplies to supply the neighborhood. I keep looking through stacks of papers. And then I'm missing random things—for instance, how is that we do not own a stapler?! Is that even possible?

Despite the heat, I venture into the garage, where all kinds of things are sitting in boxes, waiting to be re-discovered. I cannot find a stapler to save my life. I find many empty mason jars awaiting granola production at Thanksgiving. I even find "decorations for Fall", although, I'm on the fence about taking that down. And then, low and behold, I find an old trunk. I open it up.

Turns out, we own tons of blow-up mattresses. Who knew?

It's clearly not the same but.... I feel deeply comforted to know the kids can drop in any time. I have beds. Just in case.

Accepting Us for Where We Are

'It was the best of years, it was the worst of years', but then I wonder—really? Is that true? For sure some 'bests' were experienced—weddings, evolving love stories, animal additions to family packs, graduations, home making, gardening, baking, and cooking, lots of visits together B.C. (before Covid) And some harder parts for sure, but the worst? Let's recall and hold onto the fact that there was good health for some, or the ability to access help when health was faltering. For the lucky there were no heart attacks, cancer diagnoses, untimely deaths. For many of us, we were well fed, well cared for, remembered by loved ones.

So perhaps a reminder of the full Dickens' quote:

"It was the best of times, it was the worst of times, it was the age of wisdom, it was the age of foolishness, it was the epoch of belief, it was the epoch of incredulity, it was the season of light, it was the season of darkness, it was the spring of hope, it was the winter of despair."

And this is reminiscent of an older quote, the Biblical quote from Ecclesiastes:

"To everything (turn, turn, turn) there is a season and a purpose for everything under heaven." TO everything there is a season, and a time to every purpose under the heaven: A time to be born, and a time to die; a time to plant, and a time to pluck up that which is planted; a time to kill, and a time to heal; a time to break down, and a time to build up; a time to weep, and a time to laugh; a time to mourn, and a time to dance; a time to cast away stones, and a time to gather stones together; a time to embrace, and a time to refrain from embracing; a time to get, and a time to lose; a time to keep, and a time to cast away; a time to rend, and a time to sew; a time to keep silence, and a time to speak; a time to love, and a time to hate; a time of war, and a time of peace."

Embracing All Our Seasons

Which makes me reflect that perhaps this was not the 'worst' of times for some, including me, a woman of much privilege and blessing. For many, yes. Tragedy upon tragedy. Racism, not new, but exposed repeatedly. A virus from which many are dying and suffering and which is wrecking long term havoc we cannot even begin to comprehend—economic, educational, child developmental, interpersonal, medical and psychological messes which will last for decades. Ongoing climate changes such that California is on fire most of the time and temperatures of over 120 in the valley. So yes, the worst of times in a global sense.

But on a personal sense, maybe not. There was and is joy from last year and I'm committed to continue to note it and experience it in 5781 and I invite you to join in.

The upcoming Jewish New Year is almost upon us. Literally known as 'the head of the year,' Rosh Hashana begins Friday September 18, in the evening, at sunset. It is the official kick off to something known as 'the ten days of awe.' It is a time, unlike the secular New Year (where we stay up til midnight, drink lots, karaoke lots, and have a blast), or the fiscal new year (where we get nervous, work late, turn in every piece of paperwork we've mistakenly forgotten to submit, and prepare for the next fiscal audit), and unlike the back to school new year (where we *used* to buy school supplies, worry on behalf of our children, pack lunches, and buy more school supplies and where *now* we mostly just worry on behalf of our children), this New Year is established as a time of introspection and self-reflection—a time to take stock of where we are, and to think about '*Who shall live and who shall die? Who by water and who by fire, who by sword, who by beast, who by famine, who by thirst,*

who by storm, who by plague, who by strangulation, and who by stoning?
Who will rest and who will wander, who will live in harmony and who
will be harried, who will enjoy tranquilly and who will suffer, who will
be impoverished and who will be enriched, who will be degraded and who
will be exalted?' The basic idea and metaphor are that a big book will
be written, and decisions will be made—but—and here's the catch—
apparently with REPENTANCE, PRAYER, and CHARITY we each
have the ability to remove evil of any potential decree and change our
fate for the next year. And we do so as individuals, yes, and also, as part
of a community.

How do we find community when we are cut off from people?
Where do we meet our social needs, when socializing is ill advised?

I have found that in these days, a sense of connectedness pops up
in the funniest places.

For instance, I went to get my flu shot. And it was a 'drive through'
flu shot experience. And it was fascinating, depressing, impressive
AND a bizarre connection to community. I was sad that it did not
include a double double burger and fries, as In n Out was the last drive
through experience I had, back in February, but….it had other perks.
For instance, the nurses, all pediatric for some reason, were wearing
cute medical smocks, including a Winnie the Pooh one and a Safari
themed one. They were very friendly and chatty while also efficient.
They let me know that none of them have gotten sick, that the COVID
numbers in the local ICU were down, and that they were preparing for
a post Labor Day increase over the next week.

I hear from my patients that if they want any social time 'at school'
(i.e., in their online classes) then they need to hop onto the Zoom 10
minutes before class. These kids are full of Zoom tips. For instance,
do NOT write anything in the chat, not even a private message, as the
teacher/school can read it all. Also, it's easy enough to look engaged
in class while having your OTHER screen/tablet/phone under the
keyboard or to the left of the webcam. Also, just about every child I've

seen of late (including littles) have told me that it is close to impossible to NOT cheat. And they note that 'it takes lots of friends to do it well', so, there you have it—friendship in the time of virtual school. Good news—these kids will be incredibly resourceful and able to hack into any computer system of the present or future while also multi-tasking nicely. Bad news—no way anyone will really learn Algebra, let alone Algebra II.

SO, a new year coming—5781. Lots of years behind. Thousands. And thousands. And many horrific events that happened, and then passed, and then people moved on and even thrived. I imagine in the course of time, that cycle will continue. But it's hard to imagine the years ahead, while stuck in the quicksand of this specific time.

Here is a story I learned this week: On days we feel superior to others we should remember we are but dust. But on other days, when we feel like dust, we should believe the world was created just for us— for you, actually. Yes, there is a corresponding responsibility—we have to help repair the world, as it is not finished yet, by any means, but hold onto the notion—the world was created for each of you, individually. You bring such promise simply by being YOU.

And so –this unusual 'holiday' speaks to me—more so even than in previous years. Can I live life more fully? Can I re-configure the words and change them into more life affirming notions? *Who shall live by sharing water with others, and who by igniting sparks of fun and imagination in others? Who shall live with pithy sword-like wit and humor and laughter, and who by playing with big dogs who look like beasts, and who by helping to sustain others so they do not feel famine of either body or soul? Who will live by remembering to pace themselves and take naps on occasion, and who will have some wanderlust and adventure—who will bring harmony to people living with conflict and who will be able to take deep breaths to help others AND themselves? Who will live with tranquility and then share that with their community, and who will find enrichment in this, of all times?*

Who will we be in the years ahead? Whomsoever it shall be, we will be together.

I leave us with this last quote: Here is the world. Beautiful and terrible things will happen. Don't be afraid. -Frederick Beuchner A year of goodness to all.

Feeling Not So Fine

Fall is officially here, as we can tell, because it is over 100 degrees, fires are burning, Santa Anas are blowing, and Costco sent out a flyer with Christmas merch. It is hard to experience loss and remain grateful and hard to do for others when feeling depleted. And yet....

I'm noticing our language patterns in these times. Perhaps it's from just a tad too much 'alone time' or perhaps just that I spend most of my day in 1:1 Zoom calls, often with kids and teens. I am conscious of what we are saying. For instance, in nice alliteration, one of my littler patients, a nine-year-old, told me, "I know the key to managing in COVID.... it's puppies, ponies, and Peloton."

Only in L.A., by the way.

I used to think a lot of things differentiated our lives in L.A. from others'. But those distinctions are fading, along with our hair roots. We still live in the land where image is important, but perhaps it's decreasing in significance during these times.... fewer eyebrow and eye lash appointments, despite being on Zoom. Plus, I'm sure that given I have figured it out, you also realized that...Zoom has a 'virtual filter' that removes years' of wrinkles from your face staring back at you in the little box on the computer screen. Just sayin....

Who else is saying what?

Lots of teens (and parents too) are talking about 'what to do in order to feel normal, even for only a little bit.' One told me 'I feel normal when I 'change classes' at home, like I did in Middle School, so I rotate from my bedroom to the kitchen to the den to the patio and back.' (I love that idea and have proposed it to others as well.) One said, "I basically do not even remember normal, which scares me. What did it look like? What did it feel like? Did I used to have more than one to two friends, or did I only THINK I had more than one to two friends?" Funny thing is, many of us did not like or appreciate 'normal' when we had it, only to nostalgically wish for it back now.

Trying to find normal is like trying to dunk the ball when you are under 5 feet. It's not 100% impossible, but it requires dedication and practice and commitment. To find normal we need to make at least one or two 'playdates' per week, whatever those may look like. (And if you are arranging these on Zoom for younger children, limit them to half an hour....more than that, and the "I WILL SO MUTE YOU WHENVER I WANNA" wars will become impressive.) Finding normal means indulging in fun treats now and then—drive through shakes instead of drive through flu shots, decorating inside and outside for Autumn instead of going into a 'house of horror,' and instead of a 'pajama day' a 'dress up in a suit and play go to a meeting in person day.' It includes spur of the moment moments as well as joyful planning for a week or so ahead. Rescue a dog. Foster a kitten. Take a painting or cooking class. Start a longer-term project.... build a car or computer with your teen, learn to code, or simply just be. It's not like you used to be busy every moment, is it? And, while at it and seeking the new normal, DO NOT feel you have to cook and then sit down to eat as a family seven of seven nights. (I will write you a note.) Shake off the 'I feel guilty for ....' and rinse in 'It will be okay if I just ....'

Last weekend I wondered if I had COVID. There was virtually no way I could have contacted it, given how small my world is, but...I ran a low-grade temp (under 101.4, but off and on for three days) and I felt achy, and I had a headache and upset stomach. B.C. (Before COVID) I would have worked my regular day and ignored it. However, in these times, I was busy trying to figure out just when I would lose my sense of smell and taste and thinking that IF I could have a mild case (please, please, please) could I then return to normal life? To seeing people in person? To traveling? To visiting with my young adult children and not so young parents? So, off we went, husband and I, for drive by COVID testing (thank you Kaiser.) Swab throat, swab nostril high enough up to touch parts of brain, drive on through. 15 minutes. Results less than 24 hours later. NEGATIVE. How nice is it to get a negative test result?

Turns out I had a light case of the flu, despite having had the flu shot, because there is no shot that is 100% preventative for the flu. I'm climbing out of it today. Less achy. Less likely to continue to have no appetite (sigh) and more likely to want to have some pumpkin spice something delivered to me (because I deserve it, right!?)

A patient in her late teens told me, 'I did not like before, and I do not like now so I am holding out for what's next, because there will be something next, right?!' While sad about her statements about her past and present, I was happy to hear optimism for the future.

There will be something next. We have to hold onto this ride and ride it out, while also remembering, there will be something next.

Can We Get Along?

I t's a funny time. Not funny 'ha ha' but funny, 'what the heck is going on? Kamala is a role model now for women everywhere. Did you see the video of her great niece asking if she can grow up to be President AND an astronaut? ('Yes,' says her aunt, 'but you have to be 35 to be President.') And who will be the role model and mentor for Kamala? I imagine she is especially sad, even amidst her joy, to not have her mom moving in with her in the days ahead. Meantime, she found out that she and "Joe" won while out jogging. And the little snippet of her reaction—her laughter, her sense of 'for real!?!?' and the fact that she looked like a natural woman, binding anxiety on a day of uncertainty, by running in the park? Priceless.

Meantime let's remember that half of the U.S. voting population voted one way, and half the other. More people voted than ever before, and the inspirational included the pollsters and polling commissioners who were working around the clock to ensure democracy by counting every vote. In fact, they are still counting the votes. We all now know geography tons better than a week ago, including the names of little counties in Arizona and Georgia and in particular, Pennsylvania. A time to reap and a time to sow. And while not explicitly part of the saying '….and a time to make friends with people different than ourselves.'

Our children are isolating and withdrawing, and we are worrying. We call one another—what can we do? She is so lonely. He is so sad. They are so irritable. We wonder—how do you teach a 6-year-old how to make a friend, while living during a pandemic? How do you help your senior shake off the blues and get out of their bedroom?

We say to these children of ours, "Well, be nice to the new kid. Ask if she wants a Zoom play date. See if he likes video games. Find out what they do after school for fun. See if they are in a pod, we can join for a backyard playdate. Find out if s/he likes to roller blade or bake or do arts and crafts. See if s/he likes the same movies or tv shows you like. Find out what their favorite food is. Ask them if they have brothers or sisters. Ask if they grew up in this area or if they moved here at some point." We advise, "Use your sense of humor. Make a study date. Meet at the park for an exercise class. Talk to a friend of a friend. Call your camp pals. Bake cupcakes and drop them at their front door. Surprise them with a funny meme." We are saying…. Get to know them. Get to know them. Get to know them."

These are sound parental directives and suggestions for us to issue to our children and I hear creative ideas every week from parents who are desperately trying to help provide some normalcy in a time of topsy turvy.

And now, now is the time. A time to make a new friend. A time to reach out. A time to embrace 'other' and find the common ground. Outside our own bubbles, if not in person, then at least online, on zoom, on social media. Embrace. The. Other.

Listen. Most of us live in pockets of people with whom we share similarities, and the 'other' is not our actual neighbor. Likely we voted the same as many on our block. That's ok. Let's remember though, we all have relatives in Arkansas and Kansas and a Dakota state. Now is a good time to call, check in, see how they are holding up. Let's be respectful and not act smug or superior while making a new friend or deepening a connection with an old friend. Let's see what we have in common (tough raising a kid when they have to do zoom school all day—yup—me too…. worried about ever getting to travel to see grandchildren again—yup, me too….garden coming along ok—mosquitos all taking over—yup, me too, worried about my aging parents—yup, me too….dog getting into messes in this weather—yup, me too.)

Humans are wired to categorize and organize. We intuitively like to put things together, looking for the pattern and trying to forcefully design one if it is not readily apparent. We tend toward what looks and feels familiar. However, when we break it down, we can see we are each distinctly individuals and we are also all part of a larger whole. A whole that is much bigger than the sum of its parts, which you probably recall from recently teaching math to your twins.

As Simon and Garfunkel eloquently reminded us decades ago, we're all on a quest to look for America.

Counting on Pandemic Math

Many of us are busy doing math these days. How much money do we have in savings? Should we pay car insurance if we are not driving anywhere? Can we cancel memberships without sustaining fines? Should we purchase ANY new clothes when our closets are seeing no action and our yoga pants really do last a long time? And what shall we do regarding December gifting, given our traditions from years of yore, given our realities of problems of pandemic? How shall we make it from here til January, keeping ourselves and loved ones safe, but also finding and celebrating joy, somewhere somehow?

There is a kind of math upon which we can focus, which maybe will be helpful. Let's call it 'mom math', or even, 'family math.'

Family math is not too complicated; repeat after me:

The WHOLE is greater than the SUM of its parts.

Aristotle is credited with coming up with this equation. Smart guy, that Aristotle. He undoubtedly was using this concept to explain important aspects of geometry, and I'm sure he succeeded. For me, however, since learning about this in what we then called junior high school, I have always thought of it as 'family math' because it is the best explanation, I can think of to describe family. As individuals, we all have unique things to contribute to life and to the planet and to one another. We have our ups our downs, our niceties, and our absurdities. But—if you add us all up, if you quantify us and then do the math—every single time, good or bad- we are much greater than what you'd expect. Indeed, our whole is greater than the sum or our parts.

This is applicable to all forms of families.... families of origin, blended and extended families, friend families, foster families, adopted families, and even, our newest constellation of family, 'the pod family.' Pulitzer Prize winning author and mom, Anna Quindlen, once wrote:

Raising children is presented at first as a true-false test, then becomes multiple choice, until finally, far along, you realize that it is an endless essay.

She wrote that in 2000. She also said:

Every part of raising children is humbling. Believe me, mistakes were made. They have all been enshrined in the 'Remember-When-Mom-Did' Hall of Fame. The outbursts, the temper tantrums, the bad language—mine, not theirs. The times the baby fell off the bed. The times I arrived late for preschool pickup. The nightmare sleepover. The horrible summer camp. The day when the youngest came barreling out of the classroom with a 98 on her geography test, and I responded, "What did you get wrong?" (She insisted I include that here.) The time I ordered food at the McDonald's drive-through speaker and then drove away without picking it up from the window. (They all insisted I include that.) I did not allow them to watch the Simpsons for the first two seasons. What was I thinking? But the biggest mistake I made is the one that most of us make while doing this. I did not live in the moment enough.

2020 has been full of struggle, uncertainty, and loss and we are not out of it yet and it is not done with us yet. We are nervous, worried, anxious. It feels like all we DO is live in the moment. Our littles are having a hard time sleeping. Our bigs are withdrawing and becoming expert video gamers while their grades drop, and their missing assignments sheets grow. Young adults are 'on hold.' Parents are beyond exhausted. Working people are grateful for work and also overwhelmed with Zoom fatigue and the juggle of myriad responsibilities. Aging adults are doing their best to master technology and interact with their grandchildren virtually. It is almost impossible to thrive during this time. Living in the moment often feels painful. However, there are choices we can make, even in times of adversity. Living in the moment with our families can have long-term positive implications, believe it or not, as noted by Ms. Quindlen, if we can find that hidden strength to make the moment meaningful.

There is time, even in the gray of the uncertainty, to make something out of nothing and to reach for whimsy and fun.

Let's do the math.

First, find joy. Search for it and create it, even as it alludes us. What's a memory you have that can be recreated? A family photo from ten years ago? From twenty years ago? Go for it! Model the little modes of joy for your children by striving to NOT strive to have a perfect Thanksgiving dinner. Commit to it, own it, say it aloud—this year we are planning and preparing for an IMPERFECT holiday season.

Plan for an adequate meal, not an over the top one. Unless you are inviting Martha Stewart for dinner, don't sweat if your napkins don't match your plates and if your dessert is not the cover of Bon Appetit magazine. Watch some cooking and baking shows and focus on their failures—it's so comforting when those bakers take something out of the oven that is not baked all the way through or that falls over when they try to decorate it. Consider a 50-50 meal ... 50% brought in and prepared by someone else (Whole Foods, for instance!) and 50% prepared by you.

Meantime decorate, decorate, decorate. Have a family meeting. Choose a theme. Choose a few themes. Make paper chains and cut out snowflakes. Let your family decorate placemats. Collect pinecones or order some online. (Note—do NOT put glitter on them—you will regret it for sure!) Go through old photos and make paper frames for them and hang them around the house. Start a family tree on one wall, using photos or maps. Make a circles of friend poster. Check out Pinterest or Google or your sister in law's Facebook page. Do NOT take on something aggravating though. Aim for average. This is not the year to be the overachiever of the group. Aim for fun. Aim for festive. Aim for being in the moment and counting the blessings, not the losses.

Consider creating new traditions mixed with old. Let the sports enthusiasts watch sports, but also have music playing and TVs and screens turned off for some portion of the day. Dance. Make a family tik tok. Go for a walk outside. Call loved ones. Make individual holiday cards, starting this week, to mail in a few weeks. What are manageable things you have yet to try? Have you ever made jam? Granola? Pickles? Mini loaves of bread? Your own tamales? This is the time. Have you gone for a family drive up the coast? Down the coast? Have you made decorations for outside the house, for all the walkers in the neighborhood to enjoy? Do not sweat the little stuff but do invest in a little sweat for a few little projects. Nothing huge. Just an in the moment, hold onto happiness, little things.

Me? Well—we are down to two for Thanksgiving—a first—myself and my husband. So, I will of course set the table with some beanie baby bears. And also, make my cupcake turkeys. And then drop those off at others' houses. Because really, how many cupcakes do we need?

Sitting at This Little Table

A t this little table, the décor is mostly missing. In fact, the table is full of missing leaves, extra chairs, doubled tablecloths. There is no overflow of food, one starch favorite per child, resulting in sweet potatoes and marshmallows, mashed potatoes and gravy, stuffing (two varieties), corn bread, rolls, biscuits, and sometimes homemade mac n cheese in addition. There are no songbooks, stained from years of use, generated first decades ago, when the eldest started kindergarten and all wanted to 'sing with Sammy.' There are no chocolate turkeys, no See's candy at each seat, no turkey hats, and no pinecone turkeys.

At this little table, the loved ones are mostly missing. The young adult children and their loves, in town visiting for the UCLA-USC game and the holiday, they are missing. Missing also are the nephews, home fresh from afar, as well as the two Muppet Men brothers-in-law, who perfected the art of frying turkeys, drinking beer, holding court with kids, not burning down the house, and feigning grumpiness.

At this little table, the cacophony of sounds of reunion, relaxation, reconnection—they are missing. The traditions are missing. The laughter, giddiness, shouting. It is all missing. At this little table, the abundance of family and food and overflowing desserts moved to another table, are all missing.

However, at this little table, sits a husband and wife, with 40 years behind them, and hopefully, many ahead. At this little table, the center piece is a two-way memory window…it shows the past and predicts the future, and the photos of what was and what will yet to be are both full of love and blessing. At this little table, we recognize many have much less in their lives, and there is nothing unique about us. It is just that it is, for this moment, just us.

At this little table, we are on pause. We are at a moment in history, waiting for less loss and more hope and life ahead.

At this little table, despite all that is not, we recognize all the blessings that are.

WINTERING
OUR WOES

Doing Things

Lots and lots of ideas of how to fill our time, in these times, however your brain and heart operate. I've been trying to pay attention to new behaviors rather than become overwhelmed by new offers (listen to Elton John from home, work out with famous personal trainer, do yoga with goats, and just imagine the goats while putting your Sonos on a goat playlist rotation....) For instance, while not signing on to all that is offered online, here is a (not complete) list of **"Things we've started doing in our house:"**

1) Taking multivitamins (found some gummy Flintstone vitamins in the cupboard, sure they are still good)

2) Letting the dog tear up old magazines to entertain us because, why not?

3) Using that tall, long dust brush thingy purchased years ago that was only collecting dust sitting in the garage...turns out that even short people can dust their vents and tops of door frames and boy, does dust ever collect up there!

4) Eating down the freezer (discovering there is an ice maker deep down in there) and googling how many things you can make with frozen chopped spinach because apparently at one point, we must have had many coupons for those!

5) Taking beginner's piano lessons with the 'first book of piano' last used by our now 28-year-old in 1996 (while also trying to convince my young adult kids they need to sit through a recital once I master 10 songs, but so far, no one sounds excited...this, after me sitting through gazillions of hours of their sports, bands, orchestra concerts, and even the occasional dance presentation!) Hmpf!

6)　READING those New Yorker magazines that stack up and typically mock us—for that matter, also reading Bon Appetite and Easy Recipes, magazines that magically showed up a few years back and heretofore went quickly into the recycling bins.

To be fair, there are also lots of things on the list of **"Things we've stopped doing in our house."**

1)　Brushing hair—because, what's the point, really?
2)　Having happy hour inside our neighbor's house (nothing stops us from doing it outdoors, across the lawn/fence, mind you...) because who knows where her visiting relatives have been?
3)　Reading every first alert received on the phone (because alert fatigue set in last week and at this point, perhaps no news is really better than new news)
4)　Pretending to eat only healthy foods because, really, what better excuse is there for comfort food than a world-wide pandemic.
5)　Wondering if PAN in pandemic comes from *PAN*DEMONIUM or from *PAN*DA bear because I looked it up and was sad to see it's the same pan in 'pandemic' and 'pandemonium' ("pan" coming from the Greek for ALL...whereas Panda Bear coming from a Nepalese word meaning eater of bamboo.) So, mystery solved there.

Meantime, little lessons are learned daily, and in no particular order. **Be kind**, it's free and as contagious as a, well, virus. **Be funny**, it's even more contagious than kindness if you can imagine. **Be conscientious**, because without the same ole structure and routine, it's easy to really get lost and while some free floating is good, too much free floating will drown us. And **be gentle**—with yourself, with your family, with your friends....in these times, we really can slow down the pace, plant a garden, and enjoy the parts of our nests often ignored. This time will pass, I promise. But for now, as they say, simply be here now.

Being Part of the Pack

Are we starting to adjust to this as a 'new normal?' I'd say 'no', and that's fine. This is still very new, and there is absolutely nothing normal about these times. Every day presents its own unique challenges and opportunities, so the 'one day at a time' plan is the one to which to subscribe. In this brave new world, I find myself initiating new behaviors as well as ceasing activities, sometimes in the span of a short time period. For example:

Things I've started doing in these times	Things I've stopped doing in these times.
Jogging	Jogging
Weeding garden	Weeding Garden
Making mo-in-law's fudge recipe	Making mo-in-law's fudge recipe
Watching more news	Watching more news
No sugar during the day	No sugar during the day

You get the idea! It's a lovely time to try something new, but it's not necessarily true that given all this 'free time' (is it really? free?) we can get good at something just because we try it. Let's keep things in perspective and really embrace our mastery on the micro-level. Were you nice to your spouse even when you were seething because s/he keeps asking Alexa to turn up the volume and you would like peace and quiet? Were you sweet to your teen even when s/he was snarky to you and said, "I cannot stand being cooped up with you people for one more second!?" Have you figured out ZOOM and google hangouts and

WhatsApp and Facebook video? Did you not only do the laundry, but also fold it AND put it back into drawers? Then pat yourself on the back, for each and every one of these accomplishments. You got this!

There are, however, some things worth taking on in these challenging times. Here is dTip of the day. Yes, dTip: DON'T TAKE IT PERSONALLY. Nope. Even though *it seems it is about you*, and even though *it is directed at you*, it's not really all about you. Although it feels like it, when your four-year-old has her fourth tantrum, it is not about you. When your 12-year-old refuses to build a complicated Lego set you spent hours ordering online and managing to get delivered against all odds, because your 12-year-old LOVES complicated Lego sets, it's not about you. When your 17-year-old will not schedule in a weekly call to grandma, even given his/her love for grandma, it's not about you.

We are all navigating through each day to the best of our ability. Our strength comes from the fact that, as they sang in HIGH SCHOOL MUSICAL, "We are all in this together." At least on some level. (Discussion of privilege held for a different day.) Do you have relatives in other countries? They are in this with us. Do your children have friends they made in camp who live somewhere else in California or the U.S.? They are in this with us. Neighbors, colleagues, the kid in high school who was always bugging you. Family, extended family? All in this together.

The great thing about us humans is that we each have some Golden Retriever DNA in us. Some of us can access it more readily—the 'YAY, it's a new day, I'm here with my pack, I hid 12 tennis balls in the yard yesterday, and I will be going on a zillion walks' mentality. If we can channel our inner golden retriever, and smile a wide grin, it helps. We can still feel our feelings of fear or loss or anger. But let's also focus on "life is good" sidewalk chalk messages for all the folks walking our streets. You can even leave a blank, "Life is Good because _____" and we can fill in those blanks. Picture if this had occurred before we had the www for instance…. life is good because of the internet! Somewhat ironic for all our hours griping about 'too much screen time' that in these times, the screens are connecting us to work, to school, to friends, to doctors…to life.

Mostly, let's remember life is good, because we have one another. We can share our experiences and our feelings and our ideas and our laughter. We can be with our pack in our den. For better for worse. For good times or bad. We are in this together.

Singing A Song

I have two melodies stuck in my head and I cannot dislodge them for the life of me…the soundtrack for this week in the pandemic.

The first is the tune my dryer plays when the cycle ends (doo da da da da da da doo) and the second is R.E.M.'s "It's the end of the world and we know it." Neither is uplifting although at least the dryer noise is practical and helpful.

In these times, it's a good idea to choose a theme song—you can do it for yourself, or your family can do it together. You can do it daily or weekly or periodically. It can be a camp song, a gospel song, a prayer or blessing, pop or country, hip hop or classic rock, or the opening from "FRIENDS." If possible, find something that is positive, inspirational, uplifting, and/or humorous. If you're doing it as a family, you can make a game of it and each time the song plays throughout the day, you all stop what you're doing and dance a little, or air guitar a bit, or execute a freeze frame contest.

Look through your playlists or your friends' playlists or any celebrities' play list. Think more Katy Perry's 'Firework' think less Mr. Lonely.

In these times, we are needing to arm ourselves with planning some joyful activities, even when challenged to think up activities we've never done before. My 90-year-old Auntie Esther said her granddaughter from Boston mailed her puzzles. "I've never done a puzzle before in my life," she told me. "And I have 300 or 1000 or 5000 pieces all on top of the table and no clue how to get started." She also told me her tv viewing has expanded to now include Netflix UNORTHODOX, Married at First Sight, and Hallmark Channel's any Christmas romance on at the moment. Eclectic to say the least.

So, plan ahead as best we can.

The good news is that we talk more with one another than perhaps ever before. So far, we have not Y2K20 crashed the internet or our various communications systems, for which I am grateful. *Physical distancing* and *social connecting* and re-connecting. Our Millennial and young adult children call more than, well, ever. Our extended family are popping up in social media fields like no one's business and it takes a moment to think, "DO I have a cousin in Russia? Toronto? Iran?" So, while our outlook and google calendars may have more blank space than previously, fill in a few spots with scheduled playdates. For us adults as well as for our kids. Nice to have something to look forward to. Nice to reach out and (virtually) touch someone.

In these times, we are all coloring outside the lines. Non sewers are sewing masks. Non bakers are baking bread. Non singers are on public singalongs.

Choose your song. Actually, Sing, In the shower. In the kitchen. In the office. Just sing.

Dog Life in the Pandemic

As dictated by Ginger Kussin-Shoptaw

My origin story as a golden retriever pup is sad, so feel free to skip to the gooder stuff.

I was living with a loving human who did not feed me. I was hungry all the time. At a very young age she had me get pregnant and deliver 12 pups who she then sold. I was not even a year old. I spent lots of my time looking for crumbs of food. I was so skinny I could fit under the bed and couch. One night I squirmed under a couch I had not yet explored. I found an old rusty thing (which I later learned, was a 'lamp.') I pulled it out and rubbed around it hoping to find food. Instead, out popped Robin Williams (which I later learned.) He was a fast-talking genie and offered me three wishes.

For my first wish, I wished to either find my biological parents OR get adopted by a nice loving forever family. The next day, I was picked up by a husband and wife. Both of their names are "DEAR" so at first this was very confusing. They drove me in a car for two hours. They did not talk quite as fast as Mr. Williams, but they were for sure chatters, especially the mom 'dear.'

For my second wish, I wished to never be hungry again. I hit the jackpot in this house. There is so much food it's unbelievable. In a month I had put on lots of weight. In another month my black teeth and gums turned out white and pink, respectively. I was fed every morning AND every night. I also got treats for doing things I had never done before—pee outside (check!), poop outside (check!), sit (check check—I'm particularly good at that), give my paw (weird one, but gets me a treat so, check.) I started going on walks two times a day and then I learned that it's NOT okay to jump up with enthusiasm to greet other walkers and their humans and it's not okay to run into the street or follow squirrels up trees. For learning these things, I got more treats. So, I keep doing them and everyone seems very happy and very proud of me.

My genie told me the third wish was unlikely to come true, and he asked me to tone it down. However, I am nothing if not persistent, so I wished for my adoptive parents to never leave the house again. And, yup, beginning a few months ago, the wish was granted. It is now pure heaven on earth in my life. There is 24/7 coverage and focus on me. I play 'tear the newspaper to smithereens' and 'bark like crazy for no reason.' One of my favorite games is "Hometown Buffet' smorgasbord. I can open a closet and choose which shoe to carry off, or nudge open a drawer and select between many of 'dear's' tie-dye shirts. It's most fun, though, to browse through my mom/dear's stuff because it gets her very excited. My dad dear says she's annoyed, but, what's the diff? She chases me to collect her not from Target exercise socks, her sweater that she saves to wear because it needs dry cleaning, and any of her 'good' yoga pants. I love this cafeteria life. The sound of "GINGER, WHAT DO YOU HAVE?!" is my favorite sound, other than the sound of crinkly paper indicating someone is about to find some food.

The wish to have my parents at home with me around the clock is seriously an amazing gift. I climb on my dad's lap constantly, especially when he is doing something called 'workfromhomezoomcalling.' I am never more than a foot away from either of them. I am living my best life. I go on tons of walks, eat often, snuggle constantly, and am the center of attention. Hopefully my parents never 'return to normal' whatever that means. From my seat, in someone's lap at all times, I see love, friendship, lovey toys, many more of mom's socks, and lots and lots of food. Thanks Genie.

Moving Bodies

S eems these days that everywhere you turn, someone is trying to convince you that exercise is good for you. It's weird, really. Exercise and healthy eating. Who would have thought? But apparently, it's all the rave. Exercise and eating healthy. I saw a recent post that pronounced that 'science proves wheat grass is good for you.' Really? Really?! Who tested that one out? And why? Did that merit a huge study? Who paid for that study? Who requested it? It's a lot to swallow.

Eating healthy notwithstanding, The New York Times (among others), is suggesting that exercise can improve brain power. Not just impacting affect and feelings and decreasing depressive and anxious symptomatology, but actually improving cognitive abilities. Really!??! From walking briskly, you can keep memory alive and vibrant? Really!??! For instance, an article by Gretchen Reynolds stated that,

"For some time, researchers have known that exercise changes the structure of the brain and affects thinking. Ten years ago, scientists at the Salk Institute in California published the groundbreaking finding that exercise stimulates the creation of new brain cells. But fundamental questions remain, like whether exercise must be strenuous to be beneficial. Should it be aerobic? What about weightlifting? And are the cognitive improvements permanent or fleeting? ...

Scientists have conducted many experiments with animals and people to suggest that aerobic exercise really makes the difference. For instance, University of Illinois researchers had elderly people assigned to a six-month program of either stretching exercises or brisk walking. The stretchers increased their flexibility but did not improve on tests of cognition. The brisk walkers did.

Why should exercise need to be aerobic to affect the brain? "It appears that various growth factors must be carried from the periphery of the body into the brain to start a molecular cascade there," creating new neurons and brain connections, says Henriette van Praag, an investigator in the Laboratory of Neurosciences at the National Institute on Aging. For that to happen, "you need a fairly dramatic change in blood flow," like the one that occurs when you run or cycle or swim. Weightlifting, on the other hand, stimulates the production of "growth factors in the muscles that stay in the muscles and aren't transported to the brain," van Praag says.

"It would be fair to say that any form of regular exercise," he says, if it is aerobic, "should be able to maintain or even increase our brain functions."

It seems to me that it's hard enough to exercise without all these incentives. I know that seems counter intuitive but hear me out....It's hard to walk briskly. Have you tried it? You get sweaty, and then later the sweat dries on you, and you get chilly. And sometimes it's hard to chat while walking briskly, which really detracts from the only good part of exercise that I can fathom—the pre-pandemic habit of socializing with others. But now, we're adding these notions that, if taken from the opposite perspective, really create guilt. It says, 'it's good for you to exercise—and—it's bad for you if you don't exercise.' And guilt, as we know, creates stress. And stress is bad for you. And one of the best ways, purportedly, to combat stress, is to exercise. Which takes us back to the beginning. So, it's a crazy loop, like the three to four times around the park I do, in the wee hours of the morning. Makes me loopy, for sure. However, in times like these, we must keep busy, keep safe, and keep sane.

On the other hand, I guess the good thing in all this is that my memory isn't so great, so I won't recall if it's improved or not. And I have no intention of drinking wheat grass. Or any other form of grass, for that matter. I'm too old. So, I can't remember to do all these things. Like aerobics.

So, I'll just adhere to my daily schedule, and walk briskly. Unfortunately, I no longer can do my 'walkie talkies' as it's too hard to walk, briskly, and shout to a pal who is walking at least six feet from me, while masked. I also learned the hard way I should not walk, briskly, while chatting on the phone. Bad combo. Bad time to fall or sprain an ankle and end up in an ER, which has NOT happened in this decade, so, note to self...just walk.

And, surprisingly, what I've discovered in the short term is that it's not too horrible to exercise every day. As long as I don't think about it too much. Why waste brain cells on the topic? As Nike (and I) have been saying for a while now...just do it!

Everything is better when you are outdoors, and the breeze is soft, and the sky is blue. Everything. Conversations. Thought processes. Relationships. Seasonal changes. Shelter in place orders. Everything.

I hate to say it—but—EVEN exercise.

Stay safe. Stay sane.

Neighboring

These are the people in my neighborhood. So sang Sesame Street for many years. Today, it's a different list. It's these are the 'people in my COVID-19 neighborhood.' Given how small our worlds are becoming, it's good to know these folks, wave at them, and stay at list 6 feet removed. Hats off though, to them all. Thanks to our postal service workers, especially the ones who walk door to door delivering and carrying our mail. And thanks to our maintenance workers who are picking up trash and many 'big item stacks' as we go through our cupboards and garages and decide it's time to 'get rid of that couch already.' Thanks also to our gardeners and those who are sweet enough to stop blowing the leaves when we walk by with our dogs. Thanks to all the various pizza people, and of course, to delivery folk everywhere—Postmates/GrubHub/Instacart/Amazon/FedEx/UPS/Ralph's/Costco/SmartnFinal and so on. Thank you thank you to the new hunters and gatherers of our tribes.

Also, thanks to the neighborhood signs and posters saying 'thanks!' or 'Happy Birthday Billy.' Lots of sidewalk chalk art and some old-fashioned hopscotch. Some streets are participating in the hide a doll or bear in the window scavenger hunt game, so kids walking by can scout them out.

My husband and I (and the rescue dog, Ginger) walk and walk. Our local retired Fire Chief keeps special treats on hand for Ginger. Our next-door neighbor keeps special treats on hand for Ginger. One of Ginger's best pals, Bailey, runs away weekly and runs straight to our yard. One neighbor recently chased after us, a little three-year-old, holding a brand new squeezy toy, obviously purchased just for Ginger. We visit with Bandit and Cocoa, Buddy and Bernie. It's a dog love dog world here. And a neighbor helping neighbor world for us all. Lovely blessings.

Little Miss

I have a friend. Let's call her Little Miss. She is more than a friend, actually. She's a grandchild I have not had, but who, along with her big sister, let's my husband and I play extras in their lives. These girls are already blessed with parents, a Grammy, and grandparents, but there has been plenty of room in all hearts for us to also have a role. And Little Miss is 'four and three quarters years old' and she is a ride unto herself.

Little Miss is full of spunk and energy. She is also full of ideas and VERY full of feelings, which she expresses loudly and at high volume. During 'story time' together on Zoom or Facebook messenger or sometimes VSee, depending on which app is working, our reading has taken a back seat to her song writing and singing. She may not get the coaches to turn four chairs on The Voice, but she sure is ardent and articulate.

Most of her songs are about how mad she is at the germs that are keeping her inside and making her miss preschool. Some songs are about her day and how her hair gets tangled up and she does not like it, and also, she does not care so why do her parents? Sometimes she sings about missing friends. Yesterday she had four songs about how AGGRAVTIN it is that she cannot go swimming and learn 'more better' than last year's lessons and how she wished she had a big girl pool and not just a pool you fill with a hose. She also had some great lines about how a bathtub is not a swimming pool, even if you wear your bathing suit in it. Very astute.

Little Miss is a beacon of light in my life. I know she is also adored by her parents and she 'can be a bit much' 24/7 with no school or playmates. Preschool on Zoom, even with the best teacher, which is what she has, is still extremely limited and is not enough to challenge her or distract her. Her mother builds her a tent in the family room so she can have some private space, but she often prefers to seek out the rest of the family who are attempting their online 4th grade classes (sister) or teaching for the Los Angeles Unified School District LAUSD (mother) or working from home (father.) Private space is not what she wants. Proximity, attachment, life back in in the uterus, those are more her cravings.

We are practicing some oldies but goodies so she can add in others' songs along with her own. The Carrot Song is a good one (especially because she can mimic the older brother spot on) and Put the Lime in the Coconut (for some reason we hit on that one) is also fun. My husband, referred to by Little Miss's mom as 'the devil' taught her the diarrhea song. If you do not know it, you are not missing anything. And if you do, I'm sorry! Don't ask. But of course, it is her all time 'bestest song' and often requested. I see 'The Witch Doctor' in our future along with perhaps, 'Hello Mudda, Hello Fadda' as she has a knack for comedy and the irreverent.

In these times, Little Miss is mastering all kinds of things, although perhaps not on the developmental timeline to which we adhere. She can put all kinds of very funny faces on herself during our virtual visits, she is able to 'barf up stars with a unicorn dancing' and she is easily able to make herself look like a very spooky creepy alien. She is working on learning more about patience than hopefully she will really ever need. She is quite able to express herself and to identify feelings. She can delay gratification. She can engage in creative play, parallel play, fantasy play. She wears a different princess dress somedays but also likes her shorts and t-shirts. She can bake and cook and is working on a garden with her family. She is an expert on the scooter and on the two-wheeler with training wheels.

Little Miss also can scream for an hour, or two or up to five a few days per week. She tries to put words to it like 'I hate meatballs' (not true) but mostly she screams to release all the frustration and confusion. Her mom is a wonderful mom and holds her for a while and then lets her cry with privacy in her room for a while and then sits with her. If it goes on too long, the parents swap out. They play music sometimes. Attempt to go for a little walk. Try a bath. But sometimes, a Little Miss has got to do what a Little Miss has got to do, and that is cry.

I used to be able to see her often, in person, full of sticky hugs and snacks and arts and crafts projects, but no longer. I miss her tremendously. I miss her hugs and how she would run across the yard/room/house and throw herself into one of us to be scooped up and lifted up. While it looked like we were doing the lifting, in fact, it was the opposite. She lifts us up.

Her mom says, "It's like the waves at the beach. Some are tough and knock me out and some are gentle. But I still love the beach and standing in the waves."

Indeed. Forces of nature: This virus. The ocean. My little Miss.

Feeling Our Triggers

D o you know your triggers? What sets you off, emotionally, surprising your consciousness? It could be for positive or negative reasons...Is it the smell of some homecooked meal from your childhood? The sight of someone in an old photo you stumbled upon while cleaning house? The taste of a particular coffee or beer you used to drink in college?

More than anything, my mind is awoken when I hear certain songs. You'd think my body would know this by now and be prepared. But nope. For instance, I watched a show on tv last night, and just the opening of the Star-Spangled Banner did me in.

You'd think I would have been prepared.

I like to prepare for things, even on a micro level.

If we were going to a concert (back when we could) I'd prepare by listening to all the old and new songs of the performer. If we were taking a vacation (back when we could) I'd start packing (and shopping for new underwear and socks because as soon as you start packing, you wonder, how is it I only own three pair?) as much as a month before. I prepare for my professional life by staying on top of taxes a quarter ahead of time, when possible. I prepare for my holidays at least three months in advance, sometimes setting a table so early in the process I have to take it down multiple times in order for us to just live our lives and use the table for regular daily usage, and then putting it back in place.

Turns out yes, I'm neurotic and also, I enjoy the process of preparing almost as much (sometimes even more) than the actual event or happenstance. This was especially true when my children were little. I loved prepping for their birthdays and life's milestones. I made each a book and updated it annually with a new chapter. This was before computers, cell phones, google photo or drop box storage, and when Kinkos charged an arm and a leg for color 'xerox.' Even my children realized (by age seven or eight) that while it was a gift for them, it really was something I did for myself. I liked reflecting on the previous year and collecting the memories. I did not scrapbook. Or write long notes. Mostly it was a photo journal of their journey through my lens.

Mostly, I think I'm doing ok in these times. Doing all the things. Walking. Trying to be helpful. Calling and connecting. Using positive self-talk. Setting low expectations for myself. Eating healthy (ok, maybe not so much....) As my friend said today, however, "I sometimes feel very emotional even when I mean not to."

Because I *think* "I'm not sad. I lead a blessed life."

And yet, there it is. Underlying sadness. Sense of loss. Mourning. Grief. Right below the surface.

Our 'baby' is graduating with his master's degree, far away in the East Coast. He has worked hard and loves his field and is excited to go out in the world and use his knowledge and skill set. There will be a 'pre-recorded virtual graduation ceremony.' He tells us he likely won't 'attend.' There are no 'in real life' festivities. The master's hood is 3.5 feet long and features a three-inch velvet trim that indicates the graduate's academic discipline (pink salmon for public health) and looks like it is out of Harry Potter. The inside of the hood, displayed on the graduate's back, shows the colors of the school from which the student is graduating (blue and white and black from Johns Hopkins.) He will not be wearing the gown or the hood or the cap or taking photos all dressed up. I will have to use my imagination. Perhaps one photo of him with his mask on, standing in front of an empty building?

Many parents are worrying about life and death scenarios, so it seems 'little' to be sad about life affirming scenarios. But we are, nonetheless. Lots of commencement ceremonies around the globe, not happening. Weddings postponed or cancelled. Lots of living is now 'on hold.'

It's okay to be sad, even if your life has other blessings. It's okay to miss people, even when you know others have it worse. It's okay to have a cry for the national anthem by the graduating high school seniors and to have a cry for "Some Good Things," with John Krasinski. It's okay to wish you were planning for the winter holidays, 'like normal times.' It's okay. It's okay.

Remember that book, *I'm Okay. You're Okay.*

Maybe we should write a new version—*I'm Not Okay. You're Not Okay. And That's Okay.*

Minding My Musings

It has been a minute (or month) since I last wrote. So much of nothing has happened and my muse got tired of it, got up, and left me. Just another loss in these times. I had become quite fond of her, however. I'm hopeful this is her, word doc bombing me today as she cannot find her way into a photo or Zoom call. Welcome back if this is you and if so, please stay a second.

I am feeling lots of feelings—some are mine, and some I take in and share with/from my patients. Loss, for sure. Anxiety. Fear. Ennui anybody? That's the worst, truly. When it hits, oy! "A feeling of listlessness." Like living in a black hole or a void of some kind. Luckily for me, it is fairly unusual, but I know it has become a constant companion for many among us. Y'know how we thought 'we are all in this together'? Turns out, we are not.

At the beginning, I held onto science and data. That is still my go to, but it is increasingly hard to find it and decipher it and figure out where it came from and who funded it. What is clear, is that LA County is currently more dangerous than it was a few months ago. Who knew we should have gone shopping in April if we wanted to take a risk and see the inside of the new Trader Joes? Meantime, we are so desperate for things to seem 'ok.'

Sometimes, though, we really want things 'like they were.' Earlier in the week I decided to throw caution to the winds, take a full day off, take my life into my hands, and meet a friend and her daughter at Descanso Gardens. This seemed like a low-risk plan for someone who has not left the house in weeks, and it would meet my social needs as well as 'change of scenery' needs. I decided to do it on the same day my husband, who also basically is not leaving the house, decided he'd go into work and pick-up mail and sign some documents, etc. Can you predict where this is headed?

I have not driven my car for many days/weeks/months. My helpful and lovely husband, however, has.

After I got myself squiggled into JEANS and a hat and a mask and put gloves in my pocket, I realized—I had no clue where my keys are. None. As the (now minus Dixie) Chicks sing in "Earls Got to Go", I searched the house high and low. Could not find them. Finally reunited with my 'spare' set—and actually, to clarify, there is no such thing as KEYS anymore, they are 'fobs.' Well, apparently, fobs run out of juice or batteries or whatever makes them unlock your car, just an fyi. Because neither back up fob would open the car. I called my husband who said, 'oops, I think I threw your keys into the back of my car.' He felt horrible and offered to turn right around, but that seemed silly.

So, in these times—what to do? What are the options? This is clearly not a life-or-death dilemma, but it stumped me for about 20 minutes. Do I get in a car with a friend? A dear friend, but someone who has been out and about in the world, cautiously, yes, but out and about. Or do I borrow a neighbor's car? And if so, how contagious is a car interior if the person last drove it yesterday? Probably not very, right? Or?? What about calling lyft or uber? Hmmmmm. I pondered this and more. By then the jeans felt suffocating and oppressive. Ponder, tug pants, ponder, ponder, ponder.

I think about all the positive life changes I've made of late. I now brush my teeth EVERY time I eat. I even use the water pik each time. I put lotion on my heels and wear sock-ies, and my feet have never been happier. I take a shower after each fight I have with my rose bushes, who do not seem happy to have me pulling weeds a few times per day, and, what's that about anyway? I take my vitamins as well as my prescribed medications and have been more compliant than usual. I walk. A lot. My dog could not be happier.

On the other hand, I also am more neurotic than usual. My worry wand is way high and mostly I use those powers for good, protecting family and friends and loved ones with it and trying to remember to take off the backpack of anxiety and give it a rest.

So, I sit and contemplate—to leave the house, or not to leave the house? That question today is similar in design to what Hamlet wondered with 'to be or not to be?'

There were many possible things I COULD have done this morning, all dressed up with nowhere to go. And most likely all were in a 'minor' risk category. I had that very talk with myself. All the while, switching jeans to yoga pants and putting away gloves and my wallet (which had also been hard to locate!)

I figure, gardens will be there in another week or month or year— whenever there is an all clear. Same is true for my friends, hopefully, assuming they all stay safe and sound and do not take undue risk.

Deep breaths. Dental hygiene. Soft feet. Weeded front yard. Check. Check. Check.

My mental health? Not bad, all things considered. Me and my imaginary friend the muse had a nice day together.

Learning from the Wisdom of Our Sage, Pooh Bear

It is just about 40 years since I met my husband, and 35 years since we married. One of the first gifts he ever gave to me was a *philosophy* book that sits next to my bed still today. Ok, maybe 'philosophy' is too high-falutin a term. But it is for sure philosophical. It is Benjamin Hoff's *THE TAO OF POOH* and if you have not read this, and you are any kind of Pooh fan, it is a must see.

Hoff beautifully captures Pooh's voice as well as those of the rest of the gang from the Hundred Acre Wood.

In these times where we clearly are confronted, daily, with the fact that we are not, it turns out, in control over our lives, we can learn a lot from Christopher Robin and his pals.

For instance: "Things just happen in the right way, at the right time. At least when you let them, when you work with circumstances instead of saying, 'This isn't supposed to be happening this way,' and trying harder to make it happen some other way." (Benjamin Hoff)

I think we have all been saying THIS ISNT SUPPOSED TO BE HAPPENING THIS WAY, lots of times, over many days and weeks and months. And of course, we are correct. And yet, this IS what is happening. Whether we like it or not (and of course, we do not.)

What is in our control? Not much. We live with the illusion we have lots under our control, and that illusion has been not only cracked, but definitely smashed to smithereens.

Turning back to Hoff's Pooh: "The main problem with this great obsession for saving time is very simple: *you can't save time*. You can only spend it. But you can spend it wisely or foolishly."

How are we spending this time, these times?

Some of us used to have impulse control. Lots of us have found that our impulse control powers have flown out the window like illegally throwing trash on the 405 when previously stuck in traffic for hours. We see that controlling impulses has gotten increasingly hard for us, for our teens, for our children. Weight is up. People have surpassed the 'freshmen 15' with the 'covid 19' and some are careening toward the covid 25, 30, 35.... Drinking is up. A nightly glass of wine is now two, or three, or wine starting at 4pm followed by a few whiskey shots at 7, 8, 9 pm. Some of us used to have nicer tones of voice with family members, only to discover accidentally (because our kids now video tape our ever move to post on their hidden Instagram account) that we are now yelling, or even screaming, more than once a week, even more than once a day.

The virus is beyond our control. Many political and economic decisions are beyond our control (although if you want to 'do something' there is a nice thank you note letter campaign to Fauci taking place that is uplifting and of course, continued participation in local community activism, however you define that, is healthy and empowering.) Schools are making the best decisions they can, given the constraints facing them. And is always true, there is no ONE RIGHT ANSWER, nor is there ONE WISE PERSON who holds all the answers for us seekers.

"You'd be surprised how many people violate this simple principle every day of their lives and try to fit square pegs into round holes, ignoring the clear reality that Things Are as They Are." (Benjamin Hoff)

Things are as they are. Ignoring the clear reality will not work. Things are as they are. Thank you, Pooh bear.

We can handle this with a little help from our friends, with bearing in mind that at this point, six months in, 'less is more' when it comes to food, alcohol, and anger. And more is more, when it comes to social connections, lists of gratitude, whimsy and humor, and time spent in the water.... pool, sprinklers, ocean, lake, shower, river, tub....

Ground control to Major Tom.

"Do you really want to be happy? You can begin by being appreciative of who you are and what you've got." (Benjamin Hoff)

I'll close with a note from an actual spiritual guide and leader, Buddha, who said, "You can only lose what you cling to." He was no Winnie the Pooh, to be fair, but, let's hold onto those words, at least for today: you can only lose what you cling to—let go of the thought that we are entitled to be in control of our universe, and make room for the thought that within a time of chaos and fear, we can gather up our sense of hope and make space in our minds for our inner coaches and cheer leaders to shout out to us: "You got this. You can handle this."

This is not what you thought it would be, but you can handle whatever this is. Appreciative of who you are. Appreciative of what you've got. You've got this.

Morphing into Someone (Something?) New

So, so much loss surrounding us. SO many IMPORTANT things to think about, that it's possible we've all also put those important things in a box under the bed, and instead, are wisely worrying about other 'stuff.'

You've probably heard of a centaur, half human, half horse. Have you heard of a KURMA, half human, half tortoise? I'm going to now have to coin a term for half human, half chair, as over these months, I've melded into my 'office chair' which is actually a chair from the den, moved into a spare bedroom, so I have somewhere to sit during the zoom hours. Yes, the chair and I are one.

I have a beloved next-door neighbor whom I had not seen in weeks, possibly months. At the beginning of the pandemic, we visited frequently, outdoors, and then it got too hot for us, and I have not seen her. Over the weekend she had a visit from eight of her nine grandkids, in her back yard, so, I walked over, mask on, to sit on the outskirts of the garden patio and visit. It was so nice. To see and hear the chaos of little kids and cousins and to experience something remotely resembling 'normalcy.' It was not only a reunion of family, it was a little oasis of an 'in real life (IRL)' moment…something that heretofore would have been a regular part of our tapestry in summertime, but in these times, is so unique as to bring tears to my eyes.

Aside from the outbursts of laughter and shared stories, the touching moments of seeing the littles reconnect with one another with giggles and squeals, the outing was very instrumental in that I learned all kinds of new things.

For instance, have you heard that in warehouses and factories and other work sites where people have to be physically close to one another, employees wear PROXIMTY SENSORS? Like from Star Trek, the early tv series, back in the day, not the hipper more current movies that came thereafter. In that series, from the 1960s, such sensors were called 'tricorders' and they were general-purpose devices used primarily to scout unfamiliar areas, make detailed examination of living things, and record and review technical data. The medical tricorder was used by doctors to help diagnose diseases and collect bodily information about a patient; the key difference between this and a standard tricorder was a detachable hand-held high-resolution scanner stored in a compartment of the tricorder when not in use. The engineering tricorder was fine-tuned for starship engineering purposes. There are also many other lesser-used varieties of the tricorders. The word "tricorder" is an abbreviation of the device's name, the "TRI-function recorder," referring to the device's primary functions: sensing, computing, and recording. I cannot find an episode, however, where the tricorders were used specifically to determine if a human being was within social distancing parameters.

Proximity sensors, it turns out, in 2020, do what their name indicates—they sense when you are within the 6-foot social distance barrier, and they then beep. (In my head, they should sound like trucks backing up, with that insistent sound, although, when I checked them out on amazon.com, that was not the case. There are many varieties, but mostly, they emit more of a robotic sensor like sound.)

Proximity sensors, notably, are so well known, that they already have their own Wikipedia page: "A **proximity sensor** is a sensor able to detect the presence of nearby *objects without any physical contact. A proximity sensor often emits an electromagnetic field or a beam of electromagnetic radiation (infrared, for instance), and looks for changes in the field or return signal. The object being sensed is often referred to as the proximity sensor's target. Different proximity sensor targets demand* *different sensors. For example, a capacitive proximity sensor or photoelectric sensor might be suitable for a plastic target; an inductive proximity sensor always requires a metal target.*

Proximity sensors can have a high reliability and long functional life because of the absence of mechanical parts and lack of physical contact between the sensor and the sensed object."

These devices were *not developed* to sense humans. The sensor's targets were set up to sense *dangerous things in the environment*, similar to how medical professionals and individuals working near nuclear waste wear radiation badges to track exposure when they are doing X-Rays and such.

However, today, we need gadgets to alert us to the most dangerous things around us, which, it turns out, are other people. What a crazy time.

There is a lid for every pot and a solution for every problem, apparently, and thus, we now have humans walking about wearing devices that will alert them if they are 5 feet within another human being. (One of the next-door grandchildren suggested an alternative— walk around with a hula hoop around your waist to keep people out of range. I like that. Perhaps it will catch on.)

Meantime, I think I've developed some neighborhood block envy, from spending way too much time on social media. No one on our street has pulled a piano onto the yard to play a concert for us yet. There have been no shared moments of honking at 7 pm or lighting a candle in honor of those we've recently lost due to police brutality. I have not encountered pretty-painted rocks on any of my many walks and I have yet to run into anyone with a teddy bear in their window. Clearly, if we are getting graded, we are failing pandemic bonding and have yet to find a spirit squad for these times. I suppose that out here in my neighborhood, proximity sensors are not necessary.

On the other hand, many neighbors do stop by and chat at our fence, some even photographing our sunflower garden, which now boasts stalks well over 15 feet, flowers following the sun every day. Our dog has made more friends than either my husband or I, and she is often invited for more front yard playdates than are possible in one day.

For me, a privileged person working remotely from home, I do not need a proximity sensor any more than I need a fit bit—I know when I'm too close to others and I also know if I've walked or not walked.

Mostly, I am only in the proximity of others when on Zoom. And like everyone else I know, I have developed 'Zoom fatigue.' Yes, that is a thing. Google it—hundreds of articles on the topic, one of my favorites in National Geographic. Turns out that staring at ourselves and others, in tiny Brady Bunch squares, is tiring. Even though we desperately need to connect, and to 'socialize,' it is hard to differentiate Zoom work calls from Zoom fun calls. The same is true for our kids—hard to distinguish between online learning and online social calls.

The boundaries between work and home and between school and home are incredibly blurry during these times. I've tried tiny tricks for distinction, such as switching out my virtual backgrounds so for 'Work Zoom' I may use stock photos (google, 'virtual backgrounds for Zoom calls) and for 'social life Zooms' I use personal photos. This worked for a few weeks, and then I acclimated, and now, it makes no difference if I have UCLA in the background or my happy dog covered in the mud she searched out and conquered on last week's walk.

If you find yourself becoming one with your chair, or, your couch, or your bed, it's probably a good idea to get up and separate yourself out from the inanimate object. It could mean necessitating an intervention, like a patio visit with old friends who wear their masks, or maybe a drive up the coast. Unless we want to re-write Greek mythology to include these new hybrid human-furniture entities, we have to make a break for it. Good luck to us!

Knowing Which Day is What

The New Yorker published a vocab list for these times. My favorite are the words now usable for days of the week: "Sunday is Someday." "Monday is Noneday." "Tuesday is WHOSEDAY?" "Wednesday is Whensday?" "Thursday is Blursday." "Friday is WHYDAY?" and "Saturday is Doesn't Matter Day."

Yup, a whole new lexicon.

What does that mean for us? For our children?

Kaiser Permanente published a national study indicating that 53% of all Americans interviewed said the pandemic has had a negative impact on their lives. Leads me to wonder—WHO ARE THE 47% who do NOT feel negatively impacted and why do I not know those peppy folks? When we wonder what the world be like in six-months, or a year, or two years, I cannot help but thinking about our collective mental health, and the unraveling tapestry in which we are residing.

With the new year coming, we have the opportunity to 'reboot.' Just like we do to do to keep our computers and phones functional, we now have the opportunity to start anew. Unplug. Rest. Plug back in. Re-set.

A nice starting point for refresher is a family chat, which can be formal or informal. Turn off all devices, which is a nice literal and metaphoric beginning. Have each person reflect on this question: "What did you learn last year?" Let each person define last year by themselves….as the last school year (2019-2020) or as the past calendar year, or the past year since their last birthday or even, the last year since the onset of COVID –19 (sometime in March 2020, for most Californians.) The time frame here is not important, just choose one. Have each person then conjure up an image of where they were 'in the beginning.' With whom were they? Where on the planet? What were they thinking? Feeling? Wearing? Eating? Is there a song identifiable from that moment?

"Where were you when the world stopped turning?" asked Alan Jackson, referring to 'that September day, 9/11/01. I seem to find myself humming it now and then, unconsciously reflecting back to March, when I first learned I should 'stay safe and stay home' and I thought, "that sounds nuts."

Ok, so each person shares their time frame and their memory of themselves at the starting line. Then take time to think about this little question:

"Since the beginning, what have you learned?"

Littles and bigs alike can engage in this reflection. It can take in person or on a family Zoom call.

I'll start because, well, right now, I'm the only one here.

What have I learned this year?

Even though I brought it up, I already feel the need to change the question.

It's not just 'what did I learn', it's more like, what am I learning, what more do I need to learn, what am I missing in my bank of knowledge? I check my CHASE accounts every morning, and lately, I check my knowledge bank frequently as well. B.C. (Before COVID) I was not as geared toward monitoring, but now it is habit. At some point I realized that I need to keep adding to my savings, even on days when I feel secure, and that the savings accounts are both financial, and socio emotional.

What did I learn last year?

Keep on keeping on. Find something meaningful and do it. Help someone else and don't overdo it. Listen to your children—these Millennials and Gen Z-ers have a lot going on.

Fire up the neurotransmitters and see if they reignite. Celebrate them and thank them when they do, and do not be too harsh on yourself or your brain when everything is taking a break.

Find new mentors or teachers and hold onto old ones. Thank all of them. Be in touch with them. Reach out to them. Ask them for advice or for a story.

Be open to new experiences, even those in cyber land. This goes for the young and the old. Kudos to all the grandparents doing tik-tok (and save those videos before this all disappears.)

Don't let fear get in the way. Where possible and safe, lean into it. Take risks and reduce your harm when doing so. And if you have to take risks, be practical up front, so you are less tempted to be impulsive in the moment.

Finally, mark time. This, more than anything, seems pertinent. In preschool and kindergarten, the morning circle always includes the 'orientation' time—children learning the day of the week, the date on the calendar, which # day it is of school (because day #100 is always celebrated) and who has a birthday.

Today may very well be NONEDAY, in the new daily vocab, but it is also SOMEDAY for each of us.

SO happy someday. May you find a someone with whom to share it, in person, on the phone, via text, or on the computer. Let's be sure to continue learning to get by with a little help from our friends. If not now, then when?

Being Sad, versus Being S.A.D.

What is the opposite of a "terrible, horrible, no good, very bad day" (Judith Viorst's fabulous story)? How many of us are able to identify and say, it was a 'wonderful, fabulous, no mess, very good day.' It used to be we found the horrible days to be the unique experience, and the great days to be more of the norm. Only now, for many, however, that has switched. The 'new normal' is the challenging days, and the exception is the terrific days. So best to pay attention and mark and name those wonderful days, as they may be far and few between, and we don't want to let them just slip by, unacknowledged.

Autumn is behind us. Leaves changed (although in my neighborhood, they waited 'til Martin Luther King weekend in January to confuse us). You could not find a can of pumpkin puree in any store after October 1 (it's almost as bad as the still elusive search for Clorox Wipes). And winds kick up. And pollen fills the air. Allergy sufferers and asthma people are in agony, made especially challenging now when you are not sure if the sniffles are a cold, flu, allergy, or COVID.

To make matters worse, as we moved from Fall and then into Winter, we had less and less access to sunshine each day. Even here in Sunny California, with our high temperatures. The days are shorter. Despite the fact that our sense of the days is that they are ENDLESS, and we are trapped in the hamster tube of our houses, not able to get out often, with our view of the world somewhat fuzzy from our own breath on those narrow windowpanes.

We spent time outside this summer, but then—heat, fires, winds, mosquitos....and as our children 'went back to school,' we moved things indoors. As numbers of the virus re-increased in various communities, we kept things majorly indoors. So even before seasons changed, we made our worlds increasingly small, and mostly hunkered down, in our houses and covered patios, and now, here we are, permanent fixtures in our 'little boxes' (thank you Melvina Reynolds and Pete Seeger.)

Fall organically steals our daylight hours and then, to make it worse, we fall backward, the last weekend in October, and we are down to barely any time of day in the sun at all.

And we are sad. Sad? Yes, we are sad.

Worse, however, is that many of us, on top of feeling sad, also suffer from S.A.D. Seasonal Affective Disorder. It's a thing. Scientific, diagnoseable, mental illness. It is nothing to panic over, but it is a thing. And you should be aware.

I was on a national webinar called 'parenting in the pandemic.' There were many little take away pearls—like—fathers are spending more time with their children these past six months than in the history of America—and—fathers are reaching out to other fathers more than ever and connecting as parenting peers.... very nice. But also, I heard a lot about the amount our children are withdrawing, socially isolating, and demanding to be 'left alone.' What's a parent to do?

Seasonal affective disorder (SAD) is a type of depression that's related to changes in seasons. SAD begins and ends at about the same time every year. If you're like most people with SAD, your symptoms start in the fall and continue into the winter months, sapping your energy and making you moody. Signs and symptoms can include feeling depressed most of the day, nearly every day, losing interest in things you used to enjoy, experiencing sleep challenges, feeling tired and drained of energy, experiencing changes in appetite or weight, having a hard time concentrating, feeling agitated/irritable, and even having a sense of hopelessness. In extreme cases S.A.D. can include suicidal thoughts. You may recognize some of this in yourself, your spouse, your teen, or even your child.

The specific causes of S.A.D. are still unknown. However, some factors that may come into play include: a change in your biological clock/circadian rhythm *due to reduced levels of sunlight* that disrupt the body's internal clock, a drop in serotonin, a brain chemical (neurotransmitter) that affects mood, that may occur *due to a decrease in sunlight* causing a drop in serotonin, and/or a disruption to the body's level of melatonin, which has a role in sleep patterns and mood.

I don't suggest we become alarmist and start self-diagnosing medical and/or psychological conditions. However, on the other hand— don't brush off that yearly feeling as simply a case of the "winter blues" or a seasonal funk that you or your partner or your parent or you child have to tough out on your own. If concerned, assess for the following: Social withdrawal, including oversleeping and not wanting to get out of bed; school or work problems; substance abuse concerns; history or presence of other mental health disorders (anxiety, eating disorders and substantial changes in appetite/weight, attentional disorders); and of most concern, suicidal thoughts or behavior.

If you or a loved one has these issues in addition to some of the signs and symptoms listed earlier, it is important to contact your family health professionals—primary care physician, pediatrician, psychologist, psychiatrist…. the people you rely on for help with medical situations.

Many of us will have 'light' cases of S.A.D. Being aware of it, and then 'just' talking about it, or venting about it, is incredibly helpful. Call a friend, a cousin with whom you have not chatted in forever, a Facebook pal—feel free to whine, complain, have a nice cry. Get it out. Write a song, paint a picture, journal…. get it out. I had a nice visit recently with a Little Miss five-year old. She told me she needed to sing some songs. There were many feeling words in her songs. And lots of dramatic flair. Some outrage expressed. Lots of "and I am NOT happy about this" and "this better stop soon." (I'm not suggesting she has S.A.D., just admiring her as a role model for saying the things that need to be said, with a fist as microphone, and belting it out while taking a walk in the neighborhood.)

Talking helps. Exercise helps. And you know what really helps? GET OUTSIDE when the sun is shining. Sit in the sun. Walk in the sun. Read a book in the sun. Garden in the sun. Visit a friend (with masks on and at the proper distance!) in the sun. Lie in the sun. Wash your hair and let it dry in the sun. We are lucky, living in California. But. We have to make use of this good luck and GET OUTSIDE. Visit the beach or a park. Ride your bike (and not your peloton, your actual outdoors bike.) Roller blade. Skateboard. Blow bubbles in the sun. Use sidewalk chalk and make a hopscotch set in front of your house. Jump rope in the sun. Wash your car in the sun. Wash your dog in the sun. Wash your patio furniture in the sun. GET OUTSIDE. It's important and it's healthy and it's necessary in decreasing the number of 'terrible horrible no good very bad' days.

When all else fails, turn up the volume and 'walk on sunshine!'

Christmas-ing in 2020

D o you listen much to Country music? I must say, my husband
drew me into it decades ago and it took root and grew a tiny
forest in me. There's lots I don't care for but, over time, it became quite
a guilty pleasure, right up there with Real Housewives of.... but even
better. And this time of year, when there is basically nothing to watch
on tv, regular or premium, there are holiday specials galore.

I won't hold it against you if it's not your cup of tea, but I WILL
encourage you to find and watch *Garth and Trisha Live—A Holiday
Christmas Event!* None of the other tv specials hold a candle to them
this year. Of course, Garth tears up and cries while singing 'Belleau
Woods', a song he co-wrote about a Christmas cease fire which took
place during World War I. Garth tells a fictional story about soldiers
on both sides of the fight putting down their weapons at Christmas
and joining together in song. Some of those lyrics include: The answer
seemed so clear, "heaven's not beyond the clouds it's just beyond the
fear...no, heaven's not beyond the clouds, it's for us to find it here." It
is haunting and beautiful and very touching. And as is the case in this
era, there has been lots of social media coverage of this.

However, the song that seems especially relevant to me today, and
to us all, whether or not you are celebrating Christmas and regardless
of your world view and beliefs, is Trisha singing "Oh Holy Night." This
is a song of hope, in a weary world, where the birth of a baby reframes
everyone's thinking....*A thrill of hope, the weary world rejoices. For yonder
breaks a new and glorious morn'*

Weary world? Check. Double check. We are ever so weary. 2020
tried to engulf us in pain, in death, in fear. It put us into tiny pods and
bubbles and restricted us from hugging our loved ones. 2020 reminded

us we are not as invincible as we'd like to think. It oriented us toward 'what stuff is really essential?', at first, and later, more significantly, 'which people are really essential?' We went from hoarding toilet paper to recognizing the value of not only health workers and scientists, but also, mail carriers, trash collectors, and for sure teachers. We pivoted to using our 'screens' as appendages and to using our appendages as if we all are professional bread makers and master chefs. We majored in IT/tech and communications and minored in house cleaning and the rules of Eloise, and we took a leave of absence in concert going and an incomplete in party planning.

And turns out, we are not quite done. 2020 is not 100% done with us. However, 2021 is on the horizon. As my cousin told me, "We are at mile 96 of a 100-mile hike…. we cannot nor do we want, to turn back, we can rest a bit, for we are not at the end, but we are getting closer every day…we need to hang in there and be safe and not risk it all, given how far we've come and how close we are to arriving." A thrill of hope. Weary souls—rejoice a little bit. We can see a new and glorious morning in our future. Be safe. Be well. Be careful. Together let's take a few deep breaths. And hum a few verses to ourselves in the shower. A thrill of hope to us all.

Making Magic Out of Nothing

I was co-leading a parenting group for parents with schizophrenia. Most lived in Board and Care facilities and had lost custody of their kids, and they were in the classes so they could apply to have visitation without monitoring, and then, ultimately, to possibly get custody of their own kids, although, in most cases, that was highly unlikely. It became apparent early on that this group of adults had themselves had challenging childhoods. They were able to articulate sad incidences from their histories and to talk about the bad parenting they'd experienced. And so, one day, I challenged them to remember ONE good thing about their parent/s. Just one. We went around the room, and each was able to bring up first one memory, and then another.

One man, in his 40s but looking as though he was in his 70s, simply could not think of any positive memory from childhood. Each session he shook his head and said, 'nope—there was no good back then, just lots and lots of bad.' However, as we went from Thanksgiving heading into the Christmas season, he seemed to get a little bit lighter and less sad. Finally, in our last group before the holidays, he shared the following story with us:

"My parents were not bad people, but they were bad parents. They didn't have any money, and they both worked a few jobs at a time. They left us kids at home alone, lots, and I was kind of on my own by the time I was ten. But I recently remembered something—once a year, every year, they made magic out of nothing. It was Christmas. We would go to bed, in our usual dreary house, and wake up to a transformation. We still didn't have 'things', mind you—no big tree with presents under it. But we had stockings made by my mother, and stuffed with fresh oranges, picked by my father. And we had big pieces of paper and colored markers to decorate the walls. And we even had homemade pancakes for breakfast. Mostly, though, we had smiles and laughter. My parents, who rarely found things in life worth smiling about, spent Christmas with me and my brothers and sisters smiling and laughing. And in this way, they truly made magic out of nothing. I hadn't thought there was any good in my childhood, but there was at least one day, every year, that was a treasure."

It was a touching and lovely story, and he told it haltingly and in a sing song voice. When he was done, I asked if remembering the story held any significance for him now. To which he answered: "I am going to make sure my children have smiles and laughter every visit they have with me—I may be worried about paying bills or about when I'll next be hospitalized, but for my kids, I want to make magic out of nothing—like my parents did for me—only I don't want to save the magic up for only one day a year, I want my kids to know that I'm generous with my smiles, laughter, and magic."

During this dreary, challenging time—let's take a page from his book and make some magic out of nothing.

Looking to the New Year

Instead of doing a retrospective of 'let's look back on 2020,' what if we decide to imagine a fast-forwarded look back as if it is currently December 2021, and we want to see how the year went. True, we already KNOW about 2020 and the myriad challenges and upside down-isms, but what if we try to figure out how the next year has gone, and let the future pull us toward what will be our past? What do you think?

Wondering about who I lost and who I found…. reminding myself to hold fast to those I love because obviously we cannot predict how a year is going to play out. The theme of lost and found is still very profound.

It's December 2021. The year was bumpy, as are they all. We moved beyond the shock of experiencing a pandemic and we collectively came together, as scientists moved into the spots heretofore reserved for celebrities and on Hollywood Blvd, we now have 'stars' for the likes of Dr. Anthony Fauci. We came to respect our own fragility and vulnerability. Our children became talented enough with technology to be hired at age 14 to work for high level government agencies and soon will be running the CIA (although not NCIS, because nothing will ever need to change there, clearly, based on the inexplicably high ratings on CBS, even still.) Our planet started some recovery of its own, aided by the many months of us all working remotely. Consumerism and retail therapy are still a big issue, although did we not learn that all we REALLY need is two pair of yoga pants and good sneakers?

It's 2021 and we have taken back our optimism, which had been stolen from us the year before. We are planning things and putting things in our google and outlook calendars and we are traveling more than ever, to wherever we can, because, well, for so long, we could not.

We are off not only to see the world, but to visit in person with all whom we Zoomed for so long.

On a lesser note, my toenails are not pretty but they are healthy and two-year pedicure-less strong. My hair is going from gray to snow white. I never for an instant believed I could be someone who went up into space and lived in the space station, isolated for months/years on end, and yet, now I know—a few tiny details notwithstanding—I *COULD* be an astronaut. So many lessons learned and retained at the end of 2021.

For instance, it is clear my children can take care of themselves, including finding lovely partners, 3:3, for leading fulfilling and meaningful lives. I learned that I now share them with many others as they create family that extends beyond 'us five.' And as a gift, my sense of family is also expanding. Thank you 2021.

It's December 2021. Some of us have moved into different developmental stages, from 'terrible twos to terrible threes' or from teenager stuck in the nest to college student actually living at college. Some have gone from young adult to adult, or from middle age to aging gracefully, and gratefully, we are much more aware of the preciousness of our health and these transitions.

It's December 2021 and there is so much good, but also, we face the problem of our very short memory, and of us ignoring lessons we learned. Already we are fighting new viruses, who apparently can outsmart us. We are pushing back against simple things we can do, daily, to keep ourselves and our loved ones safe. It's December 2021 and our homeless rates are higher than ever, and our loved ones who suffer with addiction and mental illness are sicker. We are of course still working on social justice and equality for all, holding onto Martin Luther King's belief that "the arc of the moral universe is long, but it bends toward justice." We are relieved to be out of one crisis, but not able yet to more effectively handle our chronic issues.

It's December 2021 and the powerful part we can remember is that indeed, we can move from strength to strength. Love—It's not a race –let's let it shine…we need it for the short and for the long term—for today and tomorrow, for our friends, family, neighbors, colleagues—let's let it shine. It's December 2021 and I want to say thank you to you all. Friends, community, people we meet and add to our lives, people for whom their memories are blessings. Thank you. Blessings for a healthy and happy and safer new year, 2022, for one and all.

Offering Gifts

The big bang theory aside, I like the notion that one day, the world was 'born,' and that on that day, we mark that birth. And so, in this time of thinking of a year behind us and a new one ahead, I think— it's kind of like a birth. Or a re-birth. And given that it's a birthday celebration, I decided I should be focusing less on the mishaps, and more on the blessings—less on the 'what is/was missing?'-- and more on 'what have I received/what I can be giving?'

So, I reflect…. on what a gift my husband and I have been given with our three (now rather large and in charge) children. And in return, it feels as though I should be giving a gift back, to the planet, so to speak, to say thank you for these three cubs. Of course, then it dawns on me—one gift I offer to the world (or rather, three gifts I offer), although, in many ways, they are not 'mine' to profer—is—the three cubs.

What better gift can a parent give the planet, than our children? I feel (very objectively) that mine actually are (beyond just symbols and metaphors) the very best of my husband and me combined, and the best of the ancestors for whom they were named (including 'the guy who drove the boat') and the very best of all the family and teachers and coaches and mentors they've ever had. They have the best of their great grandparents. And the best of all those others who went before them, some of whom are buried in the cemetery in Russellville and some of whom were slaughtered and 'cremated' in Germany.

But I digress. The point is—not that I have ownership of them, but rather that they and yours too, are the gifts to the planet. Indeed. I think the planet deserves them and is actually, precisely, ready for them. And they are more than ready for the world. Each brings their own unique sense of self and passion, compassion, and empathy. Each brings joy and fun and spirit, as well as seriousness and intent. They seem to have an innate ability to build community, wherever they are, as well as an ability to help community, wherever they are. This is of particular use during a world-wide pandemic. Many worry and malign the 'Millennial' and the 'Gen Z' group—me—I say, thanks so much to you all, we need you.

They bring a sense of humor, a sense of indignation, and a sense of pride, resiliency, perseverance, and civility as well. And the planet needs that. It is a win—win and a present, I am certain, that will be majorly appreciated over the next decades.

So, I realize—I am mostly done with the baking and now they are doing it on their own. It has been forever since I've seen them, hugged them, watched them look at their significant others' faces with kindness and love and wonder, heard them laugh with friends. However, I'm 'here forever' in their lives, albeit from afar, and that's true for you who are separated from yours as well.

This is all new territory, and I'm bound to make some errors. I will try to respect their need for privacy, and I will try to balance that with my need to know how they're doing. I am acutely aware that the times are a changing and have changed…and my role in their lives, during and beyond this pandemic life, that's changing too. I imagine that they are acutely aware of how deeply I love—lurf –luff– wubba them—as the preschool song went, *"I love you in the morning, and in the afternoon. I love you in the evening, and underneath the moon….skiddle a rinky dinky dink, skiddle a rinky doo—I love you!"*

My cup runneth over. And thanks to you all as well, for those precious children you are raising and bringing up and bringing forth for our future.

Saying Goodbye

L ast week was a long week and a dark week. There were too many deaths, in general, on the planet, in California, in Los Angeles County. Also, in my small circle, there were three that took my breath away, bad things coming in threes, in the rain, in the dark. Because unusually, it rained and hailed and poured and the skies were dark. And my friend Margaret's dad passed away, after struggling for years with dementia. May his memory be a blessing for her and her family. And my friend Kim's son, Jack, also known fondly as "the beast," passed away after cheating and outrunning and surprising many with his 18+ years of life with the rare disease of MPS (Hunters.) Jack and his family have touched the lives of thousands, inspirational with their joyful approach to building community and living life to the fullest and pushing against 'that is impossible' to embrace 'we will make things possible for our child.' (To learn more about MPS visit *https://mpssociety.org/*)

And then, on Friday morning, my mentor and friend of many decades, Dr. Stan Pavey, died of COVID.

I've been focused on the loss of my friend Stan. Stan did not believe in angels. Or heaven. Or religion. But he did believe in humans, and growth, and friendship. He believed in delis and diners, in the power of music and Pete Seger and Phil Ochs and Tom Paxton and Ronnie Gilbert, and he believed in the importance of life-long learning and life-long loving. And to be selfish about this, he believed in me. All who knew him and know him, who loved him and were loved by him, are enriched by our memories of him.

Stan didn't like to be the center of attention. Stan did not like a fuss made over him. For his birthdays, his friends filled up his dance card for weeks, 'one date' a day, or sometimes, even two. One year I brought him a boutonniere. I think that was for his 80ieth. He said it was the first time he'd ever had one and he wore it for a few days in a row, even as it browned a little on the edges.

Stan liked ice cream lots. He was a fan of a nice haircut and admitted to his own vanity in 'looking pretty darn good' after a fresh do. As he said, "I have great hair, need to baby it." He was a doppelganger for Andy Warhol for sure.

Stan loved diners and we frequented many, and we were very sad when Four n Twenty Pie, in Studio City closed down, victim of the pandemic, as was Stan himself, in the end.

For years earlier we tried different delis. Jerrys in multiple locations. Now also closed forever. Fromins. Four n Twenty Pie.

Most recently we frequented The Toasted Bun.

It was (is?!) a tiny little diner in Glendale, not far from Windsor, on Brand Blvd. where mostly it was Stan and I and local law enforcement in tiny vinyl red booths. It took a while for me to adjust to 'lunch with Stan' because at some point (a few years ago?) he took to 'eating' only ice-tea for lunch, due to his chronic Crohn's Disease, which meant we visited while I ate, and he watched me eat. Took a minute. But it worked for us. Some days he had a double hitter—lunch with me followed directly thereafter with lunch or dinner (linner?) with his friend Traci. He said he loved those days—he was the middle of his friends' sandwich.

I could not possibly enumerate all I learned from Stan. I started telling him (in about 1998) that I'd like to have a Vulcan Mind-Meld with him. His memory was unbelievable. He also was meticulous in his thoughts and presentations. We had occasion to teach and train together, and he would spend weeks preparing, writing out notes and note cards, developing outlines and citations. He was very scholarly. I had/have a tendency to fly by the seat of my pants as a presenter. Invariably, we were a good duo and enjoyed by students. One of our more popular topics was "BOUNDARIES." Stan was especially good at looking at issues of ethics before the rest of us encountered them, to help us understand our own sense of self and predict how we may make tough decisions in tough moments.

Stan corrected me whenever I introduced him as my mentor. "Friend." "Mentor and friend." "Friend." "Mentor and friend and teacher." And so, we went. Stan supervised and taught, trained and mentored, reviewed and edited dissertations, and never forgot a person, an idea, or a memory. He was a brilliant psychologist and therapist and managed to see patients well into his 80s.

Stan went into the hospital with COVID two weeks before he passed. Initially he was able to have his usual chatty conversations, but soon, his breathing was labored, and it became harder and harder. Later, he became disoriented, and was coherent enough to be frustrated with his confusion. In our last chat, a few days before he died, he was able to say, "I love you, my friend."

Those will be the last words I will ever hear from him, but his voice and his counsel are ingrained and internalized.

Stan left me with hundreds, if not thousands, of letters and correspondence as well as some nice video snippets. He also entrusted me with a CD (initially, a cassette tape) of 'music to play for my memorial service someday.' It was last updated about five years ago. I took it out and played it for myself yesterday. There were some very sweet and touching jazz pieces and a haunting Judy Garland song. And then, in true Stan fashion, "Stayin Alive," by the Bee Gees popped up. So, I had to smile, as I'm sure he anticipated.

And finally, the last song: "So long, it's been good to know you." Pete Seger singing Woodie Guthrie's song as a tribute. A tribute to Woody, for sure, but clearly, also to Dr. Stan Pavey. So long. It has been incredibly good to know you. What a blessing.

SPRING-ing
FORWARD

Spring, Revisited
2021

Feeling For One Another

A Round of Empathy

Maya Angelou, recipient of the Presidential Medal of Freedom, was interviewed at a conference organized by LeadingAge. Angelou, who passed away in 2014, was the author of *I Know Why the Caged Bird Sings* (and 31 other books) and a speaker of English, French, Spanish, Arabic, Italian and the West African language of Fanti.

Asked about her greatest accomplishment she said, "My greatest blessing is giving birth to my son." Asked if she has any regrets, she said: "I wish I had known more, but I didn't. I only knew as much as I did at that time. The most wonderful thing, as soon as possible, is to forgive yourself. People do only what they know what to do, not what you think they should do. Not because they were experienced or were exposed to this and went to this school and have this degree. We think they know, but not necessarily. Intellectually they might memorize certain statements, but they don't know. In fact. When I have made mistakes, I forgive myself. I forgive anyone who comes in my earshot. I try to make sure I don't make that one mistake again.

And finally, when asked **"what do you hold most dear?"** she said: "Love. I don't mean indulgent love. I mean that condition of the human spirit that is so profound that it can allow us to look at people and not eat each other up, to accord to each other some rights and to go further than that, to try to love them, whatever that mystery is. To love people who don't look like us, who have different complexions and different hair, and to love them. To feel empathy for pets and wildlife. It's amazing."

In these times, it's nice for us to practice empathy and to be grateful for what we have and can hold in our hearts. Be understanding of those living with fear, some of which is irrational, and some of which is HIGHLY rational. Be respectful. You do not know what is going on inside your neighbor's house. Do not assume everyone is experiencing this crisis in the same manner. Some people are struggling with chronic health conditions unrelated to the pandemic, which are now trickier to treat. Some people are struggling with finances, even though it does not 'appear that way' to you. Some people have histories of trauma, neglect, abandonment, grief, poverty, hunger, all of which are currently being 'triggered emotionally' even if they are not in an acute crisis at this moment in time. Some people have family who call and check on them. Some do not. Some people have pending legal cases which are now up in the air. Some people have lost their jobs, are about to lose their jobs, and/or are about to lose their housing. Some people are working with those who are sick and dying or have died. And some people are sick and dying.

Although it feels like we've been 'stuck inside forever' this is only the beginning. This is a long, long marathon, not a sprint. We cannot use up all our good yet. We need to save some up. We can delay gratification.

Do you know that study, the one done with little kids—who are asked to sit and wait awhile until they can eat marshmallows. The Stanford marshmallow experiment was a study on delayed gratification in 1972 led by psychologist Walter Mischel, a professor at Stanford University. In this study, a child was offered a choice between one small but immediate reward, or two small rewards if they could manage to wait for a period of time. During this time, the researcher left the room for about 15 minutes and then returned. The reward was either a marshmallow or pretzel stick, depending on the child's preference. In follow-up studies, the researchers found that children who were able to wait longer for the preferred rewards tended to have better life outcomes. Not all of this study was replicable, but the basic principle that self-restraint can lead to positive results holds true.

Which is where we are now.

Can we handle a challenge? Can we continue to adhere to public health and safety measures? Can we focus on meeting our own needs as well as those of our neighbor? The children in the study ranged in age from THREE and a HALF to FIVE and a HALF.

I feel very confident that we, in adulthood, can take a page from their book. And wait things out. And smile on our brother. And attempt to walk in someone else's shoes. (Well, maybe not that—we'd have to wipe them down with Clorox wipes, which are still nowhere to be seen so....)

We lost John Prine to Covid-19 a few months ago. He reminded us—say hello in there, hello.

Experiencing the Not High and Not Low of 'Meh'

We need to come up with some new responses to the inevitable 'how's it goin?' and 'how are ya?' and 'how was your day?' Our auto reply list is too small: "I'm fine thanks, how are you?" "All's good." "We're fine." "Okay."

Given the new amount of 'freer' time we have, I believe we should take a beat, when asked after, and broaden our answers. We can have a continuum:

"I'm COVID fine," says my dear friend Jane. That works well. I get it.

"Not too bad for a Monday—wait, is it Monday? Ok, then, not too bad for a Wednesday."

"Okay-ish. Rough morning and afternoon, but thankfully it's 5:00 now so I can have a cocktail.... wait—it's NOT 5:00 yet....then I revise my response to it will be okay when we make it to 5 pm."

"Honestly, I am so not okay. On a 1-10 scale with 10 being the highest I am at a 29. I don't know what to do. Do you have any suggestions and if not, can we just chat for a bit or go for a walk on the phone together?"

One of my lovely young teen patients told me we should all start saying "MEH" much more often. It has such a nice ring to it, and is broad and vague, but also it does not suggest that we are all doing fine. I told you about my good friend who responds with 'I'm COVID good.' That works too.

Both are actually perfect, because there is no WAY we are okay. It's just impossible.

When we say 'we are in this together' it's interesting to note that 'we' are having bad dreams. We are not sleeping well and when we do, we have vivid, sad, scary dreams. I don't recall hearing about national dream states prior to this, not even during the 911 days. Perhaps I just forgot, which is clearly something I do very well these days. But also, I think during those days, we were all trying to 'do something.' We stood in line and gave blood. We wrote letters. We reached out and visited our friends and neighbors. We had lots of ways to interact with one another, so maybe that kept the night willies away.

Today we have many opportunities for volunteering, but many are either done remotely or at risk to ourselves, our health, or our family and roommates' health. It's not quite as easy. Although there are some clever do-gooders—the children painting rocks with sunshiny sayings and then just putting them here and there and all around the neighborhood. That's pretty cute. The teddy bear and dolly scavenger hunts in many areas. Adorable. More significantly, all those who are stocking food banks and delivering food and serving food and raising money to feed people. Amazing. All those reducing rent or reaching out to tenants to see what would be helpful. Kudos. Of course, our first responders, teachers, parents, maintenance workers. Thank you.

And yet, we also are having many sleepless nights. We toss, we turn. We get up and bake (again) and then pace around the house (again) and then watch some episode of The Office we've seen 87 times. There is a wonderful children's book "There is a Nightmare in My Closet" by Mercer Mayer. After bravely opening the closet door and coming face to face with the nightmare, the child begins crying. He is worried the nightmare will wake up his parents, so the nightmare is invited into bed and tucked in. The story ends: "I suppose there may be another nightmare in my closet, but my bed is just not big enough for three."

In these times, we may have to lean into our fears and invite them into our beds. As long as we set boundaries and don't invite more than one a night, we may be okay. And if not ok, then perhaps, MEH.

Showing Up

You know that feeling, deep in your stomach, that serves as a warning signal to your brain, but a sign that your brain cannot always de-code? Sometimes it's a 'hey you, I'm nervous' and sometimes it's a "hi up there, my feelings are hurt' and sometimes it's 'may day may day, something is wrong, but I have no idea what' and occasionally, it's 'I'm hangry, please feed me!' We also 'feel feelings' in other parts of our body. We tend to want to connect the dots between feelings and what caused them, but that's not always possible.

(By the way, fun fact, the term **"mayday"** started in 1923 as an international stress call and was officially adopted in 1948.... the term was used because it sounded like the French word m'aider, which means "help me." This, by the way, is what happens when I have too much free time—musing about word and phrase origins...)

When my youngest was little, say about 23 years ago, give or take (he's 28 now, or maybe 27 or 29, hard to say given our new concept of timelessness,) he was a serious and intense kid. He played with his older brother and sister and never complained that he was always the one injured—roller hockey in the street, basketball in the backyard, puppet theater in the den....

We did not know that he had an ear infection until he spiked a fever so high, we finally went to the pediatrician or vet, whoever had the earliest opening. We were lucky we realized when he'd broken a bone (on at least two occasions—flying off a teeter totter once and flying off a skateboard another time.) He was and remains our 'fly below the radar' self-reliant and self-sufficient child.

One year, his kindergarten teacher let us know that on a 'secret wish list' assignment, he'd included "Someday I would like to have clothes with tags on them." Apparently having an entire wardrobe of hand-me-downs from both gendered older sibs was wearing on him. (So, we took him to The Gap and let him try things on and buy brand new jeans and overalls with the tags on them and he was happy as could be and essentially has not been all that interested in purchasing new clothes since.)

Another year he told us, after we lightly interrogated him to try to figure out what was wrong, "I'm worried we will be homeless." We were/are blessed to never have to worry about homelessness, and we sat down and wrote out a list of all the families and friends who would let us live with them should we end up without a house. We hung the list in his room, and it was there for months until one day we noticed he'd taken it down.

There was also the time in first grade when he popped out of his bed around 10 pm to whisper, "Mom, I don't know why, and I don't mean to complain, but, for some reason, there is a clump in my throat." He sat on his father's lap and tears silently fell down his cheeks. He described a general sense of 'feeling bad, feeling sad, feeling scared' without being able to identify 'any reason for any of it.' We sat and talked and also were silent with him for about 15 minutes, which is a long while for a six-year-old. He said, 'it's deep down in my heart.' We went upstairs and put him back to bed and he let me sing a few songs and tickle his back before he fell asleep. By then my heart was sad deep down as well. I could not fix his angst and I had a clump, or maybe twelve.

We then went to sleep, uneasily. At 4:30 am we felt a third body in our bed. Sometime during the night, a body and heart seeking comfort silently snuggled in with us.

We do not have all the answers these days, or actually, any days. As they get older, we cannot just 'kiss it and make it better.' We just have to do our best to keep our attention on matters that really deserve it and be emotionally available for the unexpected moments when they need us. We're pretty good at being there for the moments requiring discipline or eliciting laughter. Let's up our game of accessibility for the feelings. Many mixed feelings abound, and we can hold the space for ourselves and our kids to hold this and that, sad and happy, worried and elated. We can.

In these times, we need to make sure we can be there to sit, chat, and listen to our kids and their clumps. Sometimes, that's all we can do. Sit. Listen. Show up. Be present. Hold their space, or maybe even their hand.

Preparing to Reflect

L et's start making our personal and family time capsules. Capsule? Yes, you have the time, and this is a good way to capture this unique experience in your life and in the lives of your loved ones. SO, for starters, decide on the size—Amazon box, Costco box, or Best Buy new appliance box? (Have you noticed how all the appliances are dying this month?) Next, hold a series of family meetings—perhaps one a week—to brainstorm what to put into the capsule , and to articulate why you've decided to include certain items.

I'm sure we'd LIKE to include both a roll of toilet paper AND some Clorox wipes, but it turns out those are much too important as commodities to give up for prosperity, so maybe an ad downloaded to represent them would work.

I'm sure we'd LIKE to include the invitations from our milestones these months—birthday invites, Mother's Day invites, wedding invites, Bar/Bat mitzvah invites, Quinceanera invites, anniversary invites, graduation invites.... but-- most of those were 'paperless' so it would be hard to generate a print form to include.

So perhaps we can begin by making a list of the things we *cannot* include, but would if we could:

1) Our collective anxiety. If we could make that into a form, what would it look like? Amorphous 'blob?' Slime with glitter? Spooky spikey dinosaur from the effects list on our various social media sites? Evil clown? Or a pinata of the actual corona virus?

2) Our collective grief. How to capture the immense sadness and mourning? A sheet of totally gray paper?

3) Our collective insomnia. What does that look like? A journal of our vivid pandemic dreams perhaps?

Here is what we CAN put in:

Photos

- of our pets, who love us unconditionally and who seem to enjoy their time with us altogether in the den.
- of our grandparents, who we have not been able to hug or greet with kisses for months, but who still love us and provide facetime stories and songs.
- of the garden we grew, for our first time, with shockingly yummy results.
- of the white board we used to list every Zoom appointment each family member had per day.

Crafts Projects

- like our home-made face masks.
- like our new DIY placemats.
- like the decorations for every holiday we celebrated while sheltered.
- like the family tree we created going back eight generations, put together with our free time AND access to our relatives online, across the globe.

And what about the new recipes we learned and mastered? And the multiple memes and GIFs we either made or received from our children, who now, at age seven, are master computer whiz kids who soon will be able to hack into anything, anytime. Maybe we can include the letters from the incredibly kind teacher who thought to mail missives to our children. Maybe we can include results from virus testing in which we participated, if we did (or maybe that's considered bio-hazardous, and we should not be holding onto it?) Newspaper clippings?

Fast forward a few years — picture opening the capsule, or your children opening the capsule.

It seems impossible to imagine, but we will forget aspects of staying at home and lining up at Trader Joes and memories will fade, as we go forward. Such is the nature of human nature.

In these times, that's a good thing to think about—the time when we are no longer 'in these times.'

Springing forward

Our task, from birth on, is to develop a strong sense of self (and then to help our children do the same.) To do so, we need to internalize a sense of being valued and loved AND, we need to master things. Littles are obvious in all they need to master, from communicating to choosing which of the four pair of identical leggings to wear. Acquisition of knowledge, academics, social skills, knowing which friend really DOES have your back. These are all part of childhood and adolescent tasks to overcome, in addition to myriad more. The need to master new things continues into adulthood, which is way DIY is ever so popular and why adult women want to learn to pole dance. (Although really? I never really got that one!)

During the past year+, we had ample need and opportunity, across the lifespan, to master things. And here's the good and bad news: We kicked butt and actually succeeded in life in the pandemic. We figured out how to adapt. We adjusted. We lowered expectations and raised the bar for learning technology. We figured out how to do things we do not like doing ('home' at school for our children) and things we hope to NEVER do again ('home' at school for our children.) And thus, the question—is there such a thing as too much mastery? Well, in this case, perhaps.

As the country is starting to come out from under the spell cast upon us, and as we are starting to see a light at the end of the tunnel, some of us are getting nervous. We pivoted so well, that we do not want to pivot back. We got very comfy in our bare feet or slippers, in our un-polished toe and fingernails, in our almost entirely gray head of hair. We adapted. We mastered ordering food online, and really wonder, 'why go to the market?' We mastered Zoom family gatherings, where we experienced more inclusivity than previous in-person gatherings, as we could bring together people from all over the world. We mastered indoor bike riding and outdoor executive meetings, on our picnic tables in the backyard.

Also, our children mastered the new world order. They fast realized how to stay up all night gaming with friends, and not only the new games, but also, activities from our own youth, like Dungeons and Dragons, and RISK. They shrunk their social circle down to one or two close pals. They made an actual nest in their bedroom and managed to take AP classes and participate in musical theater while in their pajamas, pretending they were not in their bed in their pajamas.

SO yes, we may have been over-achiever masterers of the pandemic. Some of us do not want to turn the page and 'go back,' whatever that may look like. Our teens are not chomping at the bit to get back to high school lunch landmines, where it's hard to know with whom to sit, and where it's hard to know if your good friend will still be your good friend by the weekend. It's hard to take a test in person, with the noises of other kids around you, chewing gum, sniffling, breathing too loudly, and the clock tick tick TOCKING in an annoying manner. It's hard to have to limit meals to certain times, versus wandering in and out of the kitchen at random times to take a snack or decide to cook a huge meal for the whole family, because why not?

Basically, though, here is a thought—we are not GOING BACK. We are not returning. We instead, are MOVING FORWARD. We are starting the next chapter, the new chapter, and it is scary. We have no clue what this journey will include.

Reminder—while difficult, we can take ownership, and write, if not the full thing, then an outline, to guide us toward this uncertain future. We can help our children and teens do so as well. What do we want to 'do next'? What is important to us? How do we mark the losses of the past twelve months, while not being consumed by them? Where do we want to wander, and with whom? How do we start reintegrating things like, social life, errands, ball games?

Probably the best bet is to consider our (bizarre) notion of daylight saving. Next week we 'spring ahead' (and last Autumn we 'fell backward.') So indeed, let's spring ahead. One hour at a time. One day at a time. One adventure at a time. There is no need to go backward, or to go back, or to return to something that is no longer relevant. Instead—imagine a new day, month, season, era. And let's head out and see what it is. We've mastered the past; we will master the future.

Finding Faith

When we are no longer able to change a situation,
we are challenged to change ourselves.
—Viktor Frankl

B etween 1942 and 1945 Viktor Frankl labored in four different concentration camps, including Auschwitz, while his parents, brother, and pregnant wife perished. Based on his own experience and the experiences of others he treated later in his practice, Frankl argues that we cannot avoid suffering, but we can choose how to cope with it, find meaning in it, and move forward with renewed purpose. Frankl's theory--known as logotherapy, from the Greek word logos ("meaning")--holds that our primary drive-in life is not pleasure, as Freud maintained, but the discovery and pursuit of what we personally find meaningful.

We thankfully are not currently living through a period of genocide (in the U.S.), and we are not in Concentration Camps. Even more so, then, Dr. Frankl's words are applicable—we are driven to make meaning in our lives, and the harder the times, the less we understand in our world, the greater the effort to seek to make sense of it.

A long, long time ago....

I was a young professor in a doctoral program, teaching Psycho-Diagnostic Assessment. At that time, I believed I knew lots and was imparting important information to many a psychologist in training. I took my work incredibly seriously. I did not tolerate tardiness, procrastination, or lack of curiosity. I adored my students and spent a million hours preparing for each class. I was gifted with Teaching

Assistants and support, but still wanted to read and grade most papers and assignments. I taught about bias and sensitivity and limitations in 'testing people' as well as basics regarding administration, scoring, interpretation, and writing integrated reports. I also taught professional development and how it all comes down to two things: relationships and reputation.

I had no idea that those many years of teaching would yield life-long lessons and friendships for ME. Incredible, really, thinking back on it. Such blessings, these alumni (and now decades' long) friendships.

In these times of the pandemic, I've tried all kinds of new learning activities. I worked on piano skills, guitar skills, choral singing skills, cooking and baking skills, and even bike-riding skills. All in all, I had not 'found my passion' in seeking meaning (and let's not kid ourselves, ways to pass time) until more recently, when a dear friend of mine suggested we have weekly discussions on the topic of 'spiritual and religious enlightenment and faith.'

My friend, Reverend Michael Weiler, S.J. is a few years my senior. He was my student 'back in the day' (1992? 1993?) and then I supervised him as a pre-doctoral intern. He is not a working psychologist, as you may have surmised. He is an ordained member of the Jesuit (Catholic) order and has served as a mentor, leader, supervisor for Novates the world over. He currently lives in Portland, Oregon, where he is sheltering and painting the house. He is fluent in Spanish and served many, in many countries, with compassion, and, from my perspective, godliness.

Mike and I connected decades ago on many planes, and in my long list of blessings, his friendship continues to be highly ranked. We've shared much and figured that this is a fine time in life to have a regularly scheduled visit and chat. Plus, we are very proud of ourselves for figuring out technology, at our 'advanced ages and stages'—Yay us!

We decided that we would have a talk about the broad topic of religion, sharing thoughts, questions, and ideas. We have no agenda and no text so basically, we meet and try to figure out the role of spirituality in our lives, present and historically, and examine both the good and the terrifying. Father Mike has actual professional credentials in this area, and me, I just like to contemplate human behavior in various contexts and try to understand us in relation to the Universe.

I'm a fan of the concept of community and being part of a larger historic context than just the here and now. So much to learn—from the curanderos (healers from the Latinx cultures) and Indigenous and Native People in their spiritual practices to the Judeo/Christian/Islamic traditions and all the Eastern spiritual beliefs and traditions.

We talk about the NONES—have you heard that term? The large percentage of (mostly Millennials in the U.S.) who indicate they are 'none of the above' when asked about their religious or spiritual world view. What, if any, are the implications? Much negative has been done 'in the name of religion' so perhaps this is a good trend. On the other hand, much good has been done, and continues to be done, be it practiced by Muslim, Hindu, Buddhists, Jews, Christians (of all denominations), Sikh, or Indigenous Spiritual People, to mention only a few.

There are many differences across us and between us, and many a book has been written about comparative religion. Father Mike and I are more interested in what brings comfort and inspiration. What is the soul? Is it consciousness? Or eternity? Or heart and mind intertwined?

In our visits with one another over the past 30 years, across continents and the U.S., we realize time and time again, that an integral way to make meaning is to establish and sustain friendships. It nurtures the soul. And the mind. And the heart. Thank God.

Living Each Day

I 've been working on a paper about philosophers of the 20th century, while also trying to take in any coherent sense of the world in which we currently live. Those philosophers lived during the era of World War II, and massive genocide, and compliance with genocide, and it shaped many of their thoughts, pre and post war, about humanity.

And then, with lots of coverage and media coverage, as there should be, we learn this year, in the 21st century, about one after another deaths/murders/killings. Black lives, lost way too young, way too violently. To mourn this, as a community and country, is somewhat comforting. To hear Supremacists speak out and threaten and wish more violence, is beyond frightening.

Anger and marching and cries of bitter anguish. It is a much-needed catharsis. Too little outrage too late, perhaps, but essential experiences of sad, sad, sad. I'm wishing I could be helpful to those with so much grieving to do. Sigh. Wishing we did not have to explain to our children what it means to kill someone while all around, others are telling you to stop, to cut it out, to take your knee off a breathing living individual's neck, to not take away their breath, their life.

You never know when your last day will be.

It's now Sunday am. I'm shifting focus to my own little world again, as my son and daughter-in-law are 'due in' this afternoon. They are also formally announcing that they are 'due' (in November.) I've been Googling prayers to say for pregnant women –and my thoughts turn to the future, while also attempting to stay present in the present.

I keep gravitating back to the importance of TIME.... we mark important occasions; we separate and differentiate between the mundane and the 'regular.' Excellent practices. What we tend to not do, however, is to embrace the present and the moment. The 'we are here now,' regardless of highs and lows. This is our life. This is our world. We are our people. Not enough tv media coverage of the phenomenal people in the world, doing good things, and not enough personal focus.

And, you never know when your last day will be.

So, this is a good time for me to remember—be kind, do not die with gossip and mean words on my lips or snarky thoughts in my mind. Show up. Do not die alone, in a hibernation cave, solely focusing on self. Stay open to relationships and put good thoughts and small acts of loving kindness into the world. Not so you receive them back, but simply, because you can.

Conscious Coupling in a Pandemic

In the journal of the American Psychologist, the scientific peer review magazine of psychologists in the U.S. and Canada, there are many full of articles about COVID-19. The one that caught my eye is entitled: *Risk and Resilience in Family Well-Being During the COVID-19 pandemic (authors Prime, Wade, and Browne.)*

The authors note that there are mediating processes within the family that can decrease or modify risk. These are known as the FAMILY RESILIENCE FRAMEWORK (Walsh, 2015) and include:

1) Communication (clear information, emotional sharing, collaborative problem solving, dyadic and family coping).
2) Organization (adaptability, connectedness, access to social and economic resources…routines, rituals and rules are of great import in this category); and
3) Belief Systems (meaning making, hope, and spirituality.)

The point of the article is to remind us that while we may all experience some post-traumatic stress (PTSD) at the 'end of all this,' some families may even experience post traumatic *growth*. Can you imagine? For example, quality of sibling relationships enhanced, service to others increased, outpouring of creativity not heretofore expressed or shared in the family rising, and many more.

This is inspirational and aspirational and not set out here to shame you into the sense of 'OMG, our family is not doing ANY of that,' but rather, to remind you, we can all work to improve a little bit, in one of the three areas, or even, in two or three of the three aforementioned areas. And back to school time is the perfect time to adopt these as our foundation and build from there. Afterall, we have to create a whole new scaffold anyway, so, why not use science as the basis?

As we begin our construction project, let's remember what we do NOT want to include. Because we have some good science on that as well. The #1 thing that does not lead to resiliency in families is parent/s who are themselves either in conflict with one another or who are deeply distressed and/or depressed. This is not to say that you need to play Mary Poppins and Polly Anna all day long, but it does suggest that grownups should be grownups and protect their children from toxicity at the adult level. Do you believe your children do not know what's going on? Think again!! They are little (or big) sponges and very few secrets are safe from them.

John Gottman studied what predicts divorce, and he developed an amazingly accurate formula. He identified "four horsemen of the apocalypse" to refer to the four aspects in a couple's relationship most likely to lead to a separation. These are: contempt, criticism, defensiveness, and stonewalling. For couples experiencing and acting out in these four areas, you may want to take a step back and re-assess, on behalf of the adults and of the children sharing space in these times.

Gottman found that not all negatives are alike. The four he identified turned out to be the biggest predictors of divorce and separation. After years of researching divorce between couples, Dr. Gottman found that *contemptuous behavior* is the number one predictor of divorce. Contempt can be expressed in forms of sarcasm, name calling, mimicking, eye rolling, and more. To fight contempt, couples must work hard to create a culture of appreciation, but more immediately to talk about yourself and not your partner. Both of you may be feeling very unappreciated in this relationship, but attacking your partner isn't the way to enhance their appreciation of your finer qualities! To change this around, the long-term goal is to actively change one's mindset. But the immediate antidote to contempt and *criticism* is to talk from your own perspective. If you point a finger as you're talking, you are likely being critical or contemptuous. Talk instead about yourself, your feelings, your desires, your frustrations. He suggests that couples forget criticism. There is no such thing as *"constructive criticism."* Go for a complaint instead.' In other words, own YOUR feelings or sense of self without putting it on your partner. "I had a long day and sure am tired. Nothing sounds good for dinner for me tonight." Versus "I can't believe you are making meat balls again. I cannot eat those one more night. For god's sake, can't you make anything else?" Regarding *defensiveness*, Gottman says, 'do not bat it back.' Consider that your partner has a point and there is something for you to consider and learn from. The "masters of marriage" accept some responsibility for what their partner is bringing to them. They don't bat it back. They don't deny all charges! Finally, the alternative to *stonewalling* is to learn to actively calm yourself down and then to re-engage in the conversation. Breaking patterns like this is easier when you have a lot of practice. In these times all adults struggle with fatigue, boredom, fear, uneasiness, and lack of balance. This shows up in our relationships with our partners, siblings, parents, and, unfortunately, our children as well.

To defeat the Four Horsemen, remember that Your Attitude and THOUGHTS matter. Not to be simplistic, because ya'know, we are living in cramped spaces with no sign of early release. However, in the long term, if you feel you can reduce the partner strife, work on your attitude. Try and view your partner's positive qualities and comment on them. Catch your partner doing something good and tell them you appreciate them for what they are doing. It can't hurt. And it can be added to the bucket of family resilience you're filling up.

Wondering, Where are We Now?

Where are we now? What, if anything, have we learned in the past year+? We have been surrounded by loss, by fear, by confusion. We have made mistakes, individually, collectively. We have been at our worse. We've cried lots, yelled more than we're proud of, eaten more than we should have. We've made promises we could not keep. We've started projects we did not finish.

And also....we've found that we are more resilient than we thought. We've spent time with our kids like never before, so much so, that we even know how to beat them at a few video games. We've connected with the kids who had turned us into empty nesters, only to discover that they know lots of things that are HELPFUL to us (making us memes on bitmoji sites, for instance) and also, they are more vulnerable than perhaps we'd remembered. Also, many empty nests filled back up, and while there were many challenges, there were also many blessings discovered in shared space.

We are over a year into this. We are cautiously optimistic about vaccines, but also worried about who can get them, and how. We do not want to jump the lines, especially when we are afraid to even leave the house, but also, we do not want to be left behind. We'd like, for the first time in 12 months, to actually be in the right place at the right time. And also, we have some ideas for vaccine distribution, like having ice cream trucks go through the neighborhoods offering vaccines AND snow cones, pushups, and chocho tacos. Or, if that does not work, then how about a few open bars, on the sidewalks, where Millennial can get a shot AND receive a shot!?

The sadness underlying our pithiness in this regard is tied to the intense disparities in our communities, where we see, time after time, that those who have, get, and those who do not, don't. Sigh. So, reminder to us and our children.... let's love our neighbors as ourselves, because to be perfectly selfish, we all need to be healthy for us to all be healthy. Let's not roll our eyes at others who long ago gave up 'seeking help,' based on years/decades/millennial of not finding anyone to be helpful. Let's decrease our judgmental minds and access our empathetic minds. Let's offer to help those who cannot access the technology to sign up for vaccines, or, who once they make an appointment, have no means of transportation. We are good neighbors. We check our 'Nextdoor app' and our 'Citizen app' and also our Facebook freebies pages. We show up for one another time and time again. We may have stopped clapping for health care workers at dusk, but for sure, we can figure this out—let's find health for one and all, not just for anyone.

Taking Back the House (from the rats…)

There is nothing like over 13 months stuck at home to help you
're-discover' things about your home, and your marriage. Everyone
knows that in marriage and families, we are in it for the long haul, 'for
better or worse.' Or so they say.

After 35 years plus of marriage, I feel we've been doing a fairly
good job of big picture life. We are not yellers or screamers or even
arguers, mostly. However, we continue to have strong differences of
opinions in a few areas, one of which is 'animals in the house.' And
when it comes to rodents in a pandemic, I feel strongly that MY
perspective is the RIGHT perspective.

It all started simply enough, as most things do. Over the years, my
husband, like Noah from the Ark story, has rescued what seem to be two
of every kind of animal. The baby goslings were not so bad, although full
grown geese living in suburbia was a tad much for everyone. The County Fair
rabbits were not horrible, but then the neighbor cats and hawks ate them,
and the whole affair turned torrid. Mammals, reptiles, fish, amphibians—
you name it, we've had them. There was the year my husband and the
kids 'saved 70 tadpoles' from a local toxic stream (think, Aliso Canyon.)
He insisted they'd all die, but nope, they survived. Do you know what 70
somewhat physically deformed frogs hopping through your house is like? I do!

There was the year the opossums took over the backyard. My
husband brought them into the house, one by one, as they visited our
yard, to show the kids. He held them up, with his (thankfully gloved)
hand, and marveled at how this species is so adaptive. Do you know
what it's like to keep seeing opossum in your kitchen? I do!

In addition, every animal catastrophe is reframed by this man as
some sort of 'cosmic happening.' "Dear, there are crickets all over the

house" I mention one evening. "Yes dear," he responds, 'You know, they are all good luck." My daughter and I shake our heads and stealth fully help them relocate outdoors, one by one.

I finally reached my limit though when I discovered the rodents living among us. The first time was when I took in the car for 'making a weird sound' and was told, 'nothing major, it's just that your rats have been eating through the cables.' My husband thought this was fascinating and exciting. I thought I'd vomit. "YOU HAVE GOT TO BE KIDDING" was my mature response to both the mechanic and the spouse. They were marveling over the cleverness of rats (and I had to wonder, 'clever to eat car cables?!') and I was wondering, 'were they also living INSIDE the car?) With investigation skills on board, we then discovered they were living in our crawl spaces. Turned out that the little scratching sounds I'd heard in the middle of the night were NOT the wind and the tree branches, but rather, were a MISCHIEF of rats. (Did you know a group of rats is called a mischief? I did not, and really wish there had been no reason for me to have acquired that tidbit of information.)

I decided we needed expert help (because left up to the spouse, I feared he'd collect them all and raise them together in the large aquarium left over from our large boa constrictor, Sandy, who 'ran away from home while sunning herself,' to the chagrin of our block.) Turns out, there are many companies who provide this kind of service, including checking out each crease and crevice in the residence. First, they set traps in the attic and tiny spaces. Then, they carried out multiple, living, rats, one box trap at a time. It was impossible to watch and impossible to turn away. Then, they identified every crevice open to clever four-legged little animals and closed them up with netting. My partner of decades walked around making a 'squeak squeak' noise, compounded by little scratching sounds like those I'd heard over head for the previous month. He thought he was funny. I thought I needed to list the house on Zillow.

On the last day, I decided to take the mature route and retire alone to take a nice, hot, bubbly bath. All worries dissipate in the water. I thought about how although I had believed I was the one influencing the children we raised, rather, it was their father, the animal whisperer who impacted them most. I've lived in a house with a tortoise who needed help hibernating, the aforementioned snake, who disappeared one day, after she had grown from a 'baby' to an adult boa, a solid length of six feet, and more rescue dogs than could fill the 'dead pet calendar' we gave my husband as a gift. We had tarantulas, geckos and bearded dragons. It was a menagerie, and I thought as empty nesters, we were essentially now down to just the two of us and the dog. Big picture? No more furry pals. Little picture, at least we sent the rats packing.

During these months, some folks are complaining of boredom and malaise. In my dwelling, every day has a new sumthin sumthin to it. Years ago, my husband gave me a card that said, "Celebrate the moments of our life with general food international coffees.' Inside, he'd written, "I would, but I'd rather celebrate with you." It's mutual— although, I'd prefer it to be just me and him, minus any critters.

Mother's Day

It's Mother's Day weekend. We are enjoying time as parents with our kids, parents to be themselves, and life is 'somewhat more normal'—although also full of challenge, fear, trepidation. My husband, a scientist/psychologist, has a tendency to say, when things are tough, "there is nothing bad here." It is a nice cognitive behavioral refrain, and a good substitute for negative intrusive thoughts, and often, it works very well. Because truly, in my life, 'there is nothing bad here.'

On the other hand—there are challenges, stressors, worries. Lots of worries. All day long, I have the privilege of listening to people with challenges, stressors, and worries. Couples who love one another, but after months trapped inside together, are feeling more disgust than delight. Teens who are happily wearing hoodies and doing 'school in bed,' even though their schools are offering in person (or hybrid) learning again. Parents who are overwhelmed and feel that no decision is the correct decision.

This week, I too feel anxiety creeping up and in. I believe it's related to the many potentialities of joy on the horizon. The more there is to look forward to, the more the anxiety walks around my mind and my body. The more I have to love, the more I have to worry about loss.

I've had time now in person with our two DC kids, visiting in person, and our daughter finally left her job at the prison, which, while meaningful to her as a clinical psychologist, was also increasingly dangerous. So, all three kids are happy and safe, nicely partnered up, doing things they enjoy doing, 'launched' so to speak. Additionally, many of my other kids, my patients, are doing better than they've been in over a year. And also, God willing, there is a baby grandson arriving in the Fall. So basically, life is good.

My children have done a good job of raising me up to be a mom. They started 34 years ago. The big one, the first one, as an easy-going baby, made it seem like I knew what I was doing, which I did not. Then the only girl, colicky, uncomfortable in her own skin, easily upset and agitated—she did the opposite, making me think I was clueless and never would figure out how to meet her needs. The third and last, our baby bird, was born premature and sick, and his journey was (is?) one of appreciation and worry, worry and appreciation. A huge part of my learning curve was realizing, at some point, 'this is not about me'—this is their journey, life, path—not mine—I can be here as support, and hopefully as a role model, and I can enhance their lives when possible, and I can provide an 'lifetime guarantee contract, based on love'—and then, turns out, they are free to live their lives. They are full owners of their own lives. I'm honored to be a passenger sometimes, and others, a passer-byer.

So much learning to do in this area and this regard—figuring out how to be a good mom, or any kind of mom, for that matter—and this, after studying parenting since about 1984…. I know less now than I knew then, that's for sure. On a good day, I think—where there is a foundation of love and a stated contract (I-Thou), the rest will all follow as it should. And on a bad day…. I have cardiac distress that may or may not be related to my thoughts and feelings. And on those days, I am getting better at remembering that as it turns out, my worry does NOT protect them. They are good to go. Fully formed them. Put down the backpack of worry and the world, and our kids, are still ok.

Keeping to the Slower Pace

We move through our lives at an alarming pace, which is nothing compared to the alacrity with which our children pass through us. We expect immediate gratification and cannot wait even for 'one hour photo' or 'one day dry cleaning,' as that is considered too long a time-period to wait. Our impatience is impressive, but only in that it cycles us to bigger, better, faster—frenetic pace—internalized chaos. This becomes close to impossible and crazy making during a time of pandemic, when things grind to close to a halt of the whole country. And yet, when it's time to start venturing out, is it a good idea to jump right back onto the hamster wheel?

When we are not quarantined, we raise our children to anticipate and expect this speed, and then we wonder why it is that they are addicted to Red Bull, Adderall, methamphetamine. And then, all of a sudden, we came to an abrupt halt. And all slowed down, except their internal clock, which now has them up all night, plugged in, playing video games, continually living a speedy existence during a time when we are slowly slipping deeper and deeper into, ironically called, quicksand.

So, what have we been chasing? What's the gold ring or the pot at rainbow's end? The price we pay to not feel pain is that all other senses are dulled as well—moving faster than the speed of light may protect us from sadness and loneliness, but in exchange, we also dull feelings of joy, hope, happiness.

Create a good, happy, positive moment. Capture it in your mind and feel it in your heart. Visualize it. Smell it. Hold it. Breathe in. Savor it. Breathe out.

Put that away, into your cedar chest of hopes and save it for a rainy day...for a 'terrible, horrible, no good, very bad day,' like the one experienced by Alexander, in the book written by Judith Viorst. Re-create the feeling of that time and that moment. Save it and carry it, but first, find the time and space to build and design the delight. Suspend yourself. Re-live it.

Put it back, and when you do, re-arrange the memories in there to make space for a new one. Take your time. Do it slowly and carefully, mindfully, name the experience JOY, and hold on to it or wrap it carefully in tissue paper, and remember where you've put it. It's a time of transition. From 'in school' to 'school's out'.... from intakes to graduations and terminations.... beginnings end with ends but there is so very much in between....

Take time for you, take time for your friends and family, take time—steal it, save it, and savor it.

Not Commuting

I'm stuck, like you. In the house, with some privileges of going here and there, if here and there is basically within a few miles of the house. I'm not 100% stuck indoors anymore, but also, I'm not flitting here and there and anywhere I choose. And here's the funny thing about NOT driving in to work every day—I miss it, really.

Not the first few days, mind you. The first few days I managed to really rest and relax. But then came day #3 and now day #798.... And how much 'doing nothing' can a person do? So here are some of the things I learned, and some of the things I did, from what I learned.

Learned:

No one is Martha Stewart, other than Martha Stewart. However, lest you be daunted by the challenges of domesticity.... there is a food show on EVERY SINGLE HOUR of the day (who knew?) and seriously, you can learn to do ANYTHING by watching these guys and gals, as they cook, bake, and prepare food for one or one hundred.

Did:

As a result of all that viewing, I learned to cook new things (and some were even edible) AND I learned a few keen table design tricks (Xmas wooden spoons from 99 cent store anyone? Yup, just attach plastic bendy Santas or reindeer, and away you go!)

Learned:

See above on Martha—turns out, there are ALSO shows on tv, around the clock, relative to interior design. AND get this—you can actually buy ANYTHING online. And I mean anything!! (Who knew??)

Did:

As a result of spending many hours on a couch, something I don't think I'd EVER done up until now, I realized that the 'hippie bed' (so named by my almost adult children) is really dated.... Soooooo—I surfed all kinds of pages online, and ultimately bought a new bed, from overstock.com.... (Free shipping!!) It came in the mail, and the assembly was not all that difficult ('we had harder Lego sets growing up,' claimed my youngest) AND it was/is a very nice bed.

Learned:

If you change any ONE tiny thing in your house, you're gonna wanna change it all (have you read *"IF you give a mouse a cookie"*?)

Did:

Had to go buy all new bedding (comforters, sheets, pillows, things called 'shams', probably because it's a sham/e that they get you to fork out the $$ for something that is really just a pillow case....) and then realized the room needed painting....stopped there, but really am now tempted to buy new night stands, new dresser AND paint shutters (can you even do that? Who knows?! I'll have to watch some more cable tv decorating shows....)

Learned:

Even with a huge loving, extended family, and lots of friends accessible online and a husband in the same house .... being home is isolating and lonely. It's hard to really master anything here, and it's hard to feel you're contributing anything meaningful to the planet.

Did:

Watched the entirety of West Wing (inspiring). Re-organized all the closets and folded all the clothes and stored bags and bags of things to give away at some point. Read the LA Times and the New York Times and the New Yorker (and also, PEOPLE magazine—turns out there are too many people in there I've never heard of so it's not as fun as you'd think!) Finally—most important thing I finally adjusted and toned down my 'need to keep busy.'

Father's Day 2021

I t was 1972, early Spring. Every week my father dragged my sister, 10, and me, 12, out to the park to play softball. We were on a team with the honest to goodness (unfortunate) name, "The Super Chicks." I wince every time I say this, even now, as I sit writing.

The grass was green. The park was pretty. The climate was actually mild. There was no hole in the ozone layer and the San Fernando Valley still had more orange groves than housing developments. And oh! How I hated those spring evenings. I stood back in the outfield, praying and praying that no ball would come to me. I was quite the believer in those days, as rarely—if ever—could a girl hit a ball far enough to come anywhere near centerfield.

I couldn't run. I couldn't field. I was basically afraid to catch. And I never ever wanted to 'get better with practice' because I never ever wanted to play softball.

Nonetheless, on a few startling occasions, I connected the bat to the ball, and I got on base. Mostly, though, I stood around wishing I was at home, wishing I was at the library reading Anne of Green Gables or Trixie Belden or anything by Louisa May Alcott, wishing I was invisible.

I remember wondering about my father's sanity during that season. "What is he trying to accomplish?" I'd ponder with my younger sister. "Is he purposefully trying to ruin our lives?" I'd ruminate. Finally, I'd turn to my mother "Is this about HIM or about me?" My mother answered. "Both. And someday you'll understand. You'll understand why, after working 12-14 hours a day, he comes home and puts on his shorts and schleps you and your sister to the park to play ball. He hopes you'll enjoy the game and the companionship. He hopes you'll laugh and have fun. He hopes someday you'll really like playing."

At that, I'd shake my head and retire to my stack of books, thinking 'she is as nutty as he—they really deserve one another.'

In childhood, a father's relationship with his daughter depends on the temperament and attitude of both the father and the daughter. My father tried to find things for us to do together, in an attempt to bridge the nature-nurture divide. In addition to softball, he took me horseback riding in Mexico, rock climbing in Yosemite, swimming in the waves of Zuma Beach. And I feared it all—despised it mostly—and worked increasingly hard to avoid those activities. Most of the time I thought him bizarre. I did not enjoy any of what he enjoyed. I couldn't even grasp what made him enjoy it.

On some level, I believed I let him down. And on other levels, I believed he let me down. Adolescence and early adulthood found us marveling that we were related to one another at all. It was clear that my second sister was 'his,' mastering gymnastics and in constant motion—it was clear that my brother and youngest sister were 'his,' as off they went, skiing black diamonds and planning the next snow trip from aloft a dangling chair lift. But me—not sure—nothing in common, at least, nothing I could fathom at that age and stage.

Time passed. Lots and lots of time. I came to see my dad from different perspectives, and, I'd like to hope, vice-versa. I got to see my dad as a grandfather (a "Zadie", as we say in Yiddish), and he got to see me as the mother of his grandchildren. I got to see my dad as the father of adults. I got to see my dad as a husband of 60+ years. Essentially, I guess, as I aged, I got to see my father as a person, and he too, got to see me as a person too. I saw him as he drove carpools for all ten of his grandchildren, and as he attended every sporting match imaginable (yes, it had skipped a generation, and somehow, all three of my children came out as 'jocks' of one type or another.) I saw my dad in the pool in the backyard, in the rivers of Yosemite, on the bike paths of Ventura, on the slopes of Mammoth—active, busy, a big Papa Duck, with the baby grandchild ducklings all lined up behind him.

Then, a few years back, I played in the "Mothers of Jocks Memorial Day Softball Game"—not the official name of the game, mind you, but the most descriptive. I couldn't run. I couldn't field. I did not like softball. However, for some reason, I wasn't afraid of the ball. Somehow the companionship (or the margaritas) left me lacking in self-consciousness, and full of vim and vigor. I laughed so hard I was sore from laughing, and I played so hard that the next day I couldn't move.

My kids came to cheer me on and offer advice ("Mom, keep your head down, your feet planted, your elbow up and your eye on the ball.") My husband came to take photos and to enjoy the show. ("Yep, that's my wife out there, in her baseball ready position. Just wait until I take hundreds of pictures of her in action. She will be so happy for me to have captured this for entirety!")

I hung out in the dugout with moms, some out of shape, some in shape (and some in exercise clothes that really can't be worn anywhere in public) ....we were cracking bubble gum and jokes in rapid succession, discussing the merits of estrogen over testosterone, and hoping fervently we would not get injured.

My last time at bat, I heard a voice from the stands: "That's a girl. You can do it." It was my dad. I swung hard and accidentally hit something closely resembling a bunt. I ran as hard as I could. I got on base, just barely (thank you jump!) and I beamed (or perspired—or both). And I could hear, above the others in the stands, my dad cheering and shouting, "You did it!" How as it that he could have been right, all those years ago? How was it that the older I got, the wiser he became?

I will never be an athlete and I'm pretty much lacking the competitive gene. I'm still terrified of horses, and I will not climb a rock. However, the waves of Zuma beckon periodically and I swim out, far beyond the horizon, and I feel exhilarated.

Even more significantly, though, over these years my dad and I have discovered one another. We don't have to share in activities to share in one another's lives. We can do that simply by being together and by sharing our selves.

Who knew? Lifetime is a long time—hopefully—for us all. And over time, we invent and re-invent ourselves, and we prioritize with whom we spend our time. Father-child relationships can blossom all the way through...on a baseball diamond, and in our hearts. Even, as it turns out, during a world-wide pandemic.

Holding Gratitude and Intention

Once upon a time, B.C. (before covid), there were many people who lived in many places who went about their daily lives as it made sense to them. Some participated in prayer—some were not affiliated with any 'organized' religion; some felt spiritual but not religious; some observed traditions and culture but not rituals; and what was true for all, was that they had tremendous freedom to walk about the planet and interact with whomever they wanted, whenever they wanted, holding their spiritual world view.

And then, in March 2020, things came to an abrupt stop. The world shut down in an attempt to control (and possibly eradicate?) a virus that was highly effective and lethal, and our collective sense of safety, connection, and adventure turned into a year+ of a collective sense of loss, isolation, loneliness, and fear. Many of us tried (and some even accomplished) all kinds of things: bread baking, gardening, masked hiking, piano practicing, garage cleaning, photo organizing.

Meantime, some of us stumbled into a wonderous and radically amazing new place and space of spiritual transformation. I was lucky enough to be one of those people, and I want to offer my gratitude and immense appreciation.

The daily Zoom prayer group started with humility. It was led by a different person each day. We gathered together, offered a word of gratitude and a word of intention (in the chat.) We had a short, 30-minutes from start to finish, service, where we offered prayers for healing and shared in sanctification and holiness to honor those we've lost. Over time, the prayer group became 'the little engine that could'—gathering steam and pushing up the mountain, carrying aboard many dreamers and mourners, singers and thinkers. As we evolved, our clergy kept us focused and on point, creating a space for Zoom connections and interactions.

Our group continued to grow and developed into a loose structure where each day tended to have its own feel and flavor. Mondays, for instance. At one point, our leader paused, looked around the zoom boxes, took in a deep breath, and said, one name at a time, "I see you _____." "I see you _____." "I see you, Jody." A few tears slid down my face as we began with morning prayers of gratitude. I was surprised to feel so surprised, so touched, by this little gesture. I had not realized I was feeling unseen, until she pointed out she could see me. Such a tiny gift, of such significance, and it stayed with me, and with us, as we moved forward over more and more days, weeks, months.

Before Covid, most of us did not know very many of the 'regulars' and in my case, I had not known one soul. Over time, though, we began to share many little moments, and those moments built a foundation that moved us and supported us. Some people pop in once in a while. Some come weekly on one particular day. And while we are not collecting data, it seems that about 30 come fairly regularly to the point that if one of us missing, someone else notes it and steps in. Healing and singing. Gathering, albeit remotely, and participating in this daily ritual.

Here is what we've learned together this past year: Saying a healing prayer for and with a 'stranger' and then moving from healing prayers to saying a prayer to sanctify a death, with that same individual, when their loved one passes—well—we were/are no longer strangers. We pray with one another and hold one another up. We are good listeners. If someone is missing, one of us mentions the name of their loved one on their behalf.

We came together from all over the planet. We learned about teatime in London. We watched one of our Ohio heroes as he gives blood, regularly, and we hold our breath when one of us is driving, biking, walking or occasionally jogging during our group time. We had a pajama day session. We learned to meditate. We said extra prayers for our country and our leaders during times of unrest and systemic racism. We shared ideas, recipes, and many words of gratitude, in the chat and in our breakout rooms. And we mourned, as family mourns, together.

Now we are slowly supporting one another to 'get back out there.' We still meet daily on Zoom, but now, some are trying to arrange to meet one another face to face. We still sing together and pray together in cyber space, but now, some are venturing out and about. We are cautious. We are interested in taking back our lives, but also, of preserving this little ritual. Starting the day with song, with gratitude, intention, together.

Find your circle. Drum. Sing. Dance. Meditate. Pray. Be together. Share an intention for the day. State something for which you are grateful. It may not fix things, but it sure can't hurt. Every day in the chat we write our gratitude—and EVERY SINGLE DAY, there in the chat, is this: "I am grateful for this group."

Thanks, Ikar!

Face to Face

As we are re-entering, we are all feeling lots of feelings at one time. One thing I keep hearing is concern for how others perceive us, as in, 'we've only met on Zoom, now, if/when we meet in person, they will discover 'the truth'—that I'm really ....short, fat, old, tall, covered in acne,' etc. It is true, that Zoom relationships (like profiles on dating apps) allowed us to put our best face forward. We were able to embed touch ups and use lighting and basically alter our appearances, not just by putting on video filters like bunny ears, but also by using video filters like, 'touch up appearance.'

Reminds me of being told, most of my childhood and adolescence, 'you have such a pretty face.' Of course, it did not take long for my ten-year-old self to realize that meant 'you have such a pretty face, too bad you're so fat.' It was one of those hostile remarks given as if it was a compliment. I did not quite 'get it' when younger, but once I did, it became a consistent and persistent hurtful comment, from friends and relatives alike, received over decades. In fact, to make better sense of it, I actually wrote my undergraduate psychology honor's thesis on the topic, entitled, 'Such a Pretty Face—Body Dysmorphia in Adolescents with Obesity.'

The idea that I was 'seen' but not 'seen' for many years was devastating. Thankfully, with many years of good therapy I made my way through and developed thicker skin and empathy for those without the ability to fully 'see' others, those who perseverate on one aspect of an individual, as if that aspect represents the whole of the person. My sensitivity toward this issue, living in the body of 'other' and then later, of becoming wholly integrated and being fully embraced by others, serves as a foundation for me, all these years later.

The first person I saw, in real life, post pandemic, whom I'd only seen on screen the past 10 months, is my friend Jill. I was very surprised to discover how tall she is, and she commented on how surprised she was to discover how short I am. (Note, I doubt either of us actually qualifies, on the actuarial charts, as tall or short…although, maaaaaybe, given my shrinkage with age, I'm now almost 'legally short'….but, it was likely just the contrast between only knowing one another from the neck up, in a tiny box on the computer, to now hugging one another, in person.) I could not help but worry 'she's really thinking, 'wow, look how large you are,' but also, I took to task those negative voices inside my head and reminded them that THEY are critical thinkers and speakers, and that Jill, is not.

I also got to meet, in person, a beloved teacher of mine, with whom I'd spent countless hours all year, learning and studying. She told me, "I actually put on some makeup and lipstick to meet you, since I did not want you to think I'm so old when you saw my face, face to face.' Of course, she's beautiful, inside and out, and I myself did not think of her as anything other than talented and loving, but even at age xx, she was worried what I would think and how I would see her.

We are not particularly vain people—me, my teacher, my friend. We are all in helping careers and oriented toward looking at others beneath the surface, and helping strengthen others' sense of self, expanding others' world views, lifting one another up. And yet, here we are, worrying about what we look like, or, more specifically, worrying about what others may THINK we look like.

Turns out, at the end of the day, we are all, each and every one of us, vulnerable. We ARE worried about what others think. We are worried about how others perceive us. We are worried we are not good enough, not smart enough, not thin enough, not wealthy enough, not smart enough. Turns out it is part of the human condition. I'm not sure at what developmental stage we find our self-consciousness, but I do know, many of us lost it, after a few weeks, while we were all 'working from home' in yoga pants and a hoodie, with knowledge of how best to frame our faces for Zoom.

We put up our own designated backdrops—mountains, Hawaii, dogs, babies, kittens, Yosemite, elephants on safari—and used the 'touch up' buttons, and then we relaxed. We embraced ourselves for who we were, or rather, for whom we could project we were. We may only have seen glimpses of one another, but also, we heard babies crying, dogs barking, leave blowers blowing. We shared more intimacy with one another than we normally would have, in 'work meetings' or in classrooms, and we stopped trying too hard to control the things in our environment beyond our control.

In real life, now it's time to actually remember to embrace the real us—all of it—bushy eyebrows, thinning hair, extra chins, asymmetrical features…It's time to own ourselves, and to be proud of our individuality—and of our distinct physical entities, housing our distinct inner sense of honor, integrity, grace.

It's time. Perhaps even past time. Let's move the focus from "how can I look the best?' to 'how can I be the best?' If I can tone down that internal critical voice, and you can tone down that internal critical voice, perhaps we all can begin to see (and hug!) what's really important—one another, warts and all.

Tip Toe-ing Out

So, the future appears to have arrived, and for some reason, despite all that time we spent trapped indoors, counting down days 'til freedom,' we are almost as ill-prepared for the present as we were for the past. How is that possible?

We are coming out of our caves, poking out our heads like Ground Hog's Day, wandering a bit farther each day, and yet, it is not a time of total joy and frivolity. We are surprised. Why are people so grouchy and irritable? (See the articles on air travel!) Why are day camps having a hard time filling their slots? (See the articles on kids and summertime) Somehow, this transition 'back' is not full of joy and frivolity.

Sometimes, having fewer options makes life simpler. During the past months, the number of decisions we had to make was as limited as the square footage in which we resided. We were not juggling social engagements. We were not figuring out our next trip, unless it was to a local spot, maybe, for a masked, social distanced, hike. We were not working on complicated kid transportation issues (how to get three kids, from the hours of 3-6 pm, to five places like soccer practice, doctor's office, tutor, tae kwan do, and piano.) We were not worrying about running errands to pick up clothes at the dry cleaners, because typically, hoodies and sweats can be washed easily at home. We did not have to figure out which markets had the best deals on fruit, because we were ordering groceries online, and just hoping for the best. (Anyone get good bananas more times than not? Or was everyone making multiple loaves of banana bread?)

But now, we have many choices. What do we do with so many possibilities and options? We become overwhelmed. And nervous. And worried. Because in addition to 'should I attend this event or that event' we have to factor in our health and safety in all decisions. Many of us used to take our health and safety for granted. And now, we don't. We can't. We have to add it in to the equation. Can we let our unvaccinated littles hug us? Can we go to an outdoor picnic and not wear a mask, if we know everyone is vaccinated? Can we? Should we? Dodger Stadium? Hollywood Bowl? What about a movie in a theater? Indoor live music?

In addition to the anxiety about these possibilities, we have to also remember that many of us are living with a sense of survivor's guilt from the trauma of what we've gone through. We soldiered on, when things were tough, and we were creative in the new routines we created. We got up each day and did the things. Cooked and baked lots. Exercised and then felt free to eat lots. We had Zoom playdates for ourselves and learned how to play online games with friends. We moved all our furniture around to create office and school space at home. We figured out how to get every single thing delivered. We built routine under bizarre circumstances, and we mastered what had to be mastered.

However, underneath it all was the sense of fear, doom, and sometimes, death and loss. We tried our best to ignore lots of that in favor of making things work. We were more resilient than we thought we could be, would be. But now—now that we can be less vigilant, all that pain and suffering and grief, it's bubbling up. 600,000+ died from COVID, in this country alone. And we did not have the bandwidth to mourn or reflect too closely on those numbers. It's ironic, how in the times of pending happiness, the sadness feels free to populate our hearts and minds.

While there's an inclination to push it all back underground, it's imperative that we let this come up and out. It's okay to take that box from under the bed, and open it up, a little each day, and honor the past months and sense of dread and emptiness included. Each day, a little bit. Be okay with moments of grief and having a few good cries, ugly cries even. Be okay with acknowledging how much you missed certain things, certain people, and how for some of us, those loved ones who passed in the past months, from COVID or from old age or from illness. We could not engage in our usual rituals and traditions. We attended funerals on-line. We said prayers alone at home. Despite all the 'extra time at home' we did not/could not prioritize mourning and grief, as we were so busy attending to making it through the crisis. And we are still sad, or sad adjacent.

The crisis, at least for now, appears to be abating. Time to explore the world again, or, at a minimum, venture out beyond our daily walking zones. And also, time to allow the sadness in. Perhaps we should all engage in one large smudge ceremony, to cleanse our space. And if not, then at least, a brief ceremony, of your own making, for your own family, to say goodbye to the last months. Write out some challenges you each experienced on an index card, have a little marshmallow roast, and burn the cards—enjoy the sweetness that greets you with the crispy treats, and let the sad/bad/mad of last year go. Make a time capsule for your family—physical or digital and say your goodbyes to what you lost— people and opportunities. And also, have some rituals on behalf of those who passed, those who went un-mourned, or only partially mourned.

To embrace the future fully, let's give a moment to the past.

Accounting

I am not an accountant, but I am interested in numbers. As we are headed toward 'maybe being out of this' I see that some numbers are 'up.' Last year we had an increase in gun sales, in hate crimes, and in homicides. We had more wildfires than ever. On a less 'life and death spread sheet', numbers went up regarding the amount of screen time in our daily lives, regarding the number of households who can access the internet, and regarding the efficacy in our children being able to hack into the Pentagon by age five.

On the other hand, some numbers went down. We saw DUIs decrease, we saw flus and colds decrease and we saw designer shoe sales decrease. Most significantly, due to science and medicine, we managed a dramatic decrease in the number of cases of COVID, in the number of COVID hospitalizations, and ultimately, in the number of COVID deaths.

So now, here we are. We are here. We are right where we are. And as it turns out, we are not as joyful as you'd think. On our spread sheet of revenue and expenses, you'd think we'd have more in the column of happiness than sadness, more 'pluses than minuses.' Instead, that's not what we are seeing.

On our freeways, where traffic is now 'almost back to normal', what is NOT normal, is the number of infractions—people cutting one another off, people speeding, people ignoring rules for entering and exiting carpool lanes, people flagrantly holding their phones and texting, and people yelling at one another through their glass windows. Road rage is making a re-appearance, and it's not an attractive sight. It seems that while we are all mostly happy to be 'getting back', there is also a lot of (barely) underlying rage being played out on the 405 or 101.

It turns out that it is easier for us to access anger than it is to access, experience, carry, hold, process...fear and depression. Anger projected onto others feels kinda good. It's why we (somewhat) enjoy the occasional moments we scream at our partner/child/neighbor. We release lots of energy into the world, mostly negative, when we get mad. On the contrary, with feelings of sadness and anxiety, we hold onto them and wrap ourselves in them and sink down deeper. Depression is often thought of, actually, as anger turned against ourselves.

What to do with all these feelings, some repressed, some expressed?

How to change the balance on our balance sheets?

Take a moment, or two or three. Take a breath. Reflect back over all these months. What bubbles up? Some gratitude, for things that went well, for lives that are still here, for resilience you perhaps had not realized you had. Yes. Also—a profound sense of uncertainty that the world will ever really be safe again, that you and your family and friends and community can be carefree. And the losses—the losses column is packed full. Lost lives. Lost opportunities. Lost jobs. Loss of in-person schooling where teachers and students interacted and knew one another, mask less. Loss of friendships. Loss of economic stability. Loss of a year plus. Loss of innocence. Loss of developmental milestones and celebrations and traditions and holidays and travel. We lost so much. So so much.

So, acknowledge it, identify it, name it—and feel sad about it. Have a cry (or two.) Say a prayer (or two.) Talk with a friend or partner or sister about it. Feel sad. Be sad. It's okay. And it's more than a one-time visit to that land—be prepared—it comes in waves, and it's okay. It's not only okay, but also healthy, to be sad, feel sad, talk about the sadness. Give it it's due.

The same for our anxiety. Acknowledge it. Identify it. Name it. And be nervous. Feel the butterflies in your stomach, don't ignore them.

Feel the worry, the sweaty palms, don't 'wine it away' every evening. Talk with a friend or partner or sister about it. This too will come in waves and will not simply disappear. It WAS a nerve-wracking time. It is still a time of worry. But it is not the same worry it was.

In addition to experiencing the feelings, talk back to them. Talk back to sadness and anxiety and remind them of reality. Facts versus feelings after you've let the feelings have their time! We ARE moving in the right direction. Things ARE better. We are NOT in the same place we were in March 2020, or November 2020, or even March 2021. We are getting better, stronger, safer, every day.

In accounting for who we are, and where we are, we're right where we should be. Friends, neighbors, family, communities, all of us, taking one day at a time and counting our blessings and adding them up. We do not need to create obstacle courses of enraged virtual reality road maps on our freeways. We do not need to impatiently nudge the person in front of us in line now that we're not social distanced six feet everywhere we go. We can work on our patience and appreciation for others, assuming positive intention, or at minimum, attempting to assume positive intention—of others, of ourselves.

It's a new world ahead of us. We can bubble big now, bigger by far than what we could do the past months. We can and should keep adding to our revenue column. We've earned it.

Living in The Moment

Remember a long time ago when we believed we could 'catch up on sleep'? We had the notion that we could cram for finals and stay up around the clock and then, a week later, catch up on sleep. We had the idea that we could be up all night, for months, with a hungry, restless, possibly colicky baby, and that at some point, we would make it all up when we 'sleep while the baby sleeps.' As if.

Now that the country is 'maybe going to be okay' (and really, it's not, but...) we seem to have this internal drive to make up for vacations missed, milestone birthdays skipped, graduation ceremonies experienced solely on a tiny iPad, and many more celebrations we lost, during the pandemic. Hotels and airlines are able to increase their rates by millions of dollars (well, maybe not QUITE the much, but...) and venues for any life cycle event are not only booked and double booked, but they too, can basically charge whatever they want. Supply and demand. They are supplying it and we are demanding it.

I don't blame the businesspeople for their zealous quest to 'make up' for all the lost revenues. And I don't judge the philosophy of 'we did not spend a dime on travel for 17 months, so we can now go full throttle, whatever it costs.' It makes sense to a certain degree. My only caveat is a reminder that even IF we spend three times the amount and forgo a budget, we cannot actually make up for life events, any more than we can catch up on sleep. Somethings are gone and they have passed us by, or we have passed them by. And it's okay, as long as we acknowledge this. We cannot make up for things in the past. We do not need to make up for the past. Instead, we need to live in the present. We need to locate our strength and creativity and think about what's most important and prioritize that. We do not have to eat fast, worrying someone else will clear our plate. We can take our time, savor our lives, savor these moments, today, and tomorrow too.

We've lived through (hopefully) the worst of the worst with the pandemic. There are ongoing concerns, of course, for those unvaccinated, for children under twelve, for the Delta Variant and any new variant that could come our way. We worry about school starting, fall flu season, communities where there is tighter density of living quarters, booster shots or not. But in many instances, we are just so weary of worry, that we are throwing caution to the wind, and with a 'devil may care attitude' we are saying—I am gonna do whatever I wanna do now, because—because—because…last year I could not, but this year, I CAN!

Note to ourselves—we need to find the middle ground.

We have pandemic fatigue big time, perhaps even bigger than when we had cabin fever last Fall. This fatigue is made up of so many underlining losses, it is often too painful to reflect upon it whatsoever. So instead, we are booking flights, paying outrageous amounts for hotels and fancy dinners, and taking advantage of 'one of everything please.' We are taking our children to Disney Land and Magic Mountain and Universal Studios, all in the same week. We are attending sporting events and concerts and paying primo prices for 'the best seats in the house' because, why not? We went from zero social engagements a week to going out every night, and twice on the weekends.

I do not want to rain on our parades, and I encourage us all, as I may have mentioned previously, to bubble big this summer!! Embrace it. Hug friends. Visit new places. Meet babies who are already 18 months old, and whom you've never yet held. Drive to your grandparents' house and learn how to bake a special dish with them. Set up playdates so your children can freely roam about together. Say thanks to all those who helped you make it through the troubled times. Bake a cake, and this time, deliver it in person!

However, tiny caveat. Please hold a tiny little space aside, as well. Space to be sad and mourn the losses. Space to remember the feelings of fear, terror, depression. Space to just go out a few times next week, not eight times. Ease back in and out. You do not need to 'overdo' to live big. Sometimes walking around the block for frozen yogurt or going to Denny's is equally as beneficial as a fancy night out on a roof top hotel downtown. Sometimes a few days in a national forest is even better than a week at Disney Land. We do not need to throw budgets to the wind, we do not need to pretend that 'everything is now totally ok- totally hunky dory.' Because it's not. Life does not work that way.

We need to Celebrate new opportunities. We need to reconnect with our communities beyond the next-door neighbors and fed-ex delivery person. And also, we need to be strong, to be brave, to be joyful, to be loving, to be kind. We need to show up for one another, and slowly, bit by bit, step into the next season, and then the next, and then the next.

CPSIA information can be obtained
at www.ICGtesting.com
Printed in the USA
LVHW010938160921
697948LV00007B/155